STATE AND NATION
IN SOUTH ASIA

STATE AND NATION IN SOUTH ASIA

SWARNA RAJAGOPALAN

LYNNE
RIENNER
PUBLISHERS

BOULDER
LONDON

Published in the United States of America in 2001 by
Lynne Rienner Publishers, Inc.
1800 30th Street, Boulder, Colorado 80301
www.rienner.com

and in the United Kingdom by
Lynne Rienner Publishers, Inc.
3 Henrietta Street, Covent Garden, London WC2E 8LU

Exclusively distributed in India, Pakistan, Sri Lanka, and Bangladesh by
Viva Books Private Ltd., 4262/3 Ansari Road, New Delhi 110-002

Library of Congress Cataloging-in-Publication Data
Rajagopalan, Swarna, 1964–
    State and nation in south Asia / Swarna Rajagopalan.
        p.   cm.
    Includes bibliographical references and index.
    ISBN 1-55587-967-5 (alk. paper)
    1. Nationalism—South Asia.   2. South Asia—Politics and government—20th century.
3. South Asia—Ethnic relations—Political aspects.   I. Title.

DS341.R35   2001
323.1'54—dc21

                                                                            2001019069

British Cataloguing in Publication Data
A Cataloguing in Publication record for this book
is available from the British Library.

Printed and bound in the United States of America

The paper used in this publication meets the requirements
of the American National Standard for Permanence of
Paper for Printed Library Materials Z39.48-1984.

    5   4   3   2   1

To my parents,
who were my first teachers

Contents

Preface

Witnessing the transformation of Indian politics in the late 1980s and early 1990s forced me to consider questions about political communities, consensus, and identity. In this book I discuss these issues in a comparative South Asian context. This book was researched and drafted at the University of Illinois at Urbana-Champaign and completed at Michigan State University. Thanks to funding from the Program in Arms Control, Disarmament and International Security (ACDIS) at the University of Illinois at Urbana-Champaign, I was able to conduct research in Sri Lanka and India. The repository of South Asian materials at the University of Illinois facilitated my addition of Pakistan to the list of cases considered. This book is based on a variety of primary and secondary sources. In the Indian and Sri Lankan cases, these include interviews with opinion makers (writers, media persons, filmmakers, actors, and scholars) and political activists, primarily from the two Tamil communities but also from other ethnic backgrounds. Although these are cited, the individuals who were interviewed are unnamed out of regard for their privacy. Field research was not possible in Pakistan; Sindhi nationalist journals at the Illinois library were used instead of interviews. Additionally, legal texts, polemical writings, press clippings, opinion pieces, and scholarly works were referred to in all three cases.

In addition to the financial support I received from the University of Illinois, several organizations and individuals in South Asia made this project a reality. The Regional Centre for Strategic Studies in Colombo was my home base during the research process. The counsel and guidance of scholars and the information resources at the following institutions have been invaluable: the Centre for Policy Research and Analysis at the University of Colombo, the International Centre for Ethnic Studies (Colombo and Kandy), the Centre for Policy Research in New Delhi, the National Council for Educational Research and Training in New Delhi, the Centre for Education and Documentation in Bombay, and the Perasiriyar Library at the Anna Arivalayam in Madras.

An incomplete list of individuals who have helped me at different stages of this project would likely be longer than the book itself. My family; my professors at Illinois and my other teachers; my friends and colleagues in different parts of the world who have listened to me, read drafts, discussed the literature and other issues, submitted to interviews, participated in panels and programs I organized, allowed me access to their work, and, most important, had faith in me—all must know how I treasure them. Above all, this book would not have been possible without those individuals, particularly in Colombo and Madras, who trusted me with their stories.

—*Swarna Rajagopalan*

1

National Integration as Community Building

Through the ages, from the polis in ancient Greece and the *janapada* (realm) in ancient India to modern colonies, empires, and spheres of influence, the scale of human collectives/collectivities has varied but the question has remained the same: How might one build a political community? In the context of the modern nation-state, the equivalent questions are, What does the project of national integration entail? What are the means whereby states might achieve this end? Which of these means would enable states to achieve integration without counterproductive consequences? What are the ethical limits to the desirability of this goal?

One commonplace about colonialism is that the units it carved out were unnatural in that they were neither consistent with previous boundaries nor coterminous with the "homelands" of ethnic groups or nations or clans. Decolonization created new states whose mandates exceeded previous experiences; the prerequisite to fulfilling these expanded mandates was integration at three levels: integration of territories, integration of administrations, and integration of the various peoples who lived in new territories and under new administrations. The last level of integration is the most difficult because it challenges groups' needs to remain separate and distinct, to retain the unique markers of their identities. The tension between the state's need for integration and the need of groups to preserve their identities furnishes the setting for this book.

India, Pakistan, and Sri Lanka provide the specific contexts in which the meaning and prospects of community building are considered. South Asia, or the Indian subcontinent, is a geographically distinct region, bound on two sides by sea and the other two by mountain ranges. The region has historically been distinct enough from its environs that entry has taken conscious effort (via the sea, the Khyber Pass, or the Silk Route). Nevertheless, travel into and around the subcontinent has forged a common civilization and several periods of shared history. The last of these was the British colonial period. The British Empire included all three contemporary states in this study, bequeathing to them a common law, common ideological influences, and the beginnings of an infrastructure that connected their peoples further.

India, Pakistan, and Sri Lanka gained independence in 1947–1948 under different circumstances. Although Indian independence followed what is usually described as a nonviolent struggle, this event was also accompanied by a movement for secession from the united British Indian state by Muslim-majority provinces. Therefore, the movement for the independence of Pakistan culminated in what remain the most traumatic riots in the living memory of people in the northern part of the subcontinent. Sri Lanka's independence was accomplished without a mass movement or a bloody transfer of power. In the half-century since the three countries left the British Empire, they have followed different trajectories, sometimes straying, and straying to different degrees, from the democratic path but always returning, again to different degrees. All three have experienced the same demands—poverty alleviation, decentralization or autonomy, and cultural recognition, to name a few. They have used a range of strategies to address these issues and met with varying degrees of success.

The perspectives adopted in this book are those of three communities within these states that have all been alienated from the state at different times and to different degrees. The spectrum they define, from relative integration (Tamils in India) to a combination of integration and distraction (Sindhis in Pakistan[1]) to seemingly irremediable alienation (Sri Lankan Tamils), enables us to compare the cases, arriving inductively at a variety of positions on the questions of national integration and, more broadly, community building. A reading of the state's own perspective would enable us to judge the success of its integrative enterprise as well as the efficacy of its strategies and tools on its terms. However, in this work, the views of opinion leaders from the constituent groups are the most important source for the inductively derived understanding of national integration. I ask what the terms are upon which they will become part of a community. Further, to what integrative strategies will they accede, and are there limits to the allegiance they will extend to the state? Arguably, the state should predicate integration on consideration of these questions if integration is to be sustainable and peaceful.

The rationale behind the adoption of this perspective is at first glance similar to that of the "subaltern studies" historians—to give voice to relatively disenfranchised and silenced sections of society or, in this case, constituents of a state (Guha and Spivak 1988; Guha 1997). However, this book cannot be identified with this "subaltern" view because respondents within the studied communities are elites. Adopting in this instance Paul Brass's view of ethnic politics as the instrument of the elite (Brass 1991a), I use interview responses, writings, and otherwise documented views of members of the opinion-making elite to determine the response of the community to the state and its vision as well as the vision that the community would favor.

There is more to this choice, however. The state's vision of itself and of the place and mutual relationships of its constituents is, in each of the cases studied, well-trodden ground.[2] Those who theorize the problem of community building and national integration are therefore better acquainted with this perspective, and naturally, it informs their theories. Here, both state-centered empirical analyses and efforts at building a theory of integration and community are exposed to evidence from another quarter—those who are being integrated. We are able to appraise the utility of existing theories against a simple, practical marker: Do the people who are supposed to be integrated actually think and act in line with prevalent theories?

As stated earlier, the cases selected also represent three points on a possible continuum of integration outcomes. The most current of the three cases marks the "least successful" end of this continuum. The struggle between the Sri Lankan state and the militant self-determination movement in the north of the island now appears to have approached a point of irremediable intractability, notwithstanding the promise every now and then of a breakthrough. Despair and uncertainty characterize every interaction and every relationship in Sri Lanka today. The other end of the continuum—success—is represented by the Indian case of the Dravida movement and its transformation from a secessionist movement to a partner in the central cabinet. In 1962, the demand for secession by the Dravida Munnetra Kazhagam (DMK) was regarded by the Indian Parliament as threat enough to warrant the introduction of and intense debate over the Sixteenth

Amendment to the constitution, which outlawed secessionist activity. After eloquently disputing the merits of the bill in Parliament, in late 1962 the leadership suspended secessionist activity and raised funds for the Indian state's defense of its frontiers in the war with China. A year later, the demand was dropped completely upon the passage of the constitutional amendment. In the thirty-odd years since, the DMK and its offshoots have established a stranglehold over the politics of the state of Tamil Nadu. They have been in the forefront of regional efforts to renegotiate center-state relations and are today partners in the central government.

The Pakistani case defines a middle point on this continuum. The Sindhis are neither partners in governance nor primary threats to the continuance of the Pakistani state. In the 1980s, the nationalist movement of the Sindhis acquired two "enemies"—the Punjabi-dominated Pakistani state and the Muhajirs, who, after having sought refuge in Sind in 1947, dominated Karachi's economy. The Sindhis have sought to redress the consequence of a major demographic change and have not been very effective in staking or winning their claims.

National Integration

From a study of the social science literature on the subject (Rajagopalan 1998), the constitutions of the three countries in the study (see Chapter 2, this book), and a compilation of interview responses (Rajagopalan 1997a), I have derived three definitions of integration:

- Integration is a process whereby the cooperation over time of the several creates a more or less singular entity that in turn facilitates further action and change and in which the several repose their allegiance to a greater or lesser degree.
- Integration is the state's goal of realizing its constitutional self-image.
- Integration is a process of coming together in attitude, memory, and interest. This process derives from and contributes to the development of constitutive individuals, groups, and units. The state bears the primary responsibility for directing the integrative process, which may involve a variety of relationships among the constituent groups and between those constituents and the collective.

What are the various ways in which the state community might be envisioned, and how do they affect prospects for integration? If the state's self-definition affects prospects for national integration, then what works better—the identity-blind approach or the identity-based approach? To what extent and in what ways might the state intervene in the process of national integration? The question of force haunts this political project and will lead us also to ask if there are limits to the desirability of this goal.

The discussion of state-led integration is premised on the recognition of an empirical reality—the omnipresence of the state. This premise does not preclude a normative discussion of if, when, and how a state should or should not intervene in the community-building process within its boundaries—and indeed whether any such project should be undertaken by any agency or functionary within the state. Should the state be involved in curriculum design? Can we even discuss integration outside the context of the state? If we can, what are the normative and empirical constraints of which we must be cognizant?

State Visions and State Identity

When South Asian history is discussed, one contentious issue is the treatment of minorities. Various periods in South Asian history are described in terms of *cultural synthesis* (the twelfth to fourteenth centuries in both India and Sri Lanka), *assimilation* (which accounted for the decline of Buddhism in India from around the eighth century C.E. onward), *syncretism* (notably 1556–1605, when Akbar was the ruling Mughal), and *tolerance* or *intolerance* (the reign of Maurya emperor Asoka in India and the Sri Lankan Kingdom of Kandy, on the one hand, and on the other, Aurangzeb's rule of India from 1608 to 1707). What do these terms mean? And why do we consider them problematic in the modern context but not quite so offensive when referring to the past?

Let us begin by considering the vision of the state. Integration is either the realization of a particular vision or the reconciliation of multiple visions. Favoring a particular vision invites an exclusionary outcome; the reconciliation of multiple visions is an inclusive process. Clifford Geertz (1973) refers to four patterns of social organization: (1) There are one or more minority groups and a single group is numerically and politically dominant; (2) a single group is politically but not numerically dominant; (3) no group is numerically or politically dominant; (4) one or more groups live across state boundaries. Myron Weiner lists assimilation and "unity in diversity" as the two strategies of integration generally used; R. A. Schermerhorn calls the same strategies assimilation and "sanctioned autonomy" (Weiner 1965; Schermerhorn 1978). Bashiruddin Ahmed adds a third strategy for managing diversity: segregation (Ahmed 1979). For this discussion, I consider the five ways states/societies manage diversity: segregation, hegemony, assimilation, synthesis, and pluralism.

Segregation and Hegemony

It is hard to assign the term *integration* to an exclusionary perspective, which includes the establishment of both segregationist and hegemonic sociopolitical orders. Segregation is, by definition, not integration. However, when segregated groups live in one polity, as they did in apartheid South Africa, the state has succeeded in establishing and maintaining such an order with no claims to integration. Hegemonic patterns are integrative even if they lack the consensual base of other forms of integration. Indeed, from the perspective of the state, one must concede that stripped of its pejorative overtones, this type of integration is both the easiest to establish and to maintain in the short run. This is not to say that it is the most lasting or the most deep-rooted form of integration. The hegemonic vision could either be propagated by a relatively powerful aggregate within the polity or created and supported by a state in its quest for nationhood. The latter is the type of project undertaken by new multination states whose borders have never before had their present form and whose history does not yield a natural and obvious identity. One might describe the former Union of Soviet Socialist Republics as a polity integrated on the basis of a hegemonizing, or exclusionary, vision.

Assimilation, synthesis, and pluralism are the three varieties of inclusive visions. All three involve the reconciliation of multiple visions, differing in the degree to which the aggregates integrated remain distinct.

Assimilation

The line between hegemonic and assimilative visions is thin, and herein emerge all the objections to assimilation. Assimilation resembles hegemony in that they both require that other identities be subordinated to the one favored by the prevalent dispensation. But whereas the hegemonic vision or identity could be a new one, to which adherents are recruited, the assimilative impulse usually derives from an entity already in existence in a culture or society. The controversies surrounding assimilation stem from two issues: one, whose vision will dominate, and two, the role of the state in securing assimilation.

Historically, as many people have been assimilated as have emerged as distinct, and there is no linear imperative to this process. What is new and contentious is the conscious role of the state. Older polities may have favored assimilation but, more often than not, lacked the power to direct the process. Today, states have this power, and when they are identified with one or another section of society, the assimilative impulse is hard to resist. On the continuum of state involvement, one might plot two levels of involvement: first, where integration is regarded as part of a state's work, and second, where the state is itself identified with some vision.

Picking one vision over others would be contentious enough without the identification of the state with that vision. If assimilation is one form of reconciliation, then the involvement of the state alters the prospects for that reconciliation. On the positive side, the state may be a credible and stable guarantor of what incentives there are for being assimilated. On the negative side, the state lends the specter of coercion to the assimilative process, blurring the line between the assertion of hegemony and self-conscious assimilation. Further, resistance to assimilation comes to mean resistance to the state, meriting all the authoritative responses the state can summon. Resistance and response escalate rapidly into a spiral of hostility.

The *Random House Webster's College Dictionary* (1992) definitions of the verb *assimilate* are "1. To take in and incorporate as one's own; absorb; 2. To bring into conformity with the customs, attitudes, etc., of a dominant culture group or national culture; 3. To convert (ingested food) to substances suitable for incorporation into the body and its tissues; 4. To cause to resemble; make similar; 5. To compare; liken; 6. To modify (a sound) by assimilation; 7. To be or become absorbed; 8. To conform or adjust to the customs, attitudes, etc., of a dominant cultural group; 9. (of ingested food) to be converted into the substance of the body; 10. To bear a resemblance; 11. . . . become modified by assimilation; 12. Something that is assimilated." The array is quite telling. The same dictionary defines *assimilation* as "1. The act or process of assimilating or the state or condition of being assimilated;

. . . 3. the merging of cultural traits from previously distinct cultural groups." The last is not very different from synthesis.

The range of definitions suggests that there is, within the category of assimilation, quite a range of processes and outcomes.

Absorption. Absorption is here defined as the assimilation of smaller groups into a larger or more powerful one where the relationship is more or less unidirectional in the shorter historical context. Stated in its starkest form, absorption is what distinctive minority groups fear most. Instances of total absorption are as hard to find as instances of perfect synthesis. However, the response of caste society in India toward invading or immigrating communities might be offered as one. Typically, these communities were simply adopted as a new subcaste within the existing structure, providing them with an entrée into the social setting, whose customs and beliefs they came to adopt over a period of time. The creation of the Rajput caste as a consequence of the absorption of the Huna invaders is one example.

Mutual influence. Assimilation of smaller groups into a larger or more powerful one is not always strictly unidirectional. Indeed, the relationship is more often one of give-and-take with the larger group being considerably less transformed than the smaller. Instances of this kind of assimilation are easier to find. The absorption by Brahminism of Buddhism is classic in the context of South Asian history. Buddhism in India virtually disappeared, but not before several of its features were absorbed into Brahminical Hinduism, from philosophical doctrines to the inclusion of the Buddha in lists of Vishnu's incarnations.

Cultural permeation. Sometimes there is assimilation by society at large of the culture and practices of a smaller group that may or may not be politically powerful. South Asian history is replete with instances of this kind of assimilation. Every group has contributed to the evolution of a unique subcontinental form. The Jains are an example of a group that has not been consistently politically powerful. The only instances of Jain political power are the abdication of Chandragupta Maurya and a brief influence in the courts of the south. Jain contributions in other areas, however, are undeniable and unique. As an affluent group, the Jains have been art patrons, to say nothing of their contribution to the economy of the subcontinent. They have also been influential in Indian philosophy, and their faith played an important role in entrenching in the civilization the principles of nonviolence and the practice of vegetarianism.

It is much more commonplace to think of a politically powerful, though numerically smaller, group wielding great influence on the process of assimilation in a society. This is the nightmare of the majority. Hindutvavadi Hindus (that is, those who identify with the rhetoric of the Hindu right wing) and conservative Sinhala Buddhists both fear that their identity will be overrun by a minority that they perceive as powerful beyond its size. Perceptions apart, the groups they fear are in fact political players and players of some significance. Brahmins, Sufis, Arabs, Europeans, and Greeks are all examples of small groups influencing assimilationist outcomes in South Asia.

Synthesis

Synthesis is harder to accomplish and easier to sustain than assimilation. By synthesis, I mean the arrival at a composite, syncretist alternative vision or reality. The problem is that whereas synthesis suggests a process, arrival implies a finality that is hard to establish historically. The only way synthesis works is if we acknowledge the tragic nature of the quest and allow for infinite effort with little prospect of fruition, of arrival. That is to say, synthesis is an example of infinite, but not inevitable, progress. Thus the role of the state is considerably restricted in the process of synthesis as a form of integration. If the state intervenes to promote a particular synthetic vision, we are talking in fact about a hegemonic vision.

Synthesis is defined in the same dictionary as "1. *The combining of the constituent elements of separate material or abstract entities into a single or unified entity* . . . ; 2. a complex formed by combining; 3. The forming or building of a more complex chemical substance or compound from elements or simpler compounds" (italics added). Synthesis is an act of putting together or constructing something did not exist prior to the synthesis. In Hegelian dialectic, the mutual opposition of the thesis and antithesis is resolved through a proposition—a synthesis—that reconciles them and represents a move forward in the evolution of an idea.

In the context of national integration, synthesis means the creation of a new political community through the coming together of constituent groups and individuals. This community must be larger than the sum of its constituents and have a form somewhat different from their mere aggregation. To borrow from chemistry, perfect synthesis involves the creation of a compound community where the building blocks may be difficult to discern, if discernable at all. The Indian constitution pretends that such a community resulted with the formation of the Indian state. The amalgamated political community of Deutsch and others (1957) is also based on this idea. The entity formed thus sits outside of or apart from all other relationships, affinities, and allegiances in society.

Individuals I interviewed in India and Sri Lanka did not, however, favor this model. If they are from a minority, it threatens the survival of their identity group. If they are from a majority community, they are offended by the equalization implicit in the process; that is, they find offensive the process of reducing all the components into constituents who are equal by virtue of equal obliteration in the creation of the new entity. (An analogy that comes to mind is hydrogen molecules that are resentful of the equal status of oxygen in their compound water and would rather water resembled the greater contributor of the two—in other words, that oxygen assimilate!)

Pluralism

Although most of the people interviewed defined integration in terms of assimilation or synthesis, it seems that even given their own historical narratives, there are other paths. A pluralistic vision is one in which diversity is celebrated and diverse groups within the polity enjoy autonomy and the right to be distinct. The "unity in diversity" slogan that one hears all over South Asia sometimes refers to a pluralistic vision. Pluralism is at once the simplest of the visions to achieve and the hardest to sustain. It is simple to achieve in that it is really an acceptance by the polity of society as it is. It is hard to sustain without changing the nature and the rules of the political game altogether. If politics is the capture, the shaping and sharing, of power, then in a diverse society such a capture is impossible without the formation of coalitions or the attempt to subordinate others to the interest of one section of society. If politics is an instrument for the achievement of particular goals, the political process in a diverse society involves constantly building and reworking a consensus as to what those goals are. A pluralistic vision affords stopping short of perfect unanimity and at the same time involves constantly guarding against alienating those who do not entirely agree. The state in a pluralistic polity is a facilitator, playing a minimal role in those areas of a citizen's life that do not affect large numbers of people or the pluralistic idea itself. Requiring a fragile balance, pluralism ironically requires more skilled leadership than any other integrative vision.[3]

If multiethnic states have more in common with empires than with the ideal nation-state, it might be useful to examine the policies of several historical empires. On a continuum, one might range traditional empires toward one end and colonial empires at another, although there are cases that defy this generalization. At the assimilationist, colonial end, I would place the French and Portuguese colonial empires, which actively encouraged two types of assimilation. The French sought in their empire to inculcate their cultural system in the people they colonized. In Goa, the Portuguese encouraged intermarriage so that racial differences between conquerors and conquered would be diminished. The British, less inclined to mingle with the "natives," nevertheless consciously adopted an Anglicist education policy.

The category of traditional empires includes such varied imperial arrangements as the Maurya, Achæmanid, Sassanid, Roman, Greek, and Ottoman empires. All had one thing in common: They left in place local belief systems and personal laws. Diversity within these empires was undiminished except to the extent that membership in such a large common market permitted movement of goods, services, and ideas across vast continental stretches. Pluralism, a modern-sounding idea, underpins the relationship between groups and the state in traditional empires. Pluralism is the coming together of more-or-less equal entities into a unit that is equal to the sum of its parts. The idea of a pluralistic security community captures the experience of traditional empires.

At the level of the contemporary nation-state, in so many cases not different in size or diversity from the traditional empires, pluralism seems to take the form of unity in diversity. The constitution acknowledges the existence of differences within society, and the socialization process weaves this acknowledgment into the image that citizens learn to have of their state. Beyond that, the state intervenes as and when needed in the politics of identity and not much more than that. Increasing state involvement makes groups restive. Pluralism, although it seems an ideal system, is also the most difficult of the integration approaches to pursue because the state is made up of people, and the people who run the state at every level tend to reflect the imbalances and inequities in relationships that prevail in society. It is almost impossible for the entire state machinery to speak and act as one and impartially.

Of our three cases, India is the one that comes closest to favoring this ideal because the state does not identify with any group. But the fictional quality of this whitewashed, aloof Indian state has become increasingly clear to most Indians: In Punjab and elsewhere, the central government has played groups against each other; it has promoted Hindi over other languages, and during communal riots, local police forces have acted in a partisan manner, as in Meerut and Bhiwandi. The state, being made up of the same imperfect creatures as any other human association, is doomed to repeat the same mistakes as they and on a much larger scale.

Whether the state identifies with one or another community or sees itself as neutral is of paramount importance, as this orientation drives its orchestration of the integration process and affects how other collectives within the polity articulate their visions. Exclusive strategies such as segregation or hegemony follow from an ethnically identified state. Neutrality facilitates inclusive strategies such as assimilation, synthesis, and pluralism. Exclusive strategies are likely to spawn exclusivist responses; inclusive strategies are likely to spawn both kinds. The state's role seems most crucial in the two kinds of visions that are most different in degree of inclusivity: The state is required to maintain the boundaries of a segregated society, and if pluralism is not to be segregation, not mere sufferance of others, the state is required to constantly facilitate an amicable interaction between the distinct collectivities that make up its society.

State Intervention in National Integration

Like most nonprofit but costly undertakings, the project of national integration usually falls to the state, which has both the greatest interest and the greatest wherewithal (in terms of power and resources). National integration is also typically a self-conscious project, and the state is its most self-conscious promoter. The state expresses and propagates its self-image through an almost infinite range of media and tools. Two of these—the teaching and writing of history and internal territorial organization—furnish the basis of my analysis of state intervention in national integration as I attend to the dialogue (or lack thereof) between alternative visions (the visions of the state and those it would integrate).

Several interview respondents in India alluded to other effective influences in the creation of an Indian identity. Hindi cinema, cricket, a common market, and a common polity were repeatedly mentioned, in that order.[4] (The freedom struggle and the "values of the civilization" were also mentioned by respondents as unifying factors.)

Of these, the first three are largely outside the realm of state activity. The state assumes a social interventionist role and so intervenes in them to some extent. It selectively finances the production of cinema, taxes the sale of cinema tickets, reviews or censors the films, and then judges them for state awards. Government officials also monitor the activity of cricket selection boards. The movement of foreign teams and the travels of the national team are inextricably tied to state affairs. The common market operates under rules written by the state, is facilitated by state-built infrastructure, is secured by state enforcement and security agencies, and, in recent years, has benefited enormously from the access provided first by state-owned media networks and now by cable-satellite networks. None of these was consciously intended by the state to further integration, but integration has been an irreversible consequence. The common polity provides the overarching norms and rules of the process. It should be stressed that no one referred to the old official Films Division documentaries or the Directorate of Audio-Visual Publicity's propaganda or the National Integration books produced by the Publications Division. There was apparently nothing as inspiring here as the scores of examples that came up from the private-sector-produced popular culture.[5]

In Sri Lanka, the discussion of national integration never strayed very far from the state arena. It seemed that the state had completely monopolized the national integration business. I saw very little evidence of a popular culture that bridged the gap between communities. Cricket was divisive regarding ethnic representation on the team. The economy has not grown enough to play a role in the forging of interdependent links. A language policy that has segregated Sinhalese and Tamil children in the same school is likely to hamper the development of shared memories and common associations. This policy is also likely to promote segregation in the economy as well.

This is not to say that India has achieved national integration and Sri Lanka has failed. The Indian case is viewed through the lens of one community. What the comparison yielded was the unexpected finding that at the level that it seems to matter, the Indian state has succeeded, whereas the Sri Lankan state is still floundering—the Indian state has succeeded in failing to directly intervene in the process of integration! By so failing, it has escaped the fate of the Sri Lankan state's strategies, which have had consequences disastrous beyond expectation ("Trying to bring in integration from above is not going to work" [I1][6]).

The writing and teaching of history is an important expression of the idea of the state. The state and schools are traditionally considered important agents of political socialization. Where states run schools and write syllabi and textbooks, the school system becomes a very powerful tool for the process of national integration. The idea of the state is writ across several traditional school disciplines: history, civics, community studies, literature, and classes that promote specific moral codes. History is selected here as the focus of inquiry because when the idea of the state is contested, history is almost always evoked to substantiate this contestation. Thus we need to know the idea of the state that standard or official histories promote and how that version of history affects middle and high school children, who in their early teens are just becoming aware of their role in a larger community. How does this history portray the relationship between the whole and its parts, that is, the polity as a whole and the unit in question? What consequences does this portrayal have for the project of national integration?

As constitutional and other national visions are apt under certain circumstances to acquire a territorial dimension, the internal structure of the state is the second point of intervention studied here. Unitary or federal, most states have more than one level of government. How these levels and jurisdictions are defined depends on the state's view of itself as a whole. The negotiation of the basis of unit demarcation and the politics of that demarcation are thus also negotiations about the identity of the state. In the attempt to recast itself in a national form, the state regards contestation of its internal structure as gravely as it does contestation of its external boundaries. What basis of internal structure is most conducive to a reconciliation of multiple visions?

Normative Issues in the Integration Process

Actually, national integration is a false historical project. The project of national integration came to most of the late developing societies as the twentieth century model of the modern nation-state. It has a lot of assumptions about the nation, about sovereignty, about territoriality, political obligation, but I don't think that model of nation-state and project of national integration is valid any more. (S19)

I'm not very sure. Like you, I am suspicious of all the larger narratives. The nation itself would contain in it lots of inequalities and disparities. (S4)

It [national integration] is the integration of the Indian middle class. (I1)

National integration as it exists today, it is definitely a construct of the Indian capitalists, especially the northern ones. And in the whole shaping of modern India, its ideological role was played by Brahmins and Brahminism. (I57)

When you say national integration, my memory, my powers of language don't go beyond "Mera Bharat Mahaan" stuff that I've been watching on TV for the past decade or so almost . . . all those wonderful pink-cheeked heroines, postmen, what-not from all over India. Mera Bharat Mahaan! That's the only image of national integration that sort of visually comes to mind. . . . It is almost as though one is being told that there are all these wonderful people in different parts of India, be they cricket stars or Olympic champions or film heroes and heroines and all this wonderful music that seems to flow from one end of Bharat to the other. So the sum total of which is equal to Mera Bharat Mahaan, which is equal to India is one—the whole unhappy nation under god, so to speak. (I78)

Why, indeed, should integration be regarded as a goal? What are the benefits derived from it and are they reasonable given the costs? What costs are people willing to pay for those benefits?

The benefits of integration are easily listed in economic and administrative terms. Justifying integrative arrangements that involve any one group giving up anything—land, identity, culture, resources, power—is more difficult. One must ask in those circumstances who pays and who benefits. Further, who determines whether either the costs or benefits are justified? The state's task is not enviable.

No discussion of national integration is complete without a discussion of the role of force—by the state, by groups in society, or by outside powers—in its achievement or maintenance. Charles Tilly wrote in 1975: "War makes the state and the state makes war" (Tilly 1975a: 42). As his analyses of European history have showed, the foundation of the European nation-state lay in the promise of protection and security. In return, the state received tributes and allegiance. By this argument, the continuance of conflict becomes a precondition for the continuance of the state. Over time, the state's continuance becomes an end in itself, and the state, by the same argument, justifies the use of force to ensure its survival. In doing so, it becomes the instrument of those who dominate it.

The role of force haunted this project long before field research commenced. A variety of considerations led to its elimination from the formal research design, and the circumstances that prevailed in Sri Lanka, particularly at the time the interviews there were conducted (February-March 1996), made it seem impolitic to press the question in every case. In India, the separatism of the Dravida movement never acquired proportions such that either the state or the separatists needed to use violence. Still, analytical, political, and ethical imperatives make it impossible not to at least consider this problem.

Indeed, on both the question of coercion to achieve integration and the question of the desirability of integration, just taking the moral high ground and denouncing both is not as productive as it is tempting. People have to live their lives in the shadow of states, and in some dependence on states. States are imperfect human fabrications, but they are useful enough, and powerful enough, that denouncing them will not make them go away. The question is, How are we to construct states we can live in and live with? How are we to define and participate in the integration process in a manner that will not rebound on us? The questions of coercion and desirability are also particularly hard to answer in general terms because at their heart lie the issues of legitimacy and identity.

The Polity-People (State-Nation)
Dialectic in South Asia

The evolution of the state and the nation shows different patterns in the three countries featured in this study. Geographically finite, British control over the island of Ceylon (Sri Lanka) established the putative state in its colonial form. The consciousness of nationality was aroused in three different collectives—the Sri Lankan elite, the Sinhala Buddhists, and the Tamils. With the last two, this consciousness arose in response to the colonial and (Christian) missionary presence and then developed into a dialectical relationship with each other. Both seemed to evolve largely indifferent to the national imagination of the elite (although this was less true of the Sinhalese nationalists), to which power was ultimately transferred. The relationship between the state and the Sri Lankan elite remains close. As a creation and instrument of this class, the state is to that degree alien to the others, but the imperatives of majoritarian democracy have closed the gap between this elite creation and the majority Sinhalese nation. Thus the Sinhalese nation focuses its statist aspirations on the Sri Lankan state. The Tamil nation has been left out of this evolving relationship and, partly in response, partly in retaliation, has come to focus its hopes on the achievement of Eelam—a Tamil state in the northeastern part of the island. When the Sri Lankan state-nation has attempted to bridge the gap between itself and the Tamil nation, those who demanded a separate state out of retaliation have responded positively. Other Tamils demand separatism independent of all other developments and remain alienated.

Pakistan shows another pattern. The definition of its national base evolved over several decades and culminated in the demand for a separate state of Pakistan. En route, the leaders of this nation debated first their place in the larger society of colonial India and then different forms of representation that might benefit them. The nation was, in part, religiously defined, and the state sought a homeland on that basis: The new state of Pakistan would be a home for the Muslims of South Asia. Accordingly, a massive transfer of population accompanied the transfer of power to the state. Upon its founding, though, differences over the nature of the state surfaced. Some sought to establish a liberal state with a Muslim majority; others wanted a state based on the ideals and laws of Islam. Differences over the interpretation of both, combined with the fact that those who were powerful in the new state were leaders who had emigrated from the heartland provinces of British India, alienated sections of the population that had always lived in the regions that were now Pakistan. At least two of these had a national consciousness that predated the Pakistan idea—the Sindhis and the Bengalis. Although this consciousness had been subordinated to the ideal of a Pakistani nation-state, the subordination was too tenuous to be sustained in less-than-ideal circumstances. The Pakistani state began to adopt the language and symbols of the immigrant (Muhajir) elite as its own and in the bargain alienated the Bengali majority population and the Sindhis, the older communities of the frontier such as the Baloch and the Pathans, and finally, those for whom the state did not adequately conform to the laws of Islam. The Bengali nation, favored by geographic separation and a neighbor willing to assist, was able to secede. Sindhi national consciousness found two directions—separatism and nativism. The nativist grievance against the Muhajirs fueled the separatist strain, but the rise of Sindhi leaders in the federal arena took the intensity out of the separatist demand. As these movements were forming, the demand by the Muhajir middle class for territorial recognition as denizens of Karachi turned the tables on Sindhi nativism, resulting in the pitched battles of the 1980s and 1990s in Karachi. Muhajir ethnic consciousness now challenges Sindhi nationalism far more than Sindhi nationalism does the Pakistani state. The Pakistan case seems to illustrate the process of infinite regression that scholars associate with nationalist self-determination.

It is hard to narrate the interaction between state and nation in India because for the most part they seem to operate in parallel, unrelated to each other. But of course, this is not the case. For ease of narration, they will be treated separately here. Although the Indian subcontinent has a long political history with many types of polities, there was never anything like an Indian state with firm territorial limits until 1947. Further, none of the polities resembled the modern Indian state in terms of their territorial jurisdiction. The colonial state structure was not coterminous with the borders of the contemporary state, which includes nominally sovereign principalities that were separate from British India. The Indian state ideal finds its geographic markers in the peninsula and the two mountain ranges that frame the northeast and the northwest—the Himalayas and the Hindu Kush, respectively. These are also the borders described in ancient Indian texts. The corroboration of the texts lends credence to the argument of those who define the Indian nation in terms of the early Vedic and post-Vedic civilization of the subcontinent. The state ideal does not coincide, however, with the modern state, which stops short in the northwest and misses part of the Ganges delta in the east.

The spread of Western education, the growth of an administrative class, and the rise of an English-language press coincided with the rise of vernacular presses and movements for social reform and cultural renaissance. As a result, the idea of the Indian nation and the Bengali, Sindhi, Marathi, and Tamil nations originated at the same time. In India, much like in Sri Lanka, there was a small, westernized elite that fantasized about rising through the ranks in the British Empire. These elites used new British ideas such as liberalism and utilitarianism to seek greater representation and inclusion in the administration of the colony. The second generation of nationalists of this conviction articulated these demands in terms of another European idea—the nation.

They identified themselves as a nation and, using the idea of national self-determination, formulated and articulated their demand for independence from the British. The goal of Indian nationality was rarely contested by the adherents of this school—let us call it the Congress—but two interpretations evolved of the basis of this nationality. The first located Indian nationality in an empirically real feeling of unity in diversity and the other in the Hindu tradition.

Indian nationalism developed in parallel to the nationalism of other communities. Indeed, different works by the same writers (Bankim Chandra Chatterjee and Subramania Bharati, for instance) celebrated both. An examination of Tamil nationalism reveals that although it arose around the same time and sometimes had adherents in common with Indian nationalism, the two were mutually exclusive; it appears from the Tamil case that the evolution of such mutually exclusive strands of Indian and other national identities may be attributed to class and caste difference. This divisiveness based on caste is also substantiated by the distance in Maharashtra between the depressed classes and the Dalit movements on the one hand and other caste groups that are involved in either Congress-related or Hindutvavadi politics (both oriented toward the Indian state) on the other. Among Tamils, the equation of Brahmin-Sanskrit-Congress on the one hand and non-Brahmin–Tamil–Dravida on the other simplified the difference between the two nationalities. This simple (and simplistic) polarization precludes reconciliation, let alone coexistence, within the boundaries of a state.

The identification of pan-Indian nationalism with an existing state that encompasses adherents to other nationalities and identities orders these communities hierarchically. Those who identify with an Indian nation identify with the state, although they differ on the nature, basis, and purpose of that nation-state. They favor a community of either modern citizens or coreligionists, as outlined in the following section. Those who identify with other nations, which are regarded by Indian nationalists as regions or subnational groups, must either seek their own state or redefine the Indian state to be a community of communities. The linguistic basis of unit demarcation in India is a compromise between these two national orientations. Where the lower and intermediate castes have been unable to assume the form of a nation (almost everywhere except Tamil Nadu), they have met the fate of the depressed classes and Dalits. They lack the bargaining power that nationalist rhetoric appropriates, and they are unable to compete with the nations with which they share territory. To them, two options remain vis-à-vis the state—to forsake it altogether or to advocate a universe of organic, self-sustaining communities, a possibility discussed later in the chapter. The first is not a realistic option and the last is not easy to realize.

Given the modernity of both state and national forms of the collective or community, chronological comparisons between the two are not very useful. In all three cases studied, ideas of the polity (state) and ideas of the people (nation) have evolved and been manifested in conversation with each other.

South Asian Ideas on Community

What constitutes the bases of community or the foundations of political organization is one of the oldest subjects of political inquiry. Both South Asian and Western (read Euro-American) thinkers had an interest in this question, although they placed different values on the community.[7] Regardless of the historical context of the discussions, scholars have tended to read them as though they were located at the level of the (national) state.

This book is organized around the central question of community building. Inasmuch as the question of community is central to politics, the contemporary fields whose concerns are related address this question partially, variously, and, sometimes, at cross-purposes. Political development (Deutsch 1961; Pye and Verba 1965; Huntington 1968; Binder et al. 1971; Weiner 1965; Jacob and Toscano 1964), nationalism (Kohn 1951; Anderson 1991; Geertz 1963), security (Buzan 1991; Waever et al. 1993), political socialization (Coleman 1965; Greenstein 1965; Sigel 1970), political geography (Sack 1980; Paddison 1983a, 1983b; Sack 1986; Johnston, Knight, and Kofman 1988; Hooson 1994), and other bodies of literature offer specific insights into parts of this vast human enterprise but are each an inadequate foothold for viewing the phenomenon comprehensively. Partially to redress the problem that these works are limited in scope, partially to rectify the effects of a predominantly Euro-American perspective, and partially so that this analysis takes cognizance of the working visions that grow out of the interaction between historical learning and exposure to philosophical discourses, I sidestep the conventional academic literature review to survey instead the ideological hybrids that arose in the nineteenth and twentieth centuries among the South Asian elite.

The nationalist movements of South Asia were products of the colonial experience in more ways than one. Their leaders were creations of the colonizer—middle- and upper-class professionals educated in the English style, exposed to Western ideas and ideals, dependent on the colonial economy for a livelihood. Although the movements may be broadly categorized as those focused on socioreligious reform and revival on the one hand and those with a more self-consciously political agenda on the other, all parts of the Indian nationalist movement were reactive to the presence of the West in India at the turn of the nineteenth century (Chatterjee 1982). The first category of movements adopted elements of Western religions in their reforming zeal—rejection of idolatry, selection of one or another book as the fundamental text, establishment of clerical orders—and co-opted ideas from the West with regard to the status of women and the caste system. The second category of movements began by petitioning the colonial government for greater inclusion of Indians in its administration and ended by asking for an independent nation-state. The rhetoric and practice of South Asian nationalism showed the influence of the liberal ideas of John Stuart Mill and Jeremy Bentham in the petitions for more representation and for greater involvement by the government in public welfare, the dialectical materialism of Karl Marx and Friedrich Engels in the economic critiques of colonialism, the ideas of Henry David Thoreau and John Ruskin in Mohandas Karamchand Gandhi's techniques of resistance, and the nationalism that had swept through Europe in the nineteenth century with the growing demand for self-determination. European domination was ultimately hoisted by its own petard.

The particular forms that these ideas took show a synthesis between the European and the South Asian. Historians and biographers have shown this synthesis repeatedly in the lives of personages as removed from each other as Gandhi and Arumuga Navalar, Swami Vivekananda and Mohammed Ali Jinnah, Muhammad Iqbal and S.W.R.D. Bandaranaike. To look at just one case, we know that Gandhi was deeply influenced equally by the Vaishnavite and Jain traditions, with which he grew up, and by the writings of Leo Tolstoy, Thoreau, and John Ruskin. His ideas of nonviolent resistance bear the impress of both these worlds, although he was adept at expressing them in terms that were comprehensible to those who had access to only one of them. Gandhi's ideas about labor, trusteeship, community life, and interpersonal relations drew as much from the Bhagavad Gita as they did from any European tradition. At the same time, as a lawyer, he was able to use and subvert Anglo-Saxon principles of fairness and justice to the ends of his campaign, first for integration in South Africa and then for independence in India.

If the nationalist movements of South Asia fall along various points of an ideological spectrum, several visions of the community may be identified, almost all of them modernizing visions. Bhikhu Parekh says there were three kinds of attitudes toward modernization (1995: 23–25). Adapting these somewhat to my purpose, I have identified four visions for the national community in India, Pakistan, and Sri Lanka. The groups are based on ideal types, and two caveats are called for: (1) to outline an ideal type of vision does not suggest any expectation that it was implemented or realized; (2) all ideal types obfuscate a range of differences within the categories themselves as well as overlap, inconsistency, and changes in position. The first three are modern visions—the state is central to them, and so are its purposes of economic growth and expansion of power.

A Community of Modern Citizens

A community of modern citizens was the vision of the first leaders of the three states. The founding of a state was the culmination of the right to self-determination of the peoples it led. This state would be the instrument of development and modernization, and by this process, the narrow, parochial, and irrational loyalties of its citizens would be replaced by civic loyalty based on modern rights and equality. Nehru, Jinnah, and Don Stephen Senanayake held this view to different degrees. In Jinnah's words,

> Now, if we want to make this great State of Pakistan happy and prosperous we should wholly and solely concentrate on the well-being of the people, and especially of the masses and the poor. If you will work in cooperation, forgetting the past, burying the hatchet you are bound to succeed. If you change your past and work together in a spirit that every one of you, no matter what relations he had with you in the past, no matter what is his colour, caste or creed, is first, second, and last a citizen of this State with equal rights, privileges and obligations, there will be no end to the progress you will make.
>
> I cannot emphasize it too much. We should begin to work in that spirit and in course of time all these angularities of the majority and minority communities, the Hindu community and the Muslim com-

munity—because even as regards Muslims you have Pathans, Punjabis, Shias, Sunnis and so on and among the Hindus you have Brahmans, Visahnavas (sic), Khatris, also Bengalees, Madrasis, and so on—will vanish.

. . . We are starting with this fundamental principle that we are all citizens and equal citizens of one State.

. . . Now, I think that we should keep that in front of us as our ideal and you will find that in course of time Hindus would cease to be Hindus and Muslims would cease to be Muslims, not in the religious sense, because that is the personal faith of each individual, but in the political sense as citizens of the State. (Jinnah 1950: 3–4)

Of the three leaders mentioned, only Nehru was able to enshrine this idea in the constitution that was adopted by his country, and for a long time, this view had currency among the elite. Jinnah did not live long enough to ensure that his perspective informed constitutional design, and in the case of Senanayake, who also died soon after independence, the divergence from this vision began in his tenure with the disenfranchisement of the plantation Tamils.

A Community of Coreligionists

To those who envisioned a community based on adherence to a religious belief system, the religious values reflected by the polity should be determined by the religion of the majority. Therefore, every religious community should have a place of its own.

There are actually two variations on this theme, and the difference between them is important. The first articulation of such a view had political dimensions and consequences but not exactly a political agenda. The social and religious reform movements of the nineteenth century that arose in every religious community as a response to Western education, missionary activity, and, not least, the attempt by the British to reform Indian society were the first to call on their communities as united by religion. Their articulations of what was wrong, what needed change, who should be responsible for change, and how they should effect change, as well as the relatively monolithic communities they evoked, all bore the impress of their European other. Dayanand Saraswati and Arumuga Navalar among the Hindus in India and Ceylon/Sri Lanka, respectively; Anagarika Dharmapala among the Ceylonese/Sri Lankan Buddhists; and Sir Sayyad Ahmed Khan among

Indian Muslims, for instance, wanted to recast their communities in this mode.

> This bright, beautiful island was made into a Paradise by the Aryan Sinhalese before its destruction was brought about by the barbaric vandals. Its people did not know irreligion. The pagan beliefs of monotheism and diabolic polytheism were unknown to the people. Christianity and polytheism are responsible for the vulgar practices of killing animals, stealing, prostitution, licentiousness, lying and drunkenness. . . . This ancient, historic, refined people, under the diabolism of vicious paganism, introduced by the British administrators, ignorant of the first principles of the natural laws of evolution, have cut down primeval forests to plant tea; have introduced opium, ganja, whisky, arrack and other alcoholic poisons; have opened saloons and drinking taverns in every village; have killed all industries and made the people indolent. (Dharmapala 1965: 482)

The second articulation was a more political one. Its point of departure was the view that differences between the values of one's community and others are more or less irreconcilable. More outward-looking than the reform movements, this vision sought to assert different identities, making the case for separateness—in representation, in terms of greater autonomy, as a claim to sovereignty—from other communities. Majoritarians with this vision insisted on the assertion of their dominant status, it being incumbent upon other communities to assimilate or accept domination. Where the community in question was not in the majority, majoritarians sought separation of that community but under the domination of the larger group. The range of views in this second, more political articulation of the coreligionist vision is represented by Vinayak Damodar "Veer" Savarkar and Madhavrao Sadashiv Golwalkar; Iqbal, Rahmat Ali, and Jinnah; and Gunadasa Amarasekara and Nalin de Silva of the Jathika Chintanaya school.[8]

> You have to be a citizen of your own community and country before you profess to become a world citizen. It is the *Jathika Chinthanaya* that would give you your identity on which alone you may be able to build a world identity if the latter is to mean anything. . . . A nation will have to maintain its identity of *Jathika Chinthanaya* before it becomes a part of a global village. . . . A nation if it is to progress and work out its own destiny, will have to have its own *Jathika Chinthanaya*. (Amarasekara 1991: 13)

The red herring has been the epithet we used—Sinhala Buddhist. This epithet was used only to show the main components that have gone into its formation. It was only a statement of historical fact; the exposition of the background—the milieu that nurtured this *Chinthanaya*. . . . Our assumption that the main components of the Jathika Chinthanaya are Sinhala Buddhist in origin by no means ignores or under-estimates the fact that there are contributions to it by the Hindu-Tamil culture over thousands of years, and even the Christian culture (if that term could be used) over the last few hundred years. (Amarasekara 1991: 4)

A Community (or not) of Consenting Communities

Not very different in some ways from the previous category, the basic unit here is a community defined by ethnicity, language, caste, race, or region. It is different from the category based on a common religious belief system because adherents cannot call upon ideological differences as a basis for separation.[9] Thus the self-assertion of a unit and its call for separation are based on historical and socioeconomic differences and on political grievances. At a certain moment in its history this community could claim the status of a nation and, hence, the right to self-determination. This claim takes many forms, from special rights to provincial autonomy to statehood. For those who hold this vision, the state is legitimate only when it is a community of communities or an association of communities. Any infringement on the distinctive and separate status of each group or culture contributes to the delegitimation of the state. It is assumed that the ideal situation for each community is to have its own state, and the community is by way of a compromise effected in deference to history, geography, or economics. Instances of this vision, labeled variously as cultural nationalism, subnationalism, parochialism, and "fissiparous tendencies," are legion and are promulgated by leaders such as E. V. Ramasami for Dravida nationalism in India, Sheikh Mujibur Rehman and Nazrul Islam for Bengali nationalism in East Pakistan, G. M. Syed for Sindhi nationalism in (West) Pakistan, Sheikh Abdullah in Kashmir (India), and the Eelamists in Sri Lanka. In the words of a follower of E. V. Ramasami:

The entire Sub-continent of India cannot be ruled from Delhi by a few Aryan autocrats. We want India to be a Commonwealth or Confederation consisting of free States. What Dr. Nair and Sir

Theagaroya visualised in 1916 was that South India and North India should each have a Federal Government comprising autonomous States based on linguistic affinity or homogeneity, and that the Defence, Foreign policy, etc., of these two Federations should vest in a common Confederation or Commonwealth. (The Laputan Flapper 1959)

A Universe of Organic, Self-Sustaining Communities

Placing the accent on the primacy of small, local communities and self-government, proponents of this vision are the only ones in this discussion to resist the centralizing, modern state. The norm here is self-sufficient local communities, like the villages of traditional India, which govern themselves and whose goal is self-empowerment. The standard of *dharma* is for some thinkers the mechanism whereby this society regulates itself. The modern, industrial, centralized state intervenes to disrupt this arrangement, substituting more repressive forms of domination. Therefore, this view places the community at the center and urges membership in small communities where the individual and community evolve in tandem. Cooperation among communities yields regional, provincial, national, and global communities, but each of these draws its raison d'être and authority from the base and is therefore limited in the exercise of executive power. Gandhi's idea of trusteeship places responsibility instead at the door of every individual conscience.

Bhikhu Parekh (1995) uses the term *critical traditionalist* to describe Gandhi, who is the most prominent example of thinkers in this school. Others we might include are Jayaprakash Narayan, Vinoba Bhave, and Rajni Kothari, and the Sarvodaya movement in Sri Lanka represents one application. The most institutional expression of this vision lies in the retention in more than one South Asian state of traditional self-governing structures like those of the *panchayat*s (village councils) of India and the *jirga*s (councils of tribal leaders) of frontier Pakistan. The latter exercise far greater autonomy than the former.

Independence must begin at the bottom. Thus, every village will be a republic or *panchayat* having full powers. . . . In this structure composed of innumerable villages, there will be ever widening, never ascending circles. Life will not be a pyramid with the apex sustained by the bottom. But it will be an oceanic circle whose centre will be the individual always ready to perish for the village, the latter ready to perish for the circle of villages, till at last the whole becomes one life composed of individuals, never aggressive in their arrogance but ever humble, sharing the majesty of the oceanic circle of which they are integral units. Therefore, the outermost circumference will not wield power to crush the inner circle but will give strength to all within and derive its own strength from it. (Gandhi 1991: 347–348)

The Structure of the Book

In the chapters that follow, two issues from the previous discussion will be studied at length. The first is the nature of the state's vision of itself. In Chapter 2, I discuss whether states should be ethnically identified or neutral and the implications of either choice. Further, I spell out the relationship between the identity of the state and its territory. Finally, I suggest that the notion of a singular loyalty to the state that overrides all other affiliations is inconsistent with the reality of the citizen's experience.

Chapter 3 is a study of the second issue of state intervention in the integration process, setting aside for the moment the normative question of desirability to attend to the pragmatic question of efficacy. Two avenues of such intervention are explored—socialization and internal territorial organization—with a view to assessing the limits of the state's intervention.

Finally, from these discussions, I propose in Chapter 4 two principles that must underlie the integration process—reconciliation and accommodation. The experience of the communities studied and some other historical experiences illustrate the arguments made and also provide counterexamples.

In conclusion, the objective of this book is to understand what it is that makes a community, and as a corollary, to understand the nature of the integrative process.

Notes

1. Initially, Sindhi nationalism was directed against the British colonial and then the Pakistani states; from the 1970s onward, the leadership was distracted by the rise of Muhajir nativism and Muhajir demands related to Karachi.

2. In the standard approach to the study of comparative politics, the most common unit of analysis is the nation-state, and all discussion, even dissent-

ing, of politics assumes the nation-state collective to be the natural one. One example from each of the cases: Kothari 1970 (India); Waseem 1989 (Pakistan); Wiswa Warnapala 1993 (Sri Lanka).

3. In the "Federalist Paper No. 10," James Madison (1999) recommends that differences among factions may be accommodated by giving each of them the same liberty. A state that seeks to facilitate a pluralistic vision would act in this very fashion. Whereas Madison held that this solution is in fact impracticable because of the inherent differences in the nature of individuals and the resultant differences in their property, it is argued in the conclusion of this book that the state's judicious interventions and responsiveness render its facilitation practicable. Madison's confidence in his own union's ability to contain factions—in our context, manage diversity—must, judging by the cases in this book and for our purposes, be tempered by requiring that the central government maintain an attitude of accommodation.

4. This list I owe to one senior scholar-administrator who did not want to be quoted.

5. I acknowledge that the private sector has its own agenda, one increasingly about consumption and divisive along class lines. However, the culture it is producing is more effective in capturing the imagination of the target audience than anything the state ever came up with. Even in the period before liberalization, the appeal of "Mera Joota Hai Japaani" over the nationalist songs, sung beautifully by the Akashvani Choir at 7 p.m. on television and radio, was undeniable.

6. To respect their privacy, persons interviewed are not named. The coded attribution at the end of each quotation refers to the place the interview was conducted ("I" for India or "S" for Sri Lanka; information for Pakistan was taken from secondary sources). The number allows me to identify the person interviewed.

7. In the South Asian context, to talk of Vedic, Buddhist, and Islamic traditions is to simplify rather crudely, if expediently.

8. Both of these latter individuals would contest their inclusion in this category as opposed to the vision advocating a community of modern citizens. Although, in common with thinkers in the previous section, they question the uncritical adoption of Western ideas and practices, their insistence on cultural relativism and on the salience of one particular value system to their context is different from the synthesizing perspectives of Gandhi and Jayaprakash Narayan. Further, they have no particular quarrel with state power, whereas that is a hallmark of the universe-of-small-communities category.

9. In some ways, caste blurs this distinction. Insofar as the caste system is an ideology, politics based on differences in caste positions is ideological.

2

State, Identity, and Ethnicity

The relationship between state, identity, and ethnicity—three pillars of the political arena—is an uneasy one. The way in which the state is identified, the territorial arrangements within the state, and the requirement in different contexts that citizens choose one primary and overarching affiliation among many they may have are related to each other and have consequences for the security of state, society, and individual citizens. How does the state identify itself? How does this identification differ from the way in which it is defined by people within it? How does the difference between their definitions affect their integration into the body politic? Consideration of these questions yields, on the one hand, to a discussion of the role of territory and, on the other, to an analysis of how simple, binary notions of allegiance diminish the prospects of integration.

National Identity

The term *national identity* is commonly used, fairly uncritically, to refer to the identity of the state. Continuing "terminological chaos," to borrow Walker Connor's (1994a) memorable phrase, thus conflates ethnic identity and state self-definition, evoking for the latter the natural allegiance underpinning the former. However, it is hard to understand just why national identity is problematic unless one unpacks the term into its two referents: the nation, or *ethnie,* on the one hand and the state on the other. Hans Kohn (1951) wrote that there are two kinds of nationalism—the civic nationalism of Western Europe and the cultural nationalism of Eastern Europe. Feliks Gross (1998) describes the resultant states (nation-states) as civic and tribal states, respectively, and their respective membership principles as citizenship and ethnicity. Benedict Anderson (1991), in his description of waves of nationalism, delineates another category—the nation that grows out of the state, albeit the colonial state. Those who write theoretically about national identity associate it logically with the identity of a nation with or without a state attached (Greenfeld 1992). Empirical discussions of national identity tend to be discussions not of ethnicity and ethnic identity but of the idea and ideology of a particular state (Dijkink 1996; Radcliffe and Westwood 1996; Hooson 1994). They are always conducted in the context of nation building.

In this chapter, I differentiate between the identity of the state, as seen in its name, its constitutional self-definition, and its basic laws, and the identities of peoples within the state, as diverse and crosscutting as their allegiances may be. National integration is defined here as the reconciliation of these identity claims, which may or may not be contradictory or even mutually exclusive.

Constitutional Visions

How do the states of India, Sri Lanka, and Pakistan envision themselves? To answer this question, constitutions are used to reconstruct the state's central self-portrait. Constitutions are often the founding documents of the state. They typically contain statements of what the state is or means to be, they spell out the rights of citizens as individuals and as members of groups, and they describe the internal structure of the state. Constitutions express the vision of the state in its most idealized form. Therefore, they provide the most lucid counterpoint to other visions that are current in a society. However, states also describe themselves or describe their idealized vision of themselves in other forums. Extraconstitutional policy documents on education, state employment, language, travel, tourism, and economic planning are good examples. The state also propagates its self-image through the mass media and through any control it exercises over the education system. These two expressions (constitutional and extraconstitutional) of the vision are not necessarily identical or even similar. Typically, the extraconstitutional rhetoric is more inclusive, although here too, states can exhibit schizophrenia. For instance, the state's policy on language can be exclusionary while its tourist literature celebrates the polyglot nature of its society.

In the state rhetoric in South Asia, "national integration" is used to describe both what states see as the status quo and what they define as a conscious process. "Unity in diversity" is an expression many South Asians invoke to describe their societies. States are not exceptions, seeing themselves as political spaces occupied by people who speak different languages, follow different faiths, and have somewhat different histories (although the erasure of these different histories is a project most states pursue). They pride themselves on this diversity, and this pride comes partly from their prevalence over these differences, which is proven by their continued existence.

One of the most striking differences between the way academics and states have viewed integration is in their view of what is to be integrated. For academics the primary objective seems to be the integration or streamlining of authoritative functions and then of groups. Identity issues do not figure in this literature. For states, they are primary; people of different sorts must be brought into the whole that is the state. The national integration rhetoric of the state is therefore a rhetoric about people, culture, and identity. The conversation between the state and groups, and among groups themselves, reflects this emphasis.

Constitutions are used here as the primary source of information simply because they are available for all the states and address all the citizenry equally. Constitutional provisions that take the form "India/Sri Lanka/Pakistan is . . . " will be listed and analyzed in each state's constitutional documents. Changes or shifts over time in that core definition, as well as internal contradictions, will be highlighted.

India

The preamble of the Indian constitution tells us that on November 26, 1949, the people of India constituted themselves into a "sovereign, democratic republic." Twenty-six years later, the people of India, acting through their representatives, acquired two more attributes: "socialism" and "secularism." Having come together as *individual* citizens of a newly free India, the people then constituted one republic. The preamble also contains a description of the vision that was ostensibly theirs: a republic in which all citizens would be assured social and political justice, freedom of expression and conscience, and equality of status and opportunity, and which would promote "FRATERNITY

assuring the dignity of the individual and the unity of the Nation."
Oddly, in 1976, the words *and integrity* were added after "unity." The
preamble thus speaks for a collection of individuals, but these individuals clearly make room for their individual and collective differences
in the mandate they create for the republic. This accommodation is
implicit in the kind of liberties that are envisioned and is also clear
when one reads the provisions on justice and equality in conjunction
with some of the provisions of Part III ("Fundamental Rights").

The 1976 additions to the preamble take it a step further toward
acknowledging the diversity of these "people of India." The first addition makes the point that India is a secular (and socialist, but that is not
pertinent here[1]) republic. The second adds the promotion of the unity
and integrity of the nation to the task of assuring the dignity of the individual. One reads these two additions together, in light of the circumstances in which the Forty-second Amendment was passed, and realizes
that they indicate two things.[2] First, they confirm what we already
know from memories of the Emergency—that the consensus around
the nature of the republic was fraying. We can infer this lack of consensus from the fact that whereas the original preamble spoke primarily about individuals, one of whose attributes was their membership in
a collective, both of these additions refer directly to the idea that the
people of India are really the people*s* of India—that they belong to
many different groups. If India is not made up of individuals but
groups, then it must be a different India. When the consensus frays in
such an India, the issue is not just unity but a determined integrity, or
staying intact. Second, and this follows from the previous point, this
constitutional amendment is another milestone in a path that began
with the Sixteenth Amendment, which outlawed secessionist activity or
rhetoric. This change is significant because in the struggle to preserve
the fraying consensus, "secularism" and "unity and integrity of the
nation" became two of the fundamental arguments for actions taken in
the name of national security. During the Emergency, for instance, the
civil liberties of individuals associated with communal organizations
were violated precisely on this pretext.

In the first article of the constitution, this republic, "India, that is
Bharat," went on to describe itself as a "Union of States." This self-
definition is striking for two reasons. The first is the juxtaposition in the
English text of the constitution of both the republic's names, India and
Bharat. In the late 1990s, scholars began to use these two terms to cap-
ture the growing disparity between the westernized, urban, English-

speaking middle class, or "India," and the poor, illiterate, non-English-speaking classes of the small towns and villages, or "Bharat."[3] Second, "India . . . shall be a Union of States" suggests that the states existed prior to the union, but the next article establishes the precedence of the union over the states: New states can be formed and existing states renamed or restructured by a simple act of Parliament (Constitution of India, Articles 1, 2). Thus although the structure of government is quasi-federal, India resembles Spain rather than the United States in its origins as well as in the nature of the dialogue that seems to have taken place between the union and its constituents. India is one, constituted as such by its people, who are undistinguished in their citizenship by any primordial characteristics or affinities—so the first article of the constitution and the preamble suggest. Any differences that may arise follow the creation of the state, and therefore, in their resolution, (preserving) the state in this form takes precedence. Any rights that constituent groups or regions enjoy, they enjoy at the pleasure of the union. In one sense, this reading allows us to interpret the dialogue between the union and the regions or groups as a contest between contrasting visions of the state: The union views itself as what could be thought of as a unitary state but one that has chosen to devolve power by recasting itself in a federal mold; the regions and groups see the union as a federal state but one where the center is bent on assuming the powers that should be theirs.

The definition of "India" is also implicit in the definition of "Indian." Part II of the Indian constitution defines the terms of Indian citizenship. At the commencement of the constitution, place of birth, birthplace of parents, and naturalization were the three determinants of citizenship. There are special provisions for those who migrated from what became Pakistan, but no other provision mentions or pertains to ethnic or regional origin. Citizenship of India is thus a legal category, conditional upon domicile rather than cultural identity. This status is consistent with the India whose people, undifferentiated, constituted a union of states where the states were created by the union.

Corollaries almost of imagining Indians in this manner are the provisions specifying that Indians have no separate citizenship relative to the states and that Indian citizenship must be relinquished upon becoming the citizen of another country. In a sense, these provisions reinforce the unitary essence of the Indian state. States in India do not precede the union, they follow it. Accordingly, there is no reason to respect a prior citizenship. Separate citizenship of the federation and the federating units follows from a situation where the federating units existed before the federation and recognition of their citizenship amounts to an acknowledgment of historical reality. In this case, such recognition is not necessary.

Nevertheless, the constitution does acknowledge some differences between the people of India in its chapter on fundamental rights. It does so through the rights it sees fit to guarantee to them. The rights guaranteed in this chapter fall into distinct categories: equality, liberty, religious freedom, cultural rights, and the right to constitutional remedies. The provisions pertaining to equality, religious freedom, and cultural rights make specific mention of the diversities that might exist among the people of India. In the provisions about cultural rights, there is mention in the marginal note of minorities. Article 29 secures the rights of groups to conserve their language, script, and culture. Interestingly, the text of the provision reads "section of citizens" instead of "minorities." This substitution was made by the Drafting Committee, which held that "minorities" was used in the constitution in a wider sense than the numerical.[4] In the next article, "minorities" is used, granting to these minorities the right to establish and administer educational institutions. It also secures such institutions against discrimination by the state on grounds of the nature of their management. This assurance is tempered, though, by the equality provisions that prohibit any state-aided institution from discriminating against any Indian citizen on grounds of religion, race, caste, sex, descent, place of birth, or residence.

Take a look, then, at the interesting image that begins to form. The Indian state begins to explicitly acknowledge the different identities of its citizens only when it is defining the rights they enjoy—rights that political thought traditionally sees as both emanating from the state and as defenses against the state! Is this a clue to the relationship that will obtain between the state and the different groups within? Possibly. First, the Indian state, having been constituted by the people, reconstitutes itself as a union of states. It is the union that gets to choose the basis of unit demarcation—in other words, it is the union that recognizes as legitimate or even merely acknowledges the existence of a group vis-à-vis itself and other groups. The other instrument of such recognition is the Eighth Schedule, which lists Indian languages. Groups clamor for the recognition of their language and its inclusion in this schedule even though such inclusion provides no privileges and accords no special status. It is as if these groups do not exist legitimately until they are so included. And then, the state seems to protect them from itself by endowing them with rights, especially those that obtain against discrimination by its agents and its institutions. How is one to read such a state's vision of itself?—as mostly neutral but capable of turning partisan and therefore requiring safeguards against itself?

In Parts IV and IV-A, the Indian constitution includes directives to its agents and its citizens. In the writing on postindependence Indian politics, it is customary to depict as adversarial the relationship between the "Directive Principles of State Policy" and "Fundamental Rights" sections. This depiction is, of course, far more pertinent to socioeconomic issues, but continuing the argument of the previous paragraph, I see no reason to abandon this model in thinking about integration and diversity. Government is merely instructed to work for the creation of a uniform civil code. The state is restrained by the provisions of the section on fundamental rights but not actively enjoined to do anything. Ten fundamental duties are prescribed for every Indian citizen, however, and at least three of them allude to the diversity of the country (Constitution of India, Article 51A, clauses c, e, and f). Citizens must uphold the sovereignty, unity, and integrity of India; promote harmony and fraternity transcending the detail of diversity; and, at the same time, "value and preserve the rich heritage of our composite culture." This contrast seems to further substantiate the idea that the state does not regard itself as being touched in any way by the diversities that abound in Indian society. One might even say that the Indian state sees itself as reforming or modernizing—if only by constitutional injunction—a society unwilling or unable to shed its premodern affinities. The state seems to regard itself as largely neutral and acting upon, rather than in conjunction with, society.[5]

Finally, the constitution of India states that Hindi shall be the official language of the union. This declaration is tantamount to the only touch of color in the guise of the state and is the only place where the state identifies with any particular identity trait. Little wonder, then, that in the first thirty years of the union's existence, language was the most contentious identity issue, displaced only in the late 1970s by religious differences. To non-Hindi speakers in Tamil Nadu, this provision served as conclusive evidence that the Indian state is ethnically biased.

The Indian insistence on ignoring the diversity of its people in the self-defining statements of the constitution is indicative of the state's anxiety about disintegration. This anxiety stems from a combination of factors. One, British and nationalist historiography of India painted pre-British (premodern) India as fractious and faction-ridden. Indians were constantly conquered by outsiders because they lacked unity. This lack of unity was not merely detrimental to Indian freedom but also to those attributes of modernity that the dominant national leadership so valued.[6] The experience of Partition had reinforced this distrust of any divisions. It was as if those who drafted the constitution feared that any concession to the existence of diversity would lead to a repetition of that experience.[7]

In conclusion, according to the Indian constitution, India is a union of states, so reconstituted by the Indian people after its initial constitution as a unitary republic; this union has an official language but is for the rest resolutely devoid of identity markers.

Sri Lanka

The three constitutions of independent Sri Lanka bear witness to a transformation of the state's self-definition. The first of the three constitutions—the Soulbury Constitution—was a product of the British. The Ceylon (Constitutional) Order in Council, 1946, to give it its proper name, was in fact an extensive charter of governmental reform rather than a formal constitution. Therefore, it began with no definition of the state—neither by the naming of the state in question nor by the normative description of its vision. This omission was partly because Sri Lanka was not yet an independent state. The Soulbury Constitution was adopted in 1946, but Sri Lanka did not become independent until 1948. The Soulbury Constitution stepped out of its administrative mission in only one instance: Article 29(2). This clause restricted the legislative power of the Ceylon Parliament, prohibiting it from interfering in religious practice and from favoring one religious or other community over another.

The Soulbury Constitution prevailed until 1972. When one considers that this constitution did not "constitute" a state, one looks for other clues in quest of the state's vision of itself. Turning from the constitution, one might identify two definitive pieces of legislation that were passed between 1946 and 1972. The first of these was the Citizenship Act of 1948, which through the terms whereby it defined citizenship disenfranchised a majority of the Indian Tamils who worked in the tea plantations of the central highlands. The second was the Official Languages Act of 1956, which made Sinhala the official language of Sri Lanka. Both of these acts had the consequence that in practice the state became more identified with one community—the Sinhalese. They were both divisive if only in the sense of singling out one community—in the first instance, to disenfranchise it; in the second, to privilege one community over the others. Thus a hierarchy of sorts evolved among three Sri Lankan ethnic communities regarding their place within the state: The Sinhalese became identified with the state, Sri Lankan Tamils were the insider-other, and the Indian, or plantation, Tamils were outside the system altogether.

As characterless as the text of the Soulbury Constitution was, the 1972 constitution, the Constitution of the First Sri Lankan Republic, was rooted in the Sri Lankan context and was evocative. The English text used begins and ends with Pali benedictions (*svasti* and *siddhirastu*), and the adoption of the constitution is dated according to both the Buddhist and the Gregorian calendars. The text ends with a verse in Pali describing the Buddhist ideal for the state: "Devo vassatu kaalena / sassasampatti hetu ca / phito bhavatu loko ca / raja bhavatu dhammiko" (May the rains fall in time / May the harvest be bountiful / May the people be contented / May the king be righteous).[8] The stage is set for the transformation of the state that is to follow.

The people of Sri Lanka, "being resolved in the exercise of . . . freedom and independence as a nation," gave themselves a constitution in 1972. They did not found the state or constitute a particular type of state; the nation/state preceded the constitution. We are told that Ceylon, renamed Sri Lanka in this constitution, is a "Free, Sovereign and Independent Republic."

Article 2 clearly states that Sri Lanka is a unitary state and thus works into the constitution one of the most controversial issues surrounding the state's identity. The only place where the constitution deals with smaller units within the state is in its description of electoral districts. One tradition of Sri Lankan history holds that it has always been a unitary state. In the early years of colonization, the British favored a unitary structure over the colonial apparatus as a means of managing the Kandyan chiefs. A hundred years later the idea of federalism was advocated, first by S.W.R.D. Bandaranaike and then by the Tamil leadership. After 1948, the lines that were drawn between those in favor of federalism and those in favor of the unitary state became more defined and were largely coterminous with ethnic lines. In 1972, the state entered this dialectic on the side of the unitary structure.

Article 6 gives Buddhism the "foremost place," and it gives the Sri Lankan state responsibility for protecting and fostering Buddhism (Constitution of Sri Lanka 1972). There are two ways to look at this provision, and they are not necessarily antithetical. The first is through the lens of Western experience and thought. This lens tells us that the state is now identified with one religion and that this is somehow a bad thing. This is the progressive, secular, modernizing view, and to its proponents, the identification of the state with one religion is anathema because religion is conservative, because favoring one religion over any others favors its members over other citizens, and because the separation of church and state is one of the markers of the modern period in Europe. The other way to look at this provision is to acknowledge that it simply follows tradition. The same article ends, "while assuring to all religions the rights granted by section 18(1)(d)." In the traditional political thought of South Asia, the ruler had definite duties with regard to *dharma* or *dhamma*.[9] These duties obtained at the ethical level of being just, honest, virtuous, dutiful, but they also obtained at the level of patronage—of institutions of learning (theological and otherwise) and of places of worship. The ruler was also a performer of rituals in the interest of the state and was the giver of alms. Whether in the Hindu or Buddhist tradition, the ruler was bound by what we now call religion. The 1972 constitution may therefore also be placed in this tradition. The reason the two interpretations of the provision are not intrinsically antithetical is that the state may foster and protect all religions equally, thus meeting the mandate of the traditional view without compromising modern egalitarian norms. The problem arises when "foster and protect" applies to only one of the faiths of the land.

The definition of Sri Lanka's identity is thus almost a delimitation thereof. The final limit is put in place by the constitutional adoption of Sinhala as the official language (Constitution of Sri Lanka 1972, Article 7). The constitution provides for the use of Tamil in certain contexts and for translation, but Sinhala is the language of legislation and of government in general. By the end of the first seven articles, we have a Sri Lanka that is unitary, Buddhist, and Sinhala-speaking.

Like the Indian constitution, this one begins with self-definition, first in terms of the attributes of the state and then in terms of the relationship between the state and its citizenry. Reading the 1972 constitution, one is struck by the "interventionist" role that the state is enjoined to play in cultural affairs. If the Soulbury Constitution's one striking feature is its explicit injunction that the state should not interfere in religious affairs, this constitution moves the state to the opposite position. "The Principles of State Policy" in Chapter V lay down the objectives of the state. Following these, the state is expected to enable the full realization of individual rights and group rights. Over and above the standard injunctions related to the protection of sovereignty and integrity, the state must strengthen "National Unity by promoting coop-eration and mutual confidence between all sections of the people of Sri Lanka including the racial, religious and other groups" (Constitution of Sri Lanka 1972, Article 16[4]).

The state is first charged with "raising" the people's moral and cul-tural standards (Constitution of Sri Lanka 1972, Article 16[2][f]). Under Article 16(7), the state is enjoined to contribute to the development of culture and language. Finally, and the wording of this provision suggests the perspective we might prefer on this question, "The State shall endeavour to create the necessary economic and social environment to enable people of all religious faiths to make a living reality of their reli-gious principles" (Constitution of Sri Lanka 1972, Article 16[9]). Again, as with the issue of Buddhism, there are two ways one can look at this provision. One might question the qualifications of the state to deter-mine, let alone raise, moral and cultural standards. One might also balk at the judgments involved in the implicit hierarchy suggested by "raise." Finally, one might ask if the state should intervene in this sphere. However, when one looks at the constitution from the viewpoint of tra-ditional South Asian political practice, a moral mandate for the state fol-lows from several things. The phrase *yatha raja, tatha praja* (as the king, so the populace) sums up the relationship between morality in the highest echelons of the state and in its people. When one looks at the terms of political legitimacy, the conditions for obligation and the grounds for revolution are all couched in terms of *dharma* and *dhamma*. In India (and surely a related Sri Lankan tradition exists), the *rajadhar-ma* school of political thought is distinguished by its view of politics as a process whose goal is welfare, not merely social and economic but also moral. The importance of *rajarshis*, the value placed in historical narratives on virtuous kings and the importance of the clerical-priestly adviser, also underlines the traditional linkage between these and the creation and maintenance of sociocultural standards and morality. In other words, upholding moral standards is only what states have always done in this region.

Oddly, after assigning such a strong cultural component to the state's self-definition and the state's mandate, the chapter on funda-mental rights is no more culturally focused than that of any other con-stitution considered in this book; it includes freedom of conscience and association, freedom to promote one's culture, and the right against dis-crimination on grounds of race, religion, caste, or sex. Freedom to trav-el and reside anywhere in Sri Lanka is also guaranteed.

Sri Lanka in the 1972 constitution is a unitary, Sinhala, Buddhist state with a strong cultural mandate amid a people who, while being occasionally Tamil speakers, do not have rights that reflect the state's rather overstated response to their diversity. That is not to say they have no rights, merely that their rights are commonplace compared to the strident and unambiguous self-definition of the state.

In some ways, the Constitution of the Second Republic (1978) suggests a synthesis between the Soulbury and the 1972 constitutions. The basic definitions of state identity are consistent with 1972, but particularly after a series of amendments, the 1978 constitution moves closer to the relative inclusiveness of the Soulbury Constitution.[10] The use of Pali references and the Buddhist calendar are retained, but what is interesting is the elaborate—and somewhat inelegant—explanation of how the constitution came to be adopted: The people of Sri Lanka elected representatives, and they adopted the constitution as the "Supreme Law" of the republic.[11] The 1978 version also says that the representatives were elected to constitute Sri Lanka into a democratic socialist republic. In other words, the mandate of the representatives was to constitute a particular kind of republic and further, to adopt the law of that republic. Three things are striking about this passage: First, the delegated nature of this authority is made very explicit; second, the republic is constituted and given law by these representatives; and third, given the imperfections of the electoral process even in ideal conditions (imperfect turnout, plurality rather than unanimity), this imperfection is not finessed away but dwelled upon.

The state is still unitary, but in this constitution, in the first chapter, its administrative units are demarcated explicitly. The state is made up of twenty-four administrative districts (twenty-five after the Seventh Amendment, 1983), and their names are listed. With the Thirteenth, Fourteenth, and Fifteenth Amendments and the introduction of provincial councils and proportional representation, the unitary nature of the state was somewhat diluted, but not the rhetoric of its advocates.

Buddhism retains its foremost place, but the political content of Buddhism is emphasized. The constitution stipulates very specifically that the state must foster and protect "Buddha Sasana," not the theological, metaphysical doctrines of Buddhism. It may be argued that this direction is not very different from the Judæo-Christian principles that have shaped the nature of Western democracies or the adherence to Islamic jurisprudence in other parts of the world. In the years that have passed, Sri Lankan governments have narrowly interpreted this provision to justify their close relationship with the *sangha*, or the Buddhist clergy, but this narrow interpretation does not follow from the article itself.

Whereas two of the three basic features of Sri Lankan identity are somewhat the same as in 1972—the unitary nature of the state and the preeminence of Buddhism—the state now had one official language and two national languages. In 1987, the Thirteenth Amendment to this constitution made Tamil the second official language of the state with English as the link language. The state officially ceased to be monolingual. One might interpret the fact that the addition of Tamil was not made in the same sentence giving official status to Sinhala as a sign of the reluctance with which the state became bilingual, but that reluctance does not alter the fact.[12]

What is almost quaint and curious is the tremendous detail in which the symbols of the state are listed and described. The national flag, anthem, and day are defined, and in the case of the first two, illustrations and sheet music are introduced in a schedule of the constitution. This specificity suggests that in defining itself the state (or rather the elected representatives who "constituted" it) wanted to leave no detail to chance.

The chapters on rights and principles of state policy remained much the same. The state was still charged with the cultural and moral mandate specified in the 1972 constitution. The national unity mandate is more specific and charges the state to "take effective steps in the fields of teaching, education and information in order to eliminate discrimination and prejudice (Sri Lankan Constitution of Sri Lanka 1978, Article 27[5])." But in 1978, a provision listing the fundamental duties of citizens was included for the first time. Like Buddha Sasana, these duties seem to derive from the tradition of the region, including as they do the duty to work conscientiously in one's chosen profession, to respect the rights and freedoms of others, and to protect nature and conserve its riches.

To summarize, Sri Lanka of the 1978 constitution is a state rooted in its Buddhist tradition of governance, at least in principle, and is unitary even as its centralization is fraying and it is reluctantly bilingual. It is a state painfully conscious of its identity and piously concerned about its mandate. It is a state with a moral purpose, and it enjoins duties upon its citizenry in keeping with this self-image. The constitutional debates of today are all explained by the variations between this constitutional self-image and the reality of the respondents' visions.

In 1994, the People's Alliance (PA) was elected on a peace mandate. The twin instruments of that peace were military action and constitutional reform based on devolution of power. Between 1994 and 2000, several iterations of the initial PA devolution package were discussed. In August 2000, a new constitution was placed before Parliament for debate and vote. Although it did not pass, it merits a close reading as partial indication of where the debate on Sri Lanka's identity stands.

The 2000 constitutional proposal is structured like the 1972 and 1978 constitutions. However, there are interesting and important departures in text and tone that invite comment. The preamble to this constitution is terse and legalistic, in keeping with the objective of the "People of Sri Lanka" to "establish a stable legal order based on a Supreme Law." The constitution so adopted is intended to strengthen institutions, guarantee power sharing, enshrine "democratic values, social justice and human rights," facilitate development and promote "peace, ethnic harmony and good governance." (Interestingly, the word *governance* appears twice in the short preamble.)

In the preamble to this constitution, the Sri Lankan state is still named the Democratic Socialist Republic of Sri Lanka. Unlike in the 1978 constitution, where Article 1 tells us twice what sort of state it is, once as description and once as name, in this constitution, the first article simply states, "The Republic of Sri Lanka is one, free, sovereign and independent State consisting of the institutions of the Centre and of the Regions which shall exercise power as laid down by the Constitution." All three constitutions (1972, 1978, and 2000) state tautologically that the state is "free," "sovereign," and "independent," but this one adds "one" to that emphatic assertion. Article 2 continues this emphasis, charging the state explicitly with preserving "the independence, sovereignty, unity and the territorial integrity" of the republic and with promoting a "Sri Lankan" identity while taking into account that Sri Lankan society is "multi-ethnic, multi-lingual and multi-religious." The chapter "Principles of State Policy and Fundamental Duties" reiterates this description: Sri Lankan society is pluralistic, and national unity is to be based on cooperation, mutual trust, confidence, and understanding among all the sections of that society (Article 52[1]).

Describing the nature and scope of popular sovereignty, the first chapter of the constitution also states explicitly in Article 2(1)(d) that the people shall enjoy the fundamental rights recognized by the constitution *both individually and collectively*. The recognition that people enjoy rights as members of a collective is new in this constitution. Furthermore, there are provisions in this chapter that describe the territorial composition of Sri Lanka in the manner that the federal constitutions of India and Pakistan do: "The territory of the Republic shall consist of the Regions as set out in the First Schedule" (Article 3[1]). The usual provisions regarding the national flag, anthem, and day are also included in the first chapter.

The previous provision on Buddhism remains in this constitution, but in addition to the protection provided for "all religions," this constitution guarantees to every person the right to freedom of thought, conscience, and religion (Article 15[1]) and further, the right to practice that religion individually or as part of a group, publicly or in private. Indeed, a total of thirty-one articles elucidate the rights guaranteed to citizens by this constitution—almost triple the number in the 1978 constitution. Among these are the right to equality before the law and the right against discrimination; freedoms related to thought, conscience, and religion; and the right to "enjoy and promote culture and use of language" (Article 19). Interestingly, in addition to the more standard right of free movement within the territory of the state, the constitution explicitly grants to all "persons" the right to leave the Republic (Article 12[2]) and to all "citizens" the freedom to return (Article 13). Although these provisions reflect common immigration practice, they are unusual in that they are included in these terms in the fundamental rights charter of the constitution. They appear to be providing for a postsettlement situation in which the return of refugees must be facilitated.

There are eighteen provisions in the proposed 2000 constitution that deal with the question of language. Sinhala and Tamil are to be the official languages of the republic, whereas Sinhala, Tamil, and English are recognized as national languages. The former are to be the languages of administration, but there are several provisions that secure the use of all three national languages in a large range of administrative transactions from documentation to court business to examinations for entrance to the civil service. The elaboration of language rights is warranted by the centrality of language issues to the present conflict. However, one interesting by-product of these revisions is the appearance of English in these provisions. This constitution, in admitting English to the rank of national language, is remarkable in that it enshrines the right of the individual to education through the medium of English where it is available. With this provision, language and education policy in Sri Lanka come full circle after decades of the "Swabasha" and "Sinhala Only" slogans dominating the language debate.

The most contentious departures in this proposed constitution have, however, to do with devolution. In the very first chapter, repeated mention is made of regions and regional agencies. The First Schedule specifies three categories of regions. Part A includes six regions outside the Tamil areas. Parts B and C pertain to the arrangements for the Northern and Eastern Provinces. The constitution intends that for the first ten years the two provinces should be separate and at the end of that period a referendum should be held to ascertain whether the people of those regions favor merger. Chapter XXVIII specifies how the interim government in and for those two regions should be organized.

What, then, is the Sri Lanka that this constitution proposes to establish? Although in structure and to a great extent in style, it resembles the 1972 and 1978 constitutions, in substance it is closest to the 1948 Soulbury Constitution. The descriptions of Sri Lanka as a plural society and the state as consisting of regions, along with the numerous provisions relating to language on the one hand and the mention of both individual and collective rights on the other, constitute a lengthy and positive elaboration of Article 29(2) of the Soulbury Constitution, which was essentially a negative right. Pending the discussion and vote on this constitutional proposal, we can only say that it represents the government's position in the negotiations with those who think the proposal is altogether too liberal and those for whom it comes too late. It is still the 1978 constitution upon which we must base our reading of Sri Lankan identity.

Pakistan

Pakistan's constitutional history has been checkered. The first constitution of Pakistan was not adopted until 1956. Within three years, it was abrogated, and the Basic Democracies Order was instituted. The second constitution of Pakistan commenced in 1962. It was replaced in 1973 by the constitution that is currently operative, although it was suspended for a few years under martial law and restored only after major amendments were made to it.

In essence, those provisions in which we have sought the state's definition of itself—preamble, name, statements defining internal structure, the state's relationship with religion and language issues, and the state-citizen relationship as defined by any principles of state policy and bill of rights—have changed very little through these three constitutions, although provisions relating to government, personal law, and law enforcement have changed dramatically. There have been changes in the operation of the political system. These areas are not pertinent, however, to our current exercise, which is to identify self-defining propositions in the constitution.

In all three constitutions, the preamble reminds us that divine sovereignty is exercised in trust by the people, whose will it is to establish an "order." The state is the product of that will, and the realization of Islamic ideals at the social and personal levels is its foundation. The people who exercise this will are by implication Muslim, and they do provide for minorities "freely to profess and practise their religions and develop their cultures" (Constitution of Pakistan 1973). These minorities are assumed to be religious minorities.

The first article of all three constitutions tells us the name of the republic, whether it is unitary or federal, and what territories it comprises. In 1956, it was to be a federal republic called the Islamic Republic of Pakistan, and it comprised East and West Pakistan and territories that had acceded or might accede, that is, territories other than those in the provinces. In 1962, the republic was to have the same name, but there was no mention of whether it was federal, this being the period that the state experimented with the One Unit policy. The state comprised the provinces of East and West Pakistan and other territories. In 1973, Pakistan was a federal republic once more with the same official name and a detailed listing of territories: four provinces (Baluchistan, North-West Frontier Province [NWFP], Punjab, and Sind), the Islamabad Capital Territory, the Federally Administered Tribal Areas, and any other territories that might accede to the state. The first version of this constitution had a provision that read, "The Constitution shall be appropriately amended so as to enable the people of the Province of East Pakistan, as and when foreign aggression in that Province and its effects are eliminated, to be represented in the affairs of the Federation." That provision was removed in the First Amendment.

The state's name, the Islamic Republic of Pakistan, has remained constant through the years, but the number of supporting provisions has practically tripled—including the name provision, there were seven in 1956, fifteen in 1962, and almost twenty in 1973.

In all three constitutions, it is interesting that of all the different kinds of diversity, religion is the one most featured. The constitution distinguishes between Muslims and non-Muslims not so much in their rights but in what the state is enjoined to do for them. So in one sense, the state, which is willed into existence by a predominantly Muslim people, is enjoined to do particular things for the Muslims, whereas its role vis-à-vis others is that of a facilitator (guaranteeing their rights) and law enforcer (prohibiting forced religious taxes outside one's religion, for instance). The "Principles of Policy" in the 1973 constitution illustrates this stance: Whereas the state is enjoined to ensure and create conditions for the teaching and printing of the Quran, the organization of religious taxes, the maintenance of mosques, and the observance of moral standards, it is expected to "safeguard" the legitimate rights and interests of minorities. The state shall promote unity among the Muslims but shall "discourage parochial, racial, tribal, sectarian and provincial prejudices among the citizens" (Constitution of Pakistan 1973, Articles 31 and 33).

It should be pointed out that the 1973 constitution, for the first time, defines the terms Muslim and non-Muslim. Not part of the original text, the Second Amendment (1974) of the constitution defines who was not a Muslim. "A person *who does not believe in the absolute and unqualified finality of the Prophethood of Muhammad (Peace be upon him)* the last of the Prophets or *claims to be a Prophet* in any sense of the word or of any description whatsoever after Muhammad (Peace be upon him), *or recognizes such a claimant as a prophet or a religious reformer*, is not a Muslim for the purposes of the Constitution or law" (italics added). That the constitution should pronounce definitively on what is essentially a theological matter is striking, but that the definition is negative is also interesting. Very simply, it may be that the drafters of the amendment could not conclusively define what makes a Muslim. Those drafting the Third Amendment (1985) suffered no such inhibitions. They defined both Muslim and non-Muslim. The definition of Muslim is now affirmative. It is also theological (almost toggling all the provisions in the previous definition of non-Muslim), in contrast to the definition of non-Muslim: "'Non-Muslim' means a person who is not a Muslim and includes a person belonging to the Christian, Hindu, Sikh, Buddhist or Parsi community, a person of the Quadiani Group or the Lahori Group (who call themselves 'Ahmadis' or by any other name), or a Bahai, and a person belonging to any of the Scheduled Castes." There is no further definition of who these people are. In other words, Muslims are individuals who have a set of beliefs and non-Muslims are members of specific communities. The rights enjoyed by

Muslims are individual rights, and the rights enjoyed by non-Muslims are group rights. Further, the duties of the state to Muslims are duties to individuals, and those to non-Muslims, as we saw above, are in the way of facilitating functions. Harold J. Laski defined rights as "those conditions of social life without which no man can seek, in general, to be himself at his best."[13] If an individual's rights are tied largely to her group identity, then to what extent can she define herself as she deems best? What sorts of restrictions does this status place on her rights as an individual?[14]

An interesting question arises: What happens when the state or the constitution labels a group or groups as minorities? What relationships and interactions are automatically expected of them? How do they come to view the state and their place within it? Which notion, tolerance or sufferance, would characterize the relationship between the minority groups and the state, and does the state then become automatically identified with the majority or does it need to have a specific identity (Malay, Sinhala, Muslim) for that to happen?

On the question of national language, the Islamic Republic of Pakistan has been less consistent. In the 1956 constitution, the state languages were to be Urdu and Bengali with English continuing to be used in administrative contexts for some time. Provincial languages were acceptable in the place of English in the provinces. In the 1962 constitution, this situation changed to the extent that state languages were now designated as national languages, and—a minor but interesting point in light of the Sri Lankan case—the order in which the languages were listed was reversed to read "Bengali and Urdu." The switch from "state" to "national" is also interesting, suggesting the state's determined appropriation of nationhood. In 1973, Urdu was designated the national language of Pakistan. English would continue to be used for a short period, and in addition to Urdu, provincial languages could be used and taught. All three constitutions thus had, on the one hand, language provisions that privileged one or two languages over others and, on the other hand, guarantees to any section of the citizenry having a "distinct language, script or culture" "the right to preserve and promote the same and . . . establish institutions for that purpose" (Constitution of Pakistan 1973, Article 28).[15] Essentially, neither the state nor the constitution was overly concerned with this issue. The constitution prescribes principles of state policy and rights, but again, these did not change all that much. It seems that through all the dramatic political turns in the history of Pakistan, its self-image has remained surprisingly constant. Not for Pakistan the agonizing redefinitions of identity that have characterized Sri Lanka. And although India does not identify with any one group, its constitution has in common with Pakistan's this fundamentally unaltered basic self-definition. Insofar as the alternating civilian and military regimes in Pakistan have tinkered with its constitutional law, they have been more interested in changing the structure and distribution of power (for instance, with the Basic Democracies Order under Ayub Khan and General Pervez Musharraf's devolution scheme) within the government than in changing the nature and self-definition of the state.

So what is Pakistan according to this relatively unchanging constitutional self-definition? Pakistan is an Islamic republic that has mostly been federal and that is officially Urdu-speaking. There are non-Muslims and non-Urdu speakers in Pakistan, and the state guarantees their rights but is under no obligation to do anything in particular for them. Its positive mandate applies largely to Muslims.

Visions for Three States

The three constitutions describe the communities they enfold or represent as follows:

- India is a union of states, so reconstituted after its initial constitution as a unitary republic by the Indian people. This union has an official language but is for the rest resolutely devoid of identity markers.
- Sri Lanka of the 1978 constitution is a state rooted in its Buddhist tradition of governance, at least in principle, unitary even as its centralization is fraying, and reluctantly bilingual. It is a state painfully conscious of its identity and piously concerned about its mandate.
- Pakistan is an Islamic republic that has mostly been federal and that is officially Urdu-speaking. There are non-Muslims and non-Urdu speakers in Pakistan, and the state guarantees their rights, but its positive mandate applies largely to Muslims.

If these are the visions these countries operate with, what are the means whereby the visions are achieved? In other words, if each vision might be construed as the country's idea of "integration achieved," what might be, for each of them, the process of integration?

Let us look at them one by one. In the case of India, preserving the *union* of states is the first priority of the integrative process. Not only must the state keep the territory of the union intact—an argument for the use of force to maintain it in a particular form—but it must maintain the status of the union as prior and predominant in the union-states relationship. Prioritizing the maintenance of state integrity justifies centralization. It also justifies the resistance to demands for decentralization and autonomy. Integration also means the insistence on the official language, so that although the state might make (as it has) concessions to delay the establishment of one language, there is no room for abandonment of the project. Since the state is resolutely devoid of identity markers, there is no space for negotiation on identity issues; thus integration is also nonnegotiable. The state has a self-image, and integration is almost the "falling in place" of the populace, to be expected because they constitute the state in the first place.

Sri Lanka is also centralized and is in fact unitary, but by virtue of its self-identification with one identity group, it has left the door open for negotiation, if unintentionally. Integration here goes hand in hand with the moral mandate of the state. Therefore, as the state intervenes— in keeping with its mandate—in the cultural affairs of one community and then, either by omission or commission, intervenes in the cultural affairs of the others, it creates opportunities for demands to negotiate this mandate. When it promotes one language, it creates demands for equal status for another. If the state is identified with one group, it thereby recognizes the existence of others (in the manner in which "some clouds bear rain" implies that others do not). Integration becomes a process of constant negotiation. The state is weakened by positioning itself on one side in the negotiation rather than as the arbiter in the process. Thus on the one hand, the state might need to resort to force to maintain its right to be part of the negotiation; on the other, such resort is (even) less effective and (even) less defensible than in any other situation. It is less effective because it exacerbates the tension between the negotiating groups and makes them more intransigent. It is less defensible because when the state is identified with one group, it uses force as the instrument of that group in the integrative process. Given that states (theoretically) have a monopoly on the legitimate use of force, in what position does that leave other groups? The process of integration in Sri Lanka that follows from the state's constitutional self-definition cannot be a happy one. The state must act, for it is charged to do so. At the same time, it is weakened to a one-among-equals position by its identity, and given that it is not (all said and done) a state with a taste for genocide, it must fight bitterly to stem the fraying of its definition.

What does it take for the Islamic Republic of Pakistan to be integrated in its desired form? The suspension of constitutional government every now and then makes it hard to define integration without taking into account the impact of a coercion-based dispensation. Pakistan also has the distinction of having experienced secession in the creation of Bangladesh. Historical factors seem, since then, to have blunted the incendiary potential of a federalism that demography biases in favor of one province and of state identification with one language. Finally, the state is not entirely autonomous given the role played in its affairs by the military and, to a lesser extent, the clerical establishments.

Like the Sri Lankan state, the state of Pakistan leaves the door open for negotiation by identifying with one group. However, the unique circumstances of the establishment of the state rescue it from the prospect of a Sri Lankan–style conflict. Instead, what is contested is the state's definition of who is or is not Muslim. The constitution defines the category of non-Muslim in terms of the individual's membership in a community rather than the individual's beliefs. Almost automatically, the exclusion of certain groups becomes contentious. So it is not the definition of the state but the definition of the official majority within the state that is potentially contentious. The fact that the state commands so much coercive power and these groups so little seems to determine the course of this contestation as a dialogue of sustained protest and easily repressive response.

The inability of the state to participate autonomously in a negotiation, the demographic composition and distribution of the population, and the course of history seem to have ensured a state unable to intervene in the integration dialectic even though it is capable of tremendous coercion. Individuals in Pakistan have organized effectively against the suspension of the constitutional state but have not really contested its primary definition. Is integration in a state with Pakistan's checkered history not unlike the integration of the subcontinent during the freedom movement, an accident of the political imperatives of the time?

Perhaps we can conclude, following from the text of the constitution, that integration in Pakistan might have been a negotiated consensus on power and resource sharing, assimilative in its advocacy of one language and partial to one religious group in the fulfillment of the state's raison d'état. In the periods when there was constitutional government, this conclusion seems to hold. On the whole, integration has taken second place to other priorities: regime survival for the state and democratization for the citizenry. Any definition of integration put forth on the basis of constitutional readings is open to the critique that it does not take into account extraconstitutional politics, and in the case of Pakistan, this is very salient because constitutional government has repeatedly been suspended.

The definition of integration that is easiest to read from the three constitutions seems to be one that describes the goal rather than lays out a process: the goal of realizing the self-image of the state. The process or procedure is largely unspecified, although other features of the constitution and the political system would provide at least the limits within which the state must operate.

Ethnic Neutrality or Ethnic Identification?

There are two important questions at the heart of the debate on state visions and state intervention in national integration.[16] First, should the state be ethnically defined? Second, can the state ever be ethnicity-blind?

Ethnic Identification

Since ethnic identification is easier to pinpoint than ethnic neutrality, an exposition of its forms and components, and its consequences, may be culled from our cases. That states are ethnically identified may be read from explicit, self-defining statements. Another indication of an ethnically identified state is institutional arrangements that reinforce an ethnic bias. Another is political actors—parties, leaders, government agents, activists—who work an existing set of institutions and norms to favor their purposes regardless of what the self-definition of the state is or what its institutions are. States may be explicitly identified with one community, identified in effect through the working of the political system, or so identified as a consequence of specific political actions.

Explicit identification. This is the easiest test, and one might draw on constitutional provisions (as this work has) and other official affirmations in the audiovisual and print media, tourist information, and diplomatic postures. Sri Lanka's constitutions illustrate well this kind of identification. The increasing identification of the state with Sinhalese Buddhism is apparent from the changes in relevant provisions of the constitution.

Official self-definition, however, tells only part of the tale. In the case of Pakistan, we saw this quite clearly. Although the self-defining propositions did not change much through Pakistan's three constitutions, in fact, politics in Pakistan underwent dramatic changes—four periods of military rule, increasing Islamicization of the polity and society, major demographic changes in Sind and the North-West Frontier Province (NWFP), and escalating violence. Self-definitions in the three constitutions reflect none of these changes, and the changes from federalism to One Unit to federalism suggest perfect resolution of political problems when, in fact, Pakistan's deepest political issues remain unresolved.

Further, how does one interpret the official self-definition? The meaning of the Buddha Sasana is disputed in Sri Lanka, as is the appropriate nature of an Islamic Pakistan—a secular homeland for South Asian Muslims, as Jinnah once favored, or the Nizam-i-Mustafa that Zia ul-Haq introduced?

What are the consequences of such ethnic self-definitions? Most important, they give institutional character and legitimacy to us-them divisions. In both the Sri Lankan and Pakistani constitutions, we see that when the state defines itself in terms of one identity, provisions that distinguish (not even necessarily discriminate) among groups follow logically. In the Pakistani case, for instance, such discrimination involves definitions of Muslim and non-Muslim. The state has specific charges for the community it is identified with, and even if there were no provisions that disadvantaged the other communities, this difference already alters the equation between the them.

Identification through state institutions. A closer reading is provided by the workings of institutions set up by the state. Departing from a simple textual reading, one has, however, to take into account empirical and phenomenological evidence for this factor. What is the actual operational record of the institutions? How are they perceived to be functioning?

Laws, judicial decisions, executive actions, the workings of the electoral system, and the relationship among different agencies and levels of government demonstrate how the system has actually functioned.

Departures from the letter of self-definition are easy enough to pin down. All three cases in this study illustrate this kind of ethnic identification. In India, population-based, single-member parliamentary constituencies ensure the political dominance of the densely populated Hindi belt. Although the state is not defined as a Hindi-speaking state, for those Indians who do not speak Hindi, the adoption of Hindi as a national language confirms their view that the central government (shorthand for the Indian state) favors one kind of Indian over others. Thus the accession to prime ministership of two southerners—P. V. Narasimha Rao and H. D. Deve Gowda—was read as a sign that things were changing. In Sri Lanka, the Citizenship Act in 1948 and change in language policy in 1955, even as the Soulbury Constitution prohibited the state from playing favorites, established the state as partisan and ethnically identified in the eyes of the Tamil community.

There are two sides (at least) to the question of how institutions work—the perceptions of both those within the institutions and those outside. Thus even that which seems empirically true is not incontrovertible. Sinhalese and Tamils view the various policies and actions of the Sri Lankan government in quite different ways, the Indian reality of Tamils in Madras bears little resemblance to that of other Indians in the northern part of the country, and Sindhis and Muhajirs interpret very differently Pakistani policies with regard to Urdu and local languages. A state, then, may seem ethnically identified to one group and not others. How is one to classify such a state? That would depend very much on the issue studied and the perspective chosen.

Identification through the actions of political actors. The ambiguity of state identification is exacerbated by the ways in which humans use institutions to their advantage. Majoritarian democracy is a case in point. At least in the three South Asian cases, majoritarian democracy has been seen as the culprit, as facilitating the creation of communal groups and vote blocs. In India, this observation is made in the context of caste and ethnoreligious politics. In Sri Lanka, the growth of communal parties is traced back to the introduction of majoritarian democracy, whereupon Sinhalese and Tamil politicians set up their own parties and established a style of politics where political coalitions and alliances were more important than issues and positions. In Pakistan, majoritarian representation cut many ways. On the one hand, denying Bengalis the power that was theirs by virtue of their numerical majority in pre-1971 Pakistan broke up the state; on the other, in post-1971

Pakistan the numerically superior Punjabis dominated the state at the federal level while the Sindhi majority was eroded by Muhajirs and other settlers in Karachi and Sind. The same set of institutions can be worked differently as circumstances change by actors who seek to exploit any potential that an institution had or has to lend an ethnic identification to the state. In all three countries, the domination by one ethnic group or another of the bureaucracy, police, and armed forces has been controversial for this reason. First, in a situation of economic scarcity, government service is a highly desirable career. Although the system is not quite one of nepotism, it is usual for people to encourage and help their kith and kin find jobs in the same profession. Therefore, domination by one clan or ethnic group leads directly to deprivation of another. The grievance that Sri Lankan Tamils dominated government service must be seen in this light. Further, these networks within a bureaucracy affect decisions regarding resource allocation. Hence, the allegations that Sind or Tamil Nadu did not see as much investment as other parts of Pakistan or India stem from a perception and support an argument that the government is partial. In situations of protracted conflict, the domination by one ethnic group of the police or the armed forces has obvious negative consequences. If the conflict involves the dominant group, it is unreasonable to expect that the constable or the soldier will retain his impartiality over a long period of time. This tendency of the police or paramilitary to take sides when the conflict is protracted is seen in every one of the three cases studied.

So what can one say about the ethnic identification of a state whose institutions might lend themselves to ethnic appropriation even if their self-definition is not ethnic? Let us examine this question from the standpoint of ethnic neutrality.

Ethnic Neutrality

There are two possible manifestations of ethnic neutrality: The state may completely ignore the existence of ethnic diversity, or it may actively celebrate that diversity. These attitudes are not mutually exclusive, and states sometimes exhibit both. The ideal of secularism is now enshrined in the Indian constitution as part of India's self-definition. This ideal is interpreted in two conflicting ways. The first interpretation of secularism is that it is a Western-style separation of church (or its equivalent) and state. The second interpretation is that of those who favor a catholic acceptance of all faiths practiced in India. This acceptance is based on the idea *sarva dharma samabhaava* (the same to all faiths/all faiths are equal). In effect, the Indian state oscillates between the two interpretations. It is separate from the church in that it does not pronounce on theological matters, to the point that non-Hindus are permitted to follow their own personal laws. (The argument that Hindus are *therefore* identified with the secular Indian state is never made in this context.) Regarding the second interpretation, all Indians, equally, have the right to freedom of religion and the right to set up cultural and educational institutions. (There is a third view, and although it is presented as an interpretation of secularism, it identifies Indian society and state with one religious community and therefore cannot be included in a discussion of ethnic neutrality.)

What are the consequences of the state being ethnically identified? Let us begin with the arguments in favor. An ethnically identified state is a state in which the otherwise implicit power plays between the dominant and subordinate communities are spelled out clearly—so we have the political equivalent of calling a spade a spade. This is the argument that majoritarian Hindu or Buddhist nationalists extend for the transformation of the Indian and the Sri Lankan states. Further, an ethnically identified state is able to extend concessions and protection to other groups with greater credibility than a neutral state, which must constantly mediate among groups in society. On the negative side, first, an ethnically identified state raises the stakes in intergroup conflict. All sides have more to gain and more to lose, and so the chances of escalation are greater. Second, the state adds its coercive powers to the available arsenal in such a conflict. Third, it deprives society of a powerful arbiter in the conflict. Finally, the state's inevitable engagement in such conflicts detracts from the fulfillment of its other mandates.

In contrast, an ethnically neutral state is able to mediate and prevent escalation of conflict through the exercise of its power in the interests of peace. It is more likely to enjoy the allegiance of different sections of society and is therefore able to get on with the business of governance. As the neutrality of the Indian state has been eroded in the past fifty years, its ability to move beyond crisis management to governance has been proportionately reduced. Its responses have become harsher and resistance to them more intractable. Compare the Tamil secessionism described here, to which the Indian state responded with a constitutional amendment and language concessions, to the Punjab or Kashmir problems of the 1980s and 1990s, which elicited more coercive responses from the same state! Sri Lanka also illustrates this point. With the January 25, 1998, bombing of the Temple of the Tooth and a spate of assassination attempts and bombings in 1999, the Liberation Tigers of Tamil Eelam (LTTE) and the Sri Lankan state are at an impasse. The Sri Lankan state's reaction to the attack on a Buddhist temple is much stronger than its reaction to any earlier provocation. Further, its declaration of the intention to ban the Tamil Tigers for this act makes negotiation impossible. An ethnically identified Sri Lankan state offers no protection to Sri Lankan Tamils against the Sinhalese or the Tigers.

Ethnically neutral self-definition, institutional neutrality, and the inability of political actors to bias the system ensure the state's neutrality. Perfect ethnic neutrality is probably impossible. The nature of politics, it seems, ensures that. If politics is about conflict and the struggle for power, then the process of capturing power and asserting influence impels the creation of coalitions and alliances. The successful among their number redefine the state so that it is identified with them. If politics is about the articulation and attainment of a shared agenda, then determining what that agenda shall be and even the building of a consensus inevitably compromise the neutrality of the state.

Unit Demarcation, the Identity of the State, and National Integration

Territory is one of the essential components of states. International relations are the interactions between territorially bounded polities. The study of international relations likens such polities to sealed billiard balls encountering each other on the baize of realpolitik and pays no attention to politics within their external territorial limits. Preservation of external territorial limits and their expansion or consolidation if they are disputed are critical elements in these interactions, but nothing that happens within qualifies as worthy of study. This sanguine unconcern is disturbed by the existence of irredenta, by neighborly intervention, and by transborder communities and population movements. Prising these sealed units open, we come upon another dimension of territorial politics, another relation that these politics have with the identity of the state.

If territory is the physical embodiment of the state, the internal territorial organization of the state is its identity writ as divisions of the population, distributions of power, and natural resources. The bases of unit demarcation either write into that state identity the existence of groups within the state or obliterate them altogether. Hence it is important to trace afresh the relationship between state identity, internal unit demarcation, and the place of groups in the polity (see Rajagopalan 1999, 2000). There are several dimensions to this relationship.

The Order of Precedence

What came first, the units or the state? This question can be considered from two angles: First, historically, was the polity formed by centripetal action or did a unitary polity devolve power to units of its creation? Second, and often more politically significant, what appears first in the constitution—the polity as a whole or the polity as a union of parts? "If the people's awareness of being a separate community is one of the criteria of federalism, does it matter at all if the territorial community issues from the federal system rather than precedes it?" (Duchacek 1970: 237). In the following paragraphs, it will be suggested that each of these questions has important implications for the way in which identity politics plays out within the state.

Let us consider historical circumstances first. Units have come together to form federal states in the United States, Switzerland, Canada, and Australia, as well as in newer states such as Nigeria and Pakistan. In Pakistan, even the image of the desired homeland for the Muslims of South Asia was a composite of regions, and this aspiration was reflected in the acronym that gave the homeland its name—PAKSTAN, for Punjab, North-West Frontier Province, Kashmir, Sind, and Baluchistan. What these provinces had in common was that they were all Muslim-majority provinces. In the final negotiations that led to Partition and the transfer of power, it was determined that British India's provincial legislatures would vote to become part of the existing Constituent Assembly or to join that of the new state of Pakistan. Therefore, the decision to accede to and thereby form Pakistan was also made by provinces and not by a territorially undifferentiated electorate. In addition, Punjab and Bengal were partitioned, and Sylhet was awarded to East Pakistan, but again these were also territorial units, not an amorphous electoral college. In cases like this, the building blocks—the provinces here—have forms and histories that precede not just the legal founding of Pakistan but even its imagination. Thus Pakistan (and other states with this history) can be equal to or more than the sum of their parts but not different from what their parts are, taken together. One would expect that in the resulting state, the power equation between the whole and the parts would be colored by this historical process, and the whole would be bound by and somewhat accountable to the parts. In Pakistan, however, this did not happen. The territorially defined vision of a homeland for South Asian Muslims became a theocratically defined vision of an Islamic state in which all other differences, especially ethnoregional, would be irrelevant—and marginal.

In the centrifugal model, a unitary state devolves power to its regions, as Spain, Belgium, and the United Kingdom have done and as Sri Lanka is under pressure to do. The unitary state in Sri Lanka has its constitutional origin in the Colebrooke-Cameron Reforms of 1829. The British were the first to unite the entire island under one sovereign, and the unitary state was their means to consolidate and institutionalize this control. Notwithstanding its constitutional roots, there are those who would trace the unitary state to *ekatchhatra*, the single umbrella of the sovereign *cakravartin,* or universal ruler. Such a view of Sri Lanka as a single polity is also consistent with the story that on his deathbed, the Buddha entrusted the protection of the island, the bastion of his belief system, to Vishnu and, by extension, to contemporary Sri Lankan Buddhists. Any territorial or other division of the island would be a betrayal of that trust. The first demands for representation were electoral, legislative, and administrative, but in the 1940s, territorial claims to power made their first appearance, and although they have met with limited success, they now dominate the political agenda. The point here is that the creation of units (as an initial step in the devolution process) in a unitary state often follows decades of rhetoric and negotiation.

States such as India confound these simplistic historical generalizations. India was the successor state to the British Indian Empire, and although, like Pakistan, it was formed historically by the accession of provinces and principalities, it wrote into its constitution the illusion of an undifferentiated Indian people coming together to form the Republic of India. The significance of the constitutional fiction is the suggestion that in the act of union all past histories, all past forms, were erased forever. Although historically the other two processes, centripetal and centrifugal, might predispose us to expect that the state as a whole will either be accountable to the parts or control the manner and pace of their creation, history shows us that this scenario does not necessarily follow. Constitutions mediate and alter this simplistic cause-effect sequence. Everything about the Indian state's constitutional birth belies the realities of its conception. Whereas the colonial entity was a motley collection of provinces and principalities, the new state was constituted by the monolithic "people of India" as a single political unit—the Republic of India. This republic was then decreed to be a "Union of States," simulating the devolution process of the unitary state rather than classic federalist conventions. Thus the first few provisions of the constitution set the stage for the centralized federation—the quasi-federal state—that India has been. No unit within the Indian federation can claim precedence because none predates the polity as a whole. Half a century after the promulgation of the constitution, the units do not resemble those at the moment of independence, having been altered several times.

Locus of the Authority to Demarcate Units

Following from the order of birth of units, we are faced with the question of who might create or alter units within the state. In classic federations, the center or the state as a whole does not have this right because it is a creation of the units as they come together. If regrouping or any other changes in unit demarcation must be undertaken, they must occur with the consent of the units concerned. However, in all three states in this study, the right to demarcate units is vested to different degrees in the center.

In all three constitutions adopted by Pakistan, a constitutional amendment bill that affects the provinces must be passed also in the provincial legislatures in order to come into effect. Both the 1962 and 1973 constitutions provide that an amendment to the constitution that would define the limits of a unit in the polity must be accepted by not less than a two-thirds majority in the legislature of the concerned province before that amendment can be presented for presidential assent. However, the way in which the "One Unit" arrangement came into existence shows that there is nothing sacrosanct about such provisions. The first announcement that the provinces of West Pakistan would be merged into one unit was made by Prime Minister Mohammed Ali on November 22, 1954. Later that year, an administrative council was established for West Pakistan by decree. In March 1955, the Emergency Powers Ordinance vested in the governor-general the power, among others, to constitute the province of West Pakistan and rename East Bengal as East Pakistan. Fortunately or unfortunately, as a consequence of a developing constitutional crisis, this power was never exercised. This matter was left to Pakistan's second Constituent Assembly, which met in July 1955 and finally, on September 30, 1955, legislated the merger of the provinces of West Pakistan. Quite apart from not consulting the provincial governments, they were dismissed and subsequent dissent put down rather harshly. It could be argued that since the constitutional crisis at the time was precisely about who could legitimately make laws and whose assent was essential, the only complaint one could have was that this outcome was hardly fair to the provinces that were effaced. There was no constitutional obligation as yet to consult the assemblies. The restoration of the provinces in 1973 was accomplished as part of the new constitution.

In states where the central government decides on the basis, shape, and number of units, ratification by existing units may or may not be required. Where this power vests primarily in the central government, the power of units and the people within are obviously diminished, as the central government may legislate them out of existence or alter their shape (and hence their store of natural and human resources) without much ado. The question of the identity of the unit or the place of the people within does not arise if the unit's continued existence depends on the pleasure of the central government, or even the will of neighboring units who may be its rivals—for water resources, for instance.

The 1978 Sri Lankan and the 1950 Indian constitutions are not as generous as the Pakistani constitution. A unitary state through all its constitutional changes to date, Sri Lanka began decentralizing its development administration in the 1960s. The 1978 constitution departed from the Soulbury and 1972 constitutions in that Article 5 stated that the Sri Lankan territory comprised twenty-four districts, and the First Schedule to the constitution listed them. All amendments require a two-thirds majority of the membership of the legislature to pass, but obviously, in a unitary state, there is no other requirement. In 1987, when the Indo–Sri Lanka Accord laid the basis for creating provincial assemblies (ergo, provinces), the constitution was amended to accommodate them. The Thirteenth Amendment established provincial councils and also listed nine provinces in the Eighth Schedule. The provinces were modeled on those the British set up between 1833 and 1889 and were subsequently sidelined in favor of district administration. In all these cases, the unitary center has created and dismantled units. In the draft constitutions that are being discussed as a means of resolving the ethnic conflict, regions displace provinces and the regional governments are explicitly prohibited from initiating changes in their area, form, and even name (Draft Constitution, March 1997, and Select Committee Report, October 1997). However, it is proposed that when a constitutional amendment affects the area or powers of a region, it should be approved by the relevant regional council (Select Committee Report, October 1997). In order to deal with the mixed population in places such as Amparai, referenda have been suggested as a possible means of resolution.

The Indian Parliament can create new units or alter existing ones through the passage of a bill by a simple majority. All that is required by way of other assent is that, in the event of changes in existing units, the president refer the bill to the legislature of the unit in question for "expressing its views thereon." Parliament and the president are not required by the constitution to pay heed to such expression. Conversely, when the state legislature votes to divide the state or to carve out another unit from within, it is not incumbent upon Parliament to act upon this recommendation except at its pleasure. Indian states have found this out to their chagrin. Madras State's quest to be renamed Tamil Nadu in the early 1960s is one example. More recently, in the 1995–1999 period, the Uttar Pradesh Assembly repeatedly and to no avail affirmed its support for a new state of Uttarakhand. (Contrast this outcome to the case of Jura in Switzerland, where local feeling against its inclusion in Bern led ultimately to a referendum in 1978; all of Switzerland voted to approve the creation of a new canton—Jura.)

When the state can more or less unilaterally legislate a unit out of existence, the power equation between the two is obviously unfavorable to the unit. Even in the Pakistani case, where there is a check on the power of the federal government to demarcate units, One Unit illustrated just how ineffective this check could be. Ivo Duchacek differentiates between "administrative federalism," in which the center can restructure the units or create new ones with or without their consent, and the "federal bargain," in which units that come together to form the federation remain indestructible and unalterable within that union (1970: 240). He agrees with Leslie Lipson, whom he quotes as saying that when the union antedates the units, it is the latter that must assert themselves. When constitutions foster the illusion that the union has precedence, even ahistorically, the message is clear: All who seek the benefits of membership in this polity must leave prior affiliations and allegiances at the door. The power to create, alter, and efface units adds to the advantage that administrative federalism accords the state as a whole.

The basis on which units are demarcated can further enhance the state's position. If units have been demarcated to reflect the ethnic or cultural identity of the people in a region, that unit becomes a marker of the state's recognition of their place in the polity as a whole. Such a unit is sought and guarded as a sign that people in the unit have the right to determine their future and that they have a place—physically and politically—in the system. The state's power over the existence and shape of units directly threatens that self-determination. The existence of those groups as players within the system is dependent on the pleasure of the state. If the state can legislate them in and out of existence (within the context of the system), they are truly powerless. Whereas administratively demarcated units carry less of this baggage to start with, it is possible for them over decades to develop the same sense of territorial identity. In that case, the right of the state to alter or efface them is as much of a threat to that identity as it is to the identity of a cultural group that seeks a recognized territorial home.

The Degree of State Identification with an Ethnic Group

If states can be ethnically identified or ethnically neutral and if the power to alter the shape, form, and name of the units rests with them, what consequences might we expect in either situation? Given that in most states, the life and existence of the units is constitutionally derived from what Taussig (1997) calls the "state of the whole," it is contended that the vision of the units is derivative of the vision of the state as a whole. Where the vision of the state is contested, it is likely the vision of the unit is also contentious. To achieve reconciliation in the polity, the first task is to find a way to reconcile the competing and seemingly incompatible visions of what should constitute the unit. There are many visions of the state-of-the-whole, and many visions of its parts. It is not a simple good-versus-evil, dark-versus-light contest that is depicted here. The many visions of the state-of-the-whole may be at odds with each other, and so may the visions of the parts. Then, as many different ways to group the components of the whole as there are, so many parts may be there. Any task of reconciliation involves some consensus building across all these visions.

Each vision of the state-of-the-whole gives rise to a predictable, consistent vision of the parts of that whole; each vision of a part has a corollary vision of the state-of-the-whole. For instance, to envision the

Malaysian state as primarily a Malay state is to predetermine what the place and role of other parts shall be. To envision the United States as an English-speaking state was until recently to create a rationale for learning English and assimilating among non-English-speaking immigrants. To envision Bangladesh as Bengali is to raise questions about the identity of the non-Bengalis and their bona fides as Bangladeshis. Conversely, for Quebecois to define themselves as separate and distinct undermines the idea of Canada as a bilingual, bicultural state. For increasing numbers of Asian immigrants in the United Kingdom and North African immigrants in France to make their presence felt in the political process in the past two decades is to undermine, respectively, the primordial British and French nature of those states. For China's new region, Hong Kong, to assert its distinctive political and economic but also cultural characteristics vis-à-vis the state-of-the-whole is to call into question the state-of-the-whole itself. The territorial dimension strengthens this relationship between the identity of the parts and the state-of-the-whole. Kashmir is only the most contentious example in South Asia, symbolizing the founding argument for Pakistan and its Indian counterpart and holding the legitimacy of both those state ideologies ransom in its valleys. In all three states in this study, the vision of the state has led to certain internal dispensations that have been negotiated over the years. Sri Lanka's 1972 constitution established a state in which one religion—that practiced by a significant segment of the linguistic majority community—was accorded "the foremost place." That majority language was to be the official language. Thus the state was identified with the Sinhala Buddhist community. Insofar as Sri Lanka was in 1972 a unitary state, the question of self-determining substate units did not arise. In the 1960s and 1970s, decentralization of the development administration took place but entirely at the initiative of the Sri Lankan government. The 1978 constitution established a unitary Sri Lanka whose territory "shall consist of the twenty-four administrative districts, the names of which are set out in the First Schedule, and its territorial waters" (Article 5). In spite of the fact that there have been amendments to the official-language clause in the constitution, the state continues to be identified, in the Tamil mind, with the Sinhala Buddhist community. This identification is at least partly due to the centrality of the Sinhala Buddhist electorate to any electoral success in the Parliament at Colombo and partly because of the grudging manner in which these changes have been made. Thus identified, the state has been limited in its ability to respond to the demands that have arisen from the Tamil community for a space of its own—first, a region or province in a federal Sri Lanka and then, independence.

Since the 1987 Indo–Sri Lanka Accord, devolution has emerged as the compromise catchphrase for those seeking to reconcile the Tamil demand for independence on the one hand with the Sinhalese ideal of a unitary Sri Lankan Buddhist homeland on the other. However, because the state has been explicitly identified with the latter vision in the past, it is that much harder to advocate the compromise solution. As the conflict has come to be framed as a zero-sum game, from the Sinhalese Buddhist state's point of departure, devolution is capitulation and not compromise at all—especially because the demand is made on behalf of the Tamil-majority regions of the north and the east rather than the heterogeneous central districts or the largely Sinhalese south. It may be argued, therefore, that had the Sri Lankan state not been identified with one community, devolution (and hence the creation of units) would have seemed less like a complete capitulation to the Tamil Tigers than it now does.

The Pakistani case sheds light on another facet of ethnic identification. The Pakistani state is identified with one religion, and its ideology assumes that all other distinctions and distinguishing features are unimportant. In good times, when the regime is secure, this ideology could mean that demands for units (and hence devolution) need not threaten the state. In more insecure times, such demands unsettle the regime, which might then contend that they undermine the ideology of the state. In Pakistan's experience, demands for units have not been intended as challenges to the basic premise of Pakistan's identity—that Pakistan is the homeland of South Asian Muslims. On the contrary, in Sind, the Sindh Muslim League's primary reason for supporting the demand for Pakistan was the expectation that Pakistan would deliver greater prosperity for Sind—a prosperity that in the British period had become the preserve of wealthy non-Muslim Sindhis as well as non-Sindhis. The dissolution of West Pakistan's units into one unit was justified in the name of creating parity with East Pakistan, which was essentially one province with a population more or less equivalent to that of the four provinces of the western wing. If the state's identity was based on Islam, that made no difference to this decision. If, however, it was tacitly understood and expected that a Pakistani should be a Pathan or a Punjabi or a Sindhi or a Kashmiri and speak Urdu, then there are two more implications to be considered. First, Islam is an incomplete definition of the Pakistani state's self-definition (East Pakistanis might have argued this point), at least as West Pakistani politicians seemed to see it. Second, if these other identities are so interchangeable and indistinct, there is no need for each to have its own space. The resistance in East Pakistan to One Unit and other policies formulated by the federal government led to war and secession largely because that resistance represented a challenge to the idea that in an Islamic state all other differences were irrelevant. After the war, One Unit was rescinded in the west, and the older provinces were restored. Ironically, this easy restoration seemed to also say that in an Islamic state internal divisions are irrelevant. The provinces of Pakistan did benefit to some extent during the Z. A. Bhutto years. Even in the period of military rule and Islamicization that followed, although there has been increased centralization and control over the provinces, the shape, number, and names of units have been unaffected. In other words, the vicissitudes of unit demarcation seem not to be a consequence of the state's particular identification, although they do provide us with passkeys to understand that identification and its connotations.

The Indian state is not formally identified with any one community. Nevertheless, the dialogue between visions of the state-of-the-whole and parts of the state has been constant, resulting in revisions on all sides. Where the demarcation of units is concerned, local demographics and local concerns have had the greatest impact. The rhetoric of each of these demands evokes some dimension of the state's constitutional or the government's political position. Whereas language has been the most common issue, there have been instances, such as the demand for a Punjabi Suba, where language and religion have combined to strengthen the claim for a unit. Likewise, the separatism of the Dravida movement was phrased in terms of defying and resisting the imposition of Hindi. Native Hindi speakers occupy a preponderance of seats in the Indian Parliament. In response to the anti-Hindu agitation, the government delayed indefinitely the adoption of Hindi as the official language of India. An India that is not officially identified one way or the other is able to experiment with a number of bases of demarcation and to respond with considerable flexibility to demands for territorial representation.

Demands for representation and for units or autonomy are usually inspired by local needs. They are usually framed in terms of statewide (state-of-the-whole) issues. Such demands are both more likely to be made and less likely to be met when the identity or identification of the

state is open to challenge. Neutrality largely improves the state's bargaining position, whereas identification of the state with one or the
other group diminishes its credibility and leverage. Ethnic neutrality
lowers the state's stakes in the negotiation. The state can be more flex-
ible and accommodating in its response, permitting, for instance, a variety of bases of unit demarcation.

The Basis of Demarcation

Essentially, two rationales are offered for the demarcation of units:
administrative convenience and culture. The first is more likely to
come from changes unilaterally initiated by the state-of-the-whole.
This effort is likely to characterize the state in its early days, when control must be established and central administrators are yet to develop an
instinct for the politics of identity and local issues. Political mobilization, participation, and increased representation, and the absorption of
the idea of self-determination at levels other than the state-of-the-
whole, precede the creation of cultural units. Cultural units are seldom
the result of unilateral demarcation because every such unit contains
other groups, and the state-of-the-whole can be divided in an infinite
number of ways on this basis.

Administrative convenience. When the British partitioned Bengal in
1905, they cited administrative convenience as the reason for the partition. Their concern was with political stability, especially in the frontier
province of Assam and in politically volatile Bengal, and security
developmental considerations were vital to that stability.

What are the factors that determine administrative convenience?
Size is the first possibility. As the size—of both the population and the
territory—of a political unit grows, its capacity to enforce its writ
across a population is limited by its infrastructure. This was the problem of the Maurya empire in India after the death of Asoka, its most
eminent ruler (c. 324–187 B.C.E.). The centralized bureaucracy of the
empire could not function without a strong center. One needs to ask, If
the Maurya empire had been functioning in the context of an information revolution, would it have been as limited in the absence of a strong
central leadership? In other words, is size relevant in the information
age?

In recent years, the idea of separating the hill areas of India's
largest state, Uttar Pradesh (UP), has gained momentum. Political par-

ties at the central level favor it as much as the Uttar Pradesh legislature, which has resolved twice in favor of the creation of a new state of Uttarakhand. One of the arguments for Uttarakhand is that the large size of UP (and other states) makes it impossible for every region to develop equally.[17] There is another argument that development planners made in India in the later years of the Rajiv Gandhi government when they tried to reform the Panchayati Raj structure: Development is best planned as close to the ground as possible. The greater the distance between the beneficiary and the decisionmaker, the more remote the benefit. This is certainly the argument proffered for the creation of a separate Vidarbha state out of Maharashtra and, possibly, Madhya Pradesh. Statehood offers regions within an existing state several opportunities: greater autonomy, a larger share of revenues and the right to levy more taxes, greater political opportunities for power and patronage, and finally, a ringside seat at the center. M. N. Buch cautions against very small units, however, saying that although initially they develop as expected, they can also become personal fiefdoms. Buch is also pessimistic about the ability of the small unit to overcome any loss of loyalty or credibility (Buch 1992).

According to Eric Hobsbawm (1990: 30–31), in the nineteenth century, the relationship between size and nationhood was well articulated. The primary argument was that in order to be viable, nations had to be of a certain size. "If it fell below this threshold, it had no historical justification" (30). Hobsbawm quotes Friedrich List, saying that smallness is a handicap that cripples states (meaning nation-states). List writes, "A small state can never bring to complete perfection within its territory the various branches of production."[18] The "national half-life" scenario—where every nation subsumes enough variation that its various groups keep seeking separation into smaller and smaller units—is rejected by this generation of thinkers on nationhood. They were convinced that such disintegration—balkanization, as Nehru and others liked to put it—was counterproductive. Hobsbawm (32) states what he calls the "threshold principle": "Self-determination for nations applied only to what were considered viable nations: culturally, and certainly economically whatever exactly viability meant."[19]

Hobsbawm discusses the belief that nationalism was seen as a unifying force (Hobsbawm 1990: 33). Nations were seen as a first step toward world unity. This perspective is interesting if you look at sub-state units as nations in a multinational setting. First, if the world is moving inexorably toward unity, that process must be presumed to occur all the way down. Second, if integration is the natural law of history, smaller and smaller groups must lose their identity. Third, if there is, moreover, an ideal size for national units, presumably that ideal applies to state, nonstate, and substate national units. In this case, minorities within substate units would have to be of a certain size to matter culturally and politically. Fourth (and Hobsbawm [1990: 36–37] discusses this), if, once the process of integration was set in motion, minority groups within the state accepted the principle of viability and automatically abjured their right to self-determination, the task of the state would be merely to impress that principle upon its citizens to achieve national integration. This task, in fact, is what the national integration project in most states has been about.

Working with Hobsbawm's ideas as discussed in the previous paragraphs, one must conclude that since anything else would be anachronistic, size and administrative efficiency are sound bases for unit demarcation. This is the argument that Hobsbawm offers: Once a group accepts that it has to have a viable nation to be a "real" nation, it would follow that all cultures and languages smaller than that viable unit would inevitably disappear in the course of history (1990: 34). Once this view is commonly held and challenges to states from substate nationalities cease, states (or the largest nation within) would have no reason not to foster all languages and traditions within, if only to claim a "macro-national palette" (35). Minority and majority cultures need not be mutually exclusive in these circumstances (34–35).

Further, we might conclude that if the vision is of a multinational state, the threshold principle is pertinent whether one is demarcating units on the basis of size or culture. If the state is not culturally but politically defined, then the threshold principle and the idea of nationalism as a unifying force are relevant because they sanction to some extent assimilationist strategies of integration, and assimilationists invariably oppose cultural demarcations on similar grounds.

Geographical factors also enhance or inhibit administrative convenience. Three deserve our attention. Regions that are set apart physically are geographically natural units. Islands (Lakshadweep and the Andaman and Nicobar Islands), valleys (Kashmir in the state of Jammu and Kashmir), river deltas (Bengal), coastal areas that are demarcated by hills (Baluchistan), and remote areas cut off by rivers or mountains (the Federally Administered Tribal Areas of the Pakistani northwest) are examples. Physical impediments to their day-to-day administrative integration with the rest of the polity provide a good reason for demarcating such regions or zones as separate units.

Related to the matter of geographical isolation is the fact that needs, resources, and issues are often localized (Paddison 1983b: 25). For instance, flood management in the Brahmaputra valley is a problem of considerable magnitude that a government based in Calcutta may have neither the comprehension, the will, nor the experience to resolve. In Sri Lanka, the fact that the Tamils of Jaffna, Batticaloa, and Trincomalee on the one hand and the Tamils of the central highlands on the other often occupy different political platforms, notwithstanding their shared ethnicity, is a reflection of these differences. The issues that politicized the Tamils of the northeast (called the Sri Lankan Tamils) were representation, employment, and language policy. Although these affected the Indian Tamils, as the Tamils working in the plantations are called, their issues are arguably more fundamental—citizenship being the most important one. This divergence of interests has permitted the two communities to develop politically separate identities. An administrative unit based on the concentration of Tamils in the northeast is unlikely to make the issues of the plantation Tamils part of its agenda.

Finally, does it make a difference whether units (or parts of units) are geographically contiguous? At the level of nation-states (or the state-of-the-whole), the case of Pakistan before 1971 suggests that it does. It seems that when the state-of-the-whole is spread across discontinuous regions, its unity is not sustainable. However, at the substate level, such units are sustainable. Several of India's Union Territories include geographically discontinuous sections that have a common colonial history and were decolonized together: Goa, Daman, and Diu (before Goa attained statehood); Pondicherry, Karikal, Yanam, Mahe, and Chandranagar; and Dadra and Nagar Haveli. Chandigarh, the joint capital of Punjab and Haryana, is in Punjab but is administered as a union territory. One is forced to ask why such discontinuous units are sustainable at the substate and not state level. The same administrative and communication problems must obtain at either level. It would seem that the presence of an overarching, sovereign state with responsibility for securing and maintaining links among the segments of a unit makes all the difference to the viability of such units. However, history or some other factor, not geography, must be the basis for their demarcation as a unit.

There are also economic arguments that underscore a particular demarcation of units. Of all the ways to categorize units, center-periphery relations have received the greatest attention from political geographers (Rokkan 1981; Rokkan and Urwin 1983; Paddison 1988). Center-periphery inequalities were an important justification provided for the partition of Bengal in 1905. It was argued that Assam needed to be made independent of Bengal's largesse in order to develop. However, the argument was refuted on the grounds that Partition did not alter the status of Assam, which continued to be appended to East Bengal, a relatively prosperous province and culturally quite distinct. In Sri Lanka, as elsewhere, the center-periphery rhetoric has been appended to the self-determination platform of the Tamils to demand anything from a separate province to a separate state of their own.

In conclusion, administrative convenience as a basis of unit demarcation may be defined in terms of size, geography, or economics. It is also, however, possible that those who demand a culturally defined unit will occasionally co-opt any of these for their rhetoric.

Culture. The second broad basis on which units are demarcated is culture, under which rubric we might include language, religion, ethnicity, and even race, acknowledging that these are sociopolitical constructs and that they can be mutually unintelligible. Do cultural factors promote or obstruct administrative efficiency and national (state) unity? It would seem that they do both. After all, several states have chosen to decentralize and devolve power to units that are culturally defined as a means of conflict prevention or resolution. Province-level units in Nigeria, Spain, Belgium, India, Pakistan, and the United Kingdom are characterized by their association over the years with some ethnic group, and the province is often named after that group or that language (Oyo, Catalonia, Walloonia, Gujarat, Sind, and Scotland, to name one from each of those states).

After 1956, two new bases for statehood found their way into the structure of the Indian Union—language and ethnicity. The most important argument in favor of linguistic-based states is that they give each linguistic group (nationality?) a qualified self-determination. The demand for linguistic or other cultural bases for separate units contradicts the idea of a universalizing history. It suggests instead the importance of the particular. Linguistic units replicate at their level the structure of the state. Their ideology may, however, contrast with that of the state. Units are culturally defined as a consequence of the state's self-definition or demands from cultural subnational groups. In the former case, the political rhetoric of both the state and the units is likely to be tinged with some particularist ideas. In the latter, the political rhetoric in the units is likely to retain the militant and activist tones of the separatist struggle, and the contest in the political arena is likely to be about who is truer to the cause of group identity.

This latter rhetoric is certainly visible in the Tamil Nadu case. Tamil Nadu politics is the preserve of the successor parties of the Dravida movement. Each of these tries to establish itself in the eyes of the electorate and the intelligentsia as the most effective defender of the purity and development of the Tamil heritage, especially against the incursions of northern hegemony. The Dravida Munnetra Kazhagam (DMK) government that was elected in 1996 made it mandatory for all shop signs to be in Tamil and on October 2 renamed Madras, Chennai. This conflict within the unit is in sharp contrast to the politics of the Indian state, which still privileges a larger, all-encompassing Indian national identity. When this contrast exists, it is easy to cast questions in an either/or mode. For example, I asked Tamil respondents in Madras, "Would you pick Indian over Tamil identities in a crisis?"[20]

Such ultimatums are blunted when the basis for unit demarcation is not cultural. But when the administratively defined unit or the unit defined by size leave members of a cultural group on different sides of a border, there are several other problems. Respondents in Sri Lanka told me that linguistic states made it possible for any ethnic conflict that arose in India to be contained within the boundaries of one unit and not spill over to other parts of the country. One might argue that whereas there might be some truth to this view, it is equally plausible to attribute that effect to the size of the state and the plurality of its linguistic groups rather than to its internal structuring. In any case, let us examine this Sri Lankan view of Indian ethnic politics as a possible reason to form culturally defined units.

Culturally defined units do contain the "nationalism" of their dominant groups, but there are at least two qualifiers that come to mind. First, when regions within the unit (particularly regions on the unit border) have roughly equal populations of two or more ethnic groups or nationalities, it remains a live issue as to which unit that region should belong. Within the cases being studied, Belgaum in India (which is included in Karnataka but is occasionally and violently claimed by Maharashtrians) and the North-Eastern Province in Sri Lanka are good examples. Second, when the cultural definition of a unit satisfies the needs of the dominant group but overlooks others within the same unit, there is room to question the limits to demarcation on the basis of culture. In Sri Lanka, those who ask why Tamils and not other groups must have provinces that reflect their identity are alluding to this double standard. In the case of the Eastern Province, this question is indeed relevant: What about the Moors within that unit? Are they not entitled to fair representation? In India, Coorg (Karnataka), Gorkhaland (West Bengal), Telengana (Andhra Pradesh), Saurashtra and Kutch (Gujarat), Ladakh and Jammu (Jammu and Kashmir), to name a handful, could all make similar claims; examples in Pakistan are the Saraiki speakers in Punjab, the Muhajirs, and the Pakhtoons. There are always limits to the application of the cultural-linguistic principle, and these contain the seeds of controversy.

Devolution proposals drafted in Sri Lanka demarcate the regions of the north and east as distinct from the rest of the island and as coinciding broadly with Tamil-majority regions. Yet not one of them stipulates that those regions, either together or separately, shall be identified by the name of the majority community. In keeping with the nomenclature that the British instituted, the provinces or regions are named simply for their geographical location. This strategy defuses the act of carving out units that resemble "traditional homelands" and gives changes the air of simple administrative ones.

Every so often, the heady mix of language and land is compounded by the addition of religion. This is the Palestine problem, and it was also at one point the issue in Punjab. Historically, Punjab has been home to Hindus, Sikhs, and Muslims. Partition simplified the religious mix by dividing "Muslim" West Punjab from "Hindu-Sikh" East Punjab. After 1947, as a result of the Punjabi Suba movement, East Punjab was divided in 1966 into Punjab and Haryana with some hill areas becoming part of Himachal Pradesh. Punjab had a Sikh majority and Haryana a Hindu majority. Punjabi written in the Gurmukhi script was the official language in Punjab, and in Haryana it was Hindi, thus meeting the aspirations of Hindi speakers in the region. The Sri Lankan case is also a good example of what happens when language, land, and religion get mixed up in the political rhetoric.

The important thing to note about culture as a basis of demarcation is that states seldom applied this basis universally. In most states, only some units are defined culturally or identified with a culture. For instance, in Canada, Quebec is associated with French Canadian cultural identity, and several provinces represent English Canadian identity. Likewise, in Switzerland, the cantons crosscut linguistic and religious diversity. South Asian states are no exception. In Pakistan, Sind, Punjab, and Baluchistan are defined by culture; the North-West Frontier Province is not. In India, which began the process of linguistic reorganization in 1956, the reorganization has not been thorough, and many exceptions remain. There are linguistic groups that do not have their own province, for example, those who speak Tulu, Urdu, or even Sindhi. As provincial borders were redrawn, multilingual districts and border areas where speakers of the province's minority languages predominated were another exception (Belgaum in Karnataka, for instance). Finally, there are instances where special local considerations led to departures from the linguistic basis. The creation of a corridor through Bihar, allowing West Bengal access to its northern districts, is one example. As Joseph Schwartzberg points out, a whole complex of factors enters into decisions about unit demarcation and undercuts the adoption of one basis for all units (1978: 168–172).

Comparing bases of demarcation. All in all, it seems that there are advantages and disadvantages to administrative and cultural units. More often than not, states do not have a choice, and creating a new unit may be a first step toward reconciliation with a disgruntled group or may buy the state some time before a group goes from identifying to actualizing the embodiment of its vision as a new state. The rule of thumb, experience suggests, is flexibility. What distinguishes the Indian experience, all its failures notwithstanding, seems to be the willingness of the state-of-the-whole, by and large, to enter into ad hoc, case-by-case arrangements of its territory and polity. This flexibility has resulted in a plethora of special provisions and awkward exceptions to the neat hierarchy of administrative units, but it has kept the conflict to a minimum. It is in those instances and periods that the state has been unwilling to follow an ad hoc policy that conflict has become unmanageable.

Unit Demarcation as the Currency of State-Group Negotiation

In recent years, federalism has come to be associated with ethnic conflict resolution (Smith 1995; Horowitz 1985; Elazar 1987; Duchacek 1970). Federalism's potential as an instrument of conflict resolution lies in power-sharing benefits that accrue from federal arrangements. My primary interest is in something prior to that—the demarcation of units.

Conflicts between states and groups originate in disputes over identity, distribution of resources, access to participation, and the rightful or wrongful exercise of power, usually by the state against a group. For identity-based groups in particular, these conflicts are really negotiations about their place in the polity as a whole. Land and territorial issues may enter the state-group dialogue at any stage—as grievance, as demand, and as part of the negotiation.

The desire for a unit of one's own may arise in many circumstances. It is easiest to anticipate when a community is divided by international or internal borders (the demand for Pakhtoonistan, for instance), when it is engulfed by another community (the resistance of Sri Lankan Muslims in the Eastern Province to the idea of merging the Northern and Eastern Provinces), or when, having lived in the same region for a long time, people find themselves facing discrimination (Tamils in the north of Sri Lanka). However, the demand for a unit of one's own need not be tied to groups that are concentrated in one area. The Pakistan movement is the best example of the demand for a unit for people scattered across a subcontinent. The core of the homeland demanded would be Muslim-majority provinces, but the demand was made neither solely by them nor solely for them. In this case, lack of confidence in nonterritorial representation arrangements makes the unit—independent or simply separate within a federal structure—appear to be a more reliable solution.

The previous paragraph cites both substate and transstate examples because neither as grievance nor as demand do territorial issues respect the analytical or real confines of the state. When one considers that territorial demands can be as small as the renaming of a block, at one extreme, to secession from one or more states, at the other, this is immediately apparent. Within a unit, the quest for recognition can give rise to the demand for nonterritorial rights and privileges such as language rights, special educational concessions, or even state patronage of cultural institutions. However, it is also possible that at the local level, renaming a street or a neighborhood or the creation of a local government unit to give special voice to a community that is clustered in one area can satisfy the political aspirations of the community.

By and large, the kinds of substate territorial demands that are most often studied fall into two categories: demands for a change in the status of an existing unit and demands for changes in the name, shape, and area of an existing unit or the creation of a new one. Again, this unit may be created within or outside the state-of-the-whole. This range of

Figure 2.1   A Continuum of Territorial Demands

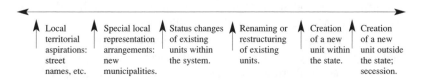

substate territorial demands is important because when the negotiation begins, the fact that there is a continuum of sorts between different kinds of territorial demands makes it possible for both states and groups to bargain. This continuum is illustrated in Figure 2.1.

When negotiations begin, the state-of-the-whole has almost by definition to resist the last demand—secession. Short of that, there is a range of positions that the various sides may discuss. Each of these represents a different degree of recognition for the identity group within the polity. Local recognition of a community may be enough if the group is small enough.

Changes of status usually are upgrades. In the context of the Indian federation, there are two categories of units, states and Union Territories. The latter are directly administered by an agent of the central government, and their autonomy is quite limited. States have their own administrative and judicial structures, and they are the true constituent units of the Union of India. Some states have special constitutional status. This constitutional arrangement was invented for Jammu and Kashmir to set it apart from the rest of the Indian Union in recognition of the special circumstances of its accession. In the past twenty years, a variety of similar arrangements have been extended to other states (Nagaland, Assam, Manipur, Arunachal Pradesh, Sikkim, and Mizoram, among others), often as part of the settlement of a long-standing conflict. These states enjoy the maximum autonomy available to units in the Indian constitution, and it has been argued that this status is a possible solution for many of India's problems (Mukarji 1992). Achieving an upgrade in status—for example, from a union territory to a state or from a state to a state with special constitutional status—involves a simple bilateral negotiation between the unit and the state-of-the-whole.

Renaming and restructuring are different issues altogether. Renaming is not difficult, although if the proposed name is an assertion of nativist sentiment in a state that does not recognize particularistic identities as politically germane, the project is seldom looked upon with favor. The central government's reluctance to rename Madras as Tamil Nadu is a case in point. Ironically, the government had previously allowed group-identity names for the new language-based states carved out of Madras; an example is Andhra Pradesh.

Restructuring involves a larger negotiation, at least politically. The endless protests against One Unit in Pakistan, the resistance to the merger of the Northern and Eastern Provinces in Sri Lanka, and the resistance to the Jharkhand movement in the Indian state of Bihar are only a few examples. Restructuring merely creates a different set of winners and losers; thus whereas it may be easy to legislate, it is hard to sell. It results also in the loss of resources to some units even as it increases the resources of others.

Merely one kind of the restructuring, the creation of a new unit is the most explicit illustration of the connection between identity and unit demarcation. It is an act of recognition whereby the state-of-the-whole acknowledges that a unique community may make some of the rules by which it lives and pursue its interests even as it has interests in common with the whole. Creation of a new unit is the most expansive negotiated gesture possible in the dialectic between the state and the group over territory. The magnitude of this gesture is the reason the Sinhalese Buddhist community is so reluctant to concede provincial autonomy to what will in effect be Tamil provinces even though, as was pointed out earlier, every set of proposals has studiously avoided identifying the units with one or the other ethnic group. Nevertheless, the demographic composition of the Northern Province makes it inevitable that it will be a Tamil-dominated, ergo Tamil, province.

Secession is essentially a unilateral act on the part of the group. In effect, the group withdraws from the dialogue and the negotiation is ended at this point. Again, the Sri Lankan case provides the best illustration. Dialogue between the Tamil Tigers, the most powerful Tamil organization, and the Sri Lankan government has long seemed almost impossible because the Tigers will settle for nothing short of independence and the Sri Lankan government cannot negotiate independence. The moderate Tamil groups that are willing to consider solutions short of independence lack the military and political clout to be credible negotiators. The independence of Bangladesh came in slightly different circumstances. There, in the first instance, the demand was not for independence but recognition within the state-of-the-whole. That proved to be non-negotiable to the Pakistan government, and so secession became the way in which the attempt to negotiate was broken off.

Closing Thoughts

In this section, I have tried to show that there is a close relationship between identity politics and unit demarcation, and by extension, unit demarcation and national integration. I have looked at five dimensions of this dialectic, spelling out the parameters of the identity-territory relationship. When states seek integration, groups seek to retain their identity to differing degrees. The importance of territory as the repository of collective remembrances, as a resource base, as home, sooner or later makes one's own territory indispensable to the group's vision of itself and its place in the polity as a whole. The tension this need creates in the political process is writ in the dialectic of unit demarcation.

Identification with the State

Subcontinental writers and scholars are fond of using cricket as a lens to the region's labyrinthine identity politics (Nandy 1985; Krishna 1993). Much as with moments of more conventional conflict, it seems as though people's loyalties are pared down to the their essences during important cricket tournaments. These scholars are not far removed from the reality of South Asian neighborhoods, where passions rise and riots are known to begin because someone had the temerity to vocally back the "wrong" side. Field research for this project was conducted in spring 1996 when the World Cup Cricket tournament was under way in South Asia. Discussions held on the ethnic conflict in Sri Lanka would lapse into heated discussions of cricket and why it was or was not possible to support a Sri Lankan team in which there was only one Tamil player. The Indian team was upheld in Colombo as the epitome of a perfectly integrated national team, notwithstanding contentions to the contrary in India. In the Indian context, it does not really matter which team one supports until the Indian team plays the most prominent of India's others—Pakistan. Those non-Muslims who anticipate that support for the two teams will fall along communal lines make that defection a part of their litany against the Muslims of India, who are often accused by Hindutvavadins of not being "Indians first," a common expression indicating a single, primary, overriding allegiance within the state.

Outside sports, in most of our everyday experiences the question of being anything first, second, or last does not arise. It is a divisive view of the state that predicates citizenship on undivided allegiance. If Muslims were not asked what they are first, they would no more have to consider the question than do Hindus, who are seldom asked to choose between their loyalties. So pressed, a Hindu Indian who is Hindu first might be construed as equally disloyal to the secular Indian state. In the case of Bangladesh, a Bengali is able to be Bengali and Bangladeshi, but if a Chakma were to say that she were Chakma and Bangladeshi, the question of prior allegiance would arise. If one could accept that conflict arises between these identities only when the state acts in a manner that forces a choice, as when it promulgates policies that push Chakmas out of their homes, then it is clear that the question is a mischievous or at least counterproductive one.

There are two levels at which one might read the individual's identification with the state. The first is citizenship itself, an overt, official expression of allegiance that is established through bureaucratic procedures, proven through the possession of official documents such as passports and identity cards, and articulated through participation in the political process. Citizenship can, however, be merely a procedural expression of identification. At the level of affect, there exist several shades of identification, ranging from allegiance to alienation, so that in the political arena, the issue is not so easily settled. Even though the state's existence is predicated on the habitual obedience of its citizenry and citizenship itself may be read as an act of tacit consent, most citizens do not habitually obey the state. We also cannot assume that their continued presence within its borders and the fact that they do not repudiate citizenship indicates allegiance or even that identification with the state is the single most important association in their minds. The contrast between the official and the affective indicators of identification form the subject of this section.

Even states that allow dual citizenship make the assumption that inhabitants prize citizenship above all other affiliations. Laski points out that such a view follows from particular historical circumstances in which Jean Bodin, Thomas Hobbes, John Austin, and others theorized sovereignty and obligation (Laski 1921: 233–234). What he considered outdated in his time is even more so almost a century later. Political pluralists such as Laski, G.D.H. Cole, and F. W. Maitland contended that individuals belonged to many groups and associations, and the state, being "an absorptive animal" (Laski 1921: 235), seeks to undermine or subsume all others. Pluralists argued that any view of the state as either the all-powerful sovereign or the sole locus of allegiance was misplaced. They cited examples such as the limits of imperial control over local affairs in the colonies, U.S. federalism, and the place of the church in Europe to show that there were real limits to the power of the state (Vincent 1987:184). Pluralists opposed both classic individualism and Hegelian statism as two sides of the same coin. Whereas individuals were easier to manipulate, resistance to the expanding powers of the state would come from groups.

Closer to our time, those who write about multiculturalism and cultural pluralism take this argument one step further. Although the political pluralists were not talking about identity groups, Charles Taylor and others are. They have used these terms to describe the realities of the late twentieth century as well as to prescribe social and political arrangements in which the potential for conflict among groups, on the one hand, and groups and the state, on the other, can be minimized. Taylor, for instance, argues that the state should recognize the cultural rights of groups within its boundaries in the context of a framework of civil and political rights for all (Taylor 1994). In any event, the understanding still seems to be that by an act of recognition or facilitation, the requisite degree of allegiance can be fostered among those otherwise on the periphery.

It was the intention of this study to look at national integration from the point of view of those being integrated into the state. Given the context of my field research in Sri Lanka, I was hesitant to limit the ways in which my respondents might identify themselves. The question that came closest to making them pick one identification was, "How would you tell me the story of your country?" (Rajagopalan 1997c). Respondents chose to narrate either a history based largely on Sinhalese legend and Pali chronicles, Tamil history and experiences, or a more secular chronology of events within what is now the Sri Lankan state. I did not probe their choice of identity, letting their stories direct my understanding of the situation as a whole. However, often in the course of the interview, the respondent who identified with Tamil or Sinhalese would speak as a Sri Lankan, and the Sri Lankan as a Tamil or Sinhalese. Just as often, my own identity in the interview would be changed; that is, in their answers, respondents would identify me in different ways—as an Indian, as a Tamil, as a Bombayite, as someone studying in the United States, as "one of us," as "one of them."

This experience and the Sinhalese refrain that Tamils in South Asia would one day unite and form a nation-state of their own led me to add a series of questions on the subject when I conducted interviews in

Madras. If there was any room to doubt that people identify themselves in more ways than one, the interviews in Madras put paid to that doubt. One of my questions suggested a rank ordering of Tamil and Indian identities, and almost universally, it met with puzzlement and then criticism. No matter how vehemently the respondent had upheld one or the other identity, the suggestion that either was primary brought on a defense of the other identity claimed. The questions about Tamil identity were asked only in India. At the end of the section, the implications and findings of this research will be discussed in the context of the other two case studies, Pakistan and Sri Lanka.

The Tamil-Indian Relationship

What is, for you, the relationship between being Tamil and being Indian? In order to illustrate what I meant by this question, I often used three Venn diagrams (Figure 2.2). Each depicts a particular relationship between being Tamil and being Indian. The first shows Indianness and Tamilness as unrelated. The second suggests that the identities intersect, showing that there are Indians who are not Tamils, Tamils who are not Indians, and some Indians who are Tamils and some Tamils who are Indians. Finally, Tamils are shown as a subset of Indians, completely absorbed by the larger identity.

In retrospect, using these diagrams restricted the range of positions that respondents could have taken. The diagrams suggest that there are only three possible relationships, each defining an absolute state of affairs. However, the responses to these diagrams suggest otherwise.

Figure 2.2   Three Depictions of the Tamil-Indian Relationship

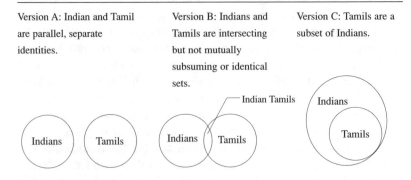

Version A: Indian and Tamil are parallel, separate identities.

Version B: Indians and Tamils are intersecting but not mutually subsuming or identical sets.

Version C: Tamils are a subset of Indians.

I think they *are* intersecting. . . . I think that I tilt more towards being a Tamilian. I mean that when that is going to come under pressure, I wouldn't take it. . . . Not actually, not that strongly but in a very mild way. *(Let's say you are more often a Tamil than anything.*[21]*)* Yes, when I think if I open up from being a Tamilian, I don't mind going international. I belong to the world, than just Indian. Somewhere, you don't have that much of a sense of belonging to the country. . . . It's not exactly . . . you can't even say that. In a way it is a subset. In a way it is not. . . . It can become a subset, but when you're going to be respected and treated well. (I28)

Respondents, as we see in the previous instance, disregarded any limits placed by the diagrams and chose instead to regard them as suggesting either an actual or normative sequence. They moved from one choice to another, saying, "This, but also that" or "This, except when that." As we see in the previous quotation, there is a suggestion of sequence or direction in these three sets. One might place the three diagrams at three points on a linear continuum, suggesting that movement from Version A to Version C represents increasing integration, where integration is assimilation of a sort.

In this sense, the national integration debate can be seen as a debate about where to place the limits on this process and how to maintain that position. If this is so, then the choice of more than one position is in fact more revealing than the choice of any one position. It indicates the degree of integration, and it also reveals the conditions of that integration.

Tamil and Indian as parallel identities. The most common interpretation of Version A was unexpected. One would expect, "There is no relationship. These are parallel, unrelated identities." However, respondents seemed to use that image to convey not just "My feelings for one are unrelated to my feelings for the other" but also "Such a question makes no sense to me." When there are two parallel identities, one might read two independent propositions: (1)"I am an Indian" and (2) "I am a Tamil." Logically, the propositions may be linked by "or" and by "and." My initial assumption was that the diagram would be read with an "or." However, more often than not, it was read with an "and." Witness:

Are you an Indian or a Tamilian? There has been a question recently. . . . I am a Tamilian who is proud of India and an Indian who is proud of being a Tamil. . . . I don't differentiate between the two in the sense that I function as a Tamil for forty-eight hours, the next ninety-six hours I am an Indian. That doesn't happen that way. You are both simultaneously. It cannot be another way. (I45)

There is no relationship. Absolutely nothing. . . . I feel I am much integrated to my counterpart in Lucknow. And Allahabad. I feel so much at home and I know people also . . . the only difference is the distance. I am in Madras, and that my friend is in Lucknow or Allahabad or Varanasi. I never feel strange when I go to these countries. Except the language. I am not very proficient in Hindi. (I82)

By virtue of living in India, I feel I am an Indian. That doesn't feel very difficult. To feel like an Indian and to feel like a Tamilian does not seem very difficult. We have got used to it. Even Subramania Bharati would say on the one hand, "Vande Mataram" [I bow down to thee, Mother], and then he would say, "We must honour this regional mother."[22] Regionalism, nationalism and then an international attitude . . . all three are not hard to combine. (I22)

In other words, the parallel relationship suggested in Version A is to be read not as suggesting distance or incompatibility between the two identities but as an absence of hierarchy between them. This is the opposite of "I am an Indian first" or "I am a Tamil first." It says, "I am both, always."

Tamil and Indian as intersecting identities. Version B yielded four logical propositions: (1) Some Tamils are Indians; (2) Some Tamils are not Indians; (3) Some Indians are Tamils; (4) Some Indians are not Tamils. Picking this version as a description of the Tamil-Indian relationship effectively says little because it lays out a range of possibilities as to the degree of intersection. How many is "some" on either side? It was simply not enough to just say that the identities intersected. What made this version interesting in spite of this limitation was the idea that the three versions might represent a progressive but reversible integration. Finally, Version B is of interest because competing allegiances are possible.

One issue that came up over and over in Sri Lanka was that of the affinity between Sri Lankan and Indian Tamils. Several Sri Lankans insisted that the independence of Eelam would be followed by a renewed secessionist demand in Tamil Nadu. The possibility of intersecting identities provided the premise for asking about a competing allegiance to non-Tamil Indians and non-Indian Tamils. The question I asked: *If you had to place your affinity with non-Tamil Indians and non-Indian Tamils on a scale, which one would carry greater weight with you?*

The Tigers are very clear about it, they are not interested in mainland Tamil Nadu at all. They have never been interested. (*Is mainland Tamil Nadu interested?*) No, we have lots of sympathies. You know, because there is so much cultural unity between us and them. We speak the same language. . . . They are very self-centred. They are not interested in the welfare of this Tamil Nadu, or getting autonomy for Tamil Nadu. They are more interested in their own cause. Apart from that, I don't think they are interested in anything else. I don't think it will spill over . . . this whole . . . that Tamils are aiming at creating a Vishal Tamizhagam that is inclusive of both the Eelam as well as Tamil Nadu. It's all bullshit. That is only canard and false propaganda of the state and the media. They are not at all interested. . . . Nor are we. I don't think we are interested. (I57)

Thamizhan, Andhran, Karnatakan, . . . we should not hesitate to accept that. To say that [one is] Thamizhan is not opposed to Indian, opposed to Indian unity. We shouldn't say that; we should say only "Indian." We should not say that. Ramalinga Pillai, a Congress freedom-fighter who was in Amaravathi jail, said something that the Dravida movement did not, "Say you are Tamilian, raise your head and stand." He sang that song. It is not a secessionist song. "Tamilian is our ethnicity, it has its own characteristics" was also sung by a Congressman. We can't call that secessionist. But today, movements that say that, that call themselves like that, are all suspect. . . . This is a country with a large number of communities, with a large number of cultures, whose people speak many languages—only if that is accepted, can all these people get together and establish a community of equals. . . . Unless that is the case, even a small thing that you do [is seen as] suppression of the Tamilian by the northerner. Or in Assam where the Assamese unite and suppress . . . the UP-ite suppresses the hill-people . . . we must accept the divisions. These are not real divisions. They bear the seal of history. Those seals cannot be erased like election ink. They treat it like election ink and try to erase it. (I75)

There were those who gave primacy to Tamil identity. They also, however, discounted the feasibility of a separate Tamil state.

After seeing . . . what happened to Yugoslavia, I strongly feel . . . I have very strong Tamil sentiments personally, I am very proud of being a Tamil, but I don't want to be atavistic. I feel that I would be impoverished if I happen to live in a separate Tamil Nadu. In a sense, culturally. Because you are always enriched. (I57)

We don't believe that Tamil can function on its own as a region. So we have to remain a part in a larger set-up. (I22)

If we said, no secession, but prepared an arsenal and prepared for an uprising, we are still secessionist. But we have to take [. . .] at their word. If you don't oppose them, nobody is secessionist in India. Everyone wants India to stay together. Today, as we speak, parties only aspire to capture power. (I75)

. . . for Tamil language it will be beneficial . . . to be part of a big India. So maintaining our separate identity need not be opposed to being part of an Indian nation. . . . I personally feel that I will be completely impoverished [by separation] because I like Hindustani music, I like Odissi dance, I like the sculptures of north, I like the miniature paintings of Rajasthan. I like the food. And you see the churidar is such a liberative thing for the Tamil girls. . . . We are not self-sufficient. We don't have a perennial river also. We can always say we can survive. [But] see what happened in Yugoslaviia. . . . So when I say there will be tension at some chance, when I feel that being Tamil is more important than being Indian, the tension will be there but still I would not think in terms of getting away from India. (I57)

Version B is also interesting in terms of another of my questions: *What is the "place" of Tamil or Tamil Nadu in the Indian context?* There are at least four ways this question can be addressed, identifying the actual and ideal places of both Tamil (as in culture) and Tamil Nadu.

THE PLACE OF TAMIL. The actual and ideal places of Tamil, even when they varied, were in fact not unlinked. The actual place of Tamil was a combination of the place it deserved by virtue of the qualities it possessed and its place in the contemporary economic and political dispensation. Prior to assessing the place of Tamil in India, several respondents chose to reflect on what they saw as its lamentable condition in Tamil Nadu.

I don't have much idea about what it should be or what it is in the Indian context because I think it is losing its place even in the state context. In this generation, how many people can speak the language, leave alone read and write it. I think that Tamilians as a whole, they think that speaking Tamil is . . . we really take pride in saying we can't. (I28)

For Tamils living in Tamil Nadu, language was one of the sensitive topics and it was a great obsession at a point of time. . . . Within Tamil Nadu, Tamil has acquired a political dimension. And so naturally, various equations exist. Pro-Tamil, anti-Tamil, the extreme Tamil-lovers, and that kind of a thing exists. Tamil as a whole, Tamil will play a role, like any other language in India, it will play its role in the modern India. My personal wish is that one generation is slowly and visibly moving out of Tamil, in the sense that because they were not taught in Tamil, they don't speak Tamil, not out of any hatred for it, because they were not trained to do so. So . . . I am worried about the place of Tamil in Tamil Nadu than about the place of Tamil in India. In India it has got a natural role to play. If India can afford to have all the languages mentioned in the Constitution as its official languages, then Tamil also can have a role to play. Otherwise, Tamil cannot play a big role outside the Tamil belt. (I34)

On the whole, consensus held that the language had declined in spite of the fuss the Dravidian movement made. This decline was partly because, as several respondents pointed out, the fuss was about keeping Hindi out and not about promoting Tamil. The decline of Tamil was in fact attributed to the adoption of the two-language system rather than the three-language system: Parents picked Hindi over Tamil as a second language because Hindi provided more opportunities to their children and because Tamil was a low-prestige option. A three-language system wherein students would study English, Tamil, and finally Hindi was the suggested alternative. Tamil became a political position rather than a language to develop for modern communication. Thus research in Tamil remained in ancient Tamil classics rather than to promote better communication. (The development of Tamil versions of programming languages was one suggestion mentioned by respondents.) As a result, Tamil is not competitive as a medium for economic activity.

In the contemporary context, they have kept it [Tamil] as one among the regional languages. In India, we have an official language, we can't accept it as a national language, it is an official language— Hindi. And there is one classical language. Only Sanskrit has that status. Then there is another classification—modern Indian languages. In that there are regional languages, and Tamil is one of them. We fought that inclusion, saying it was wrong. Tamil is in the same category as Telugu, Malayalam which are running "nuclear house-

holds," which many don't like. Tamil should be given a classical status. . . . We are not a regional language. (I22)

As far as the recent political role goes, I think there has been a lot of
injustice to the non-Hindi civilisation, non-Hindi cultures, non-Hindi
ethnic groups over the years. (I45)

Everyone agrees that Tamil deserves more respect, both within and
outside Tamil Nadu. That India should recognize Tamil as the classical
and modern language it is was an article of faith for some. Others suggested that Tamil be made an official language along with Hindi. Some
felt that the issue was not the place of Tamil but the place of any language other than English. It was suggested that modern technology be
used to make it possible to use all the languages in the Eighth Schedule
as official languages.

THE PLACE OF TAMIL NADU. Tamils in Madras are torn between the
reality of the Indian political universe and the conclusions to which
their self-image logically leads them. On the one hand, they have
learned their place within the Indian firmament—they are too strong to
be on the periphery, too weak to be in the center; too vocal to be
ignored, and too marginal to matter much. On the other hand, they see
themselves as inheritors of a proud political history, as equals in an
Indian social contract with their northern compatriots, and as unrelent-
ing crusaders in the cause of an Indian federal democracy.

[Tamil Nadu] is one of the most important regions. And one of the
most urbanised areas and also one of the best transport structure.
People can travel from any part down south to Madras anywhere. I
have not come across any state which is so well, entirely connected
through road. And in terms of economy also, Tamil Nadu stands
somewhere between first ten states. I think it's the sixth or so. And
. . . in a country like India where there are many languages, certain
imbalances are likely to continue irrespective of your own contribution to the overall economy or the overall structure. (I45)

After DMK gave up its secessionist demand, Tamil Nadu has been
accepted as a part of India by the people here too. . . . Regionalism
has come to stay at the Centre. We are getting into a kind of a loose
political federation. . . . So if that's going to be the case, probably
Tamil Nadu will again emerge as a power to reckon with. As it is, it
is not a force to reckon with and . . . India can do very well without

Tamil Nadu . . . but Tamil Nadu cannot do without India. *(Why?)* Well, its resources are very limited. . . . Tamil Nadu is not able to offer jobs to all Tamils within Tamil Nadu. Traditionally, it was not able to do so at any time. If you look at when Tamil Nadu was by and large dependent on agriculture, the people from the so-called dry belt—Ramnad, North Arcot— . . . were migrating out of Tamil Nadu. The people in the North Arcot traditionally go to military and take a job there. The people in Ramnad . . . turned into traders. They moved out of India to Sri Lanka, Malaysia, to Myanmar and all those places. Tamil Nadu cannot at any point of time offer jobs to all people in Tamil Nadu. Tamil Nadu resources are so meager. It . . . has no economic strength either. There is no big industrial baron in Tamil Nadu except one or two. So, people are naturally dependent on . . . if it remains a part of India, it can avail the resources that are not available as for example, Cauvery. [If] things settle down, probably sizeable land can be irrigated with Cauvery. So lot of small and big things. Another good example is the Tamil businessmen will get a large market resource. Whatever he makes he can go and sell up to Assam. . . . For him to sell within Tamil Nadu will become very difficult. It will not be viable for him. So Tamil Nadu cannot exist without India, but since Tamil Nadu has failed to make its presence felt in the rest of the country, people in the other parts of India may think that India can go ahead without Tamil Nadu. (I34)

I don't think [Tamil Nadu is] very important. I don't think it is as important as we think it is. I suppose its industrialisation . . . and other things. It's a very material world and it depends on what role they play in the Central politics. (I28)

Although there was dissatisfaction with Tamil Nadu's lack of significance, there was also acknowledgment that the Tamils in Tamil Nadu were better off than the Tamils of Jaffna.

The reasons for the Eelam Tamils to have their own country don't apply to the Tamils of India . . . because the Tamils of India don't need a separate country. Because the kind of oppression of Tamils here or whatever sufferings the Tamils have had to undergo under their Hindi heartland bosses are not similar to the sufferings of the Eelam Tamils under the Sinhalese flag. . . . It is not a difference of degree. Even a degree difference, makes a lot of difference. . . . My point is the differences are big. You cannot think in terms of even a United Front government in Sri Lanka today. In India you have a United Front government where the Tamil parties have a major role to play. These possibilities cannot be imagined in Sri Lankan context. So how can we say that the Indian situation is similar to the Sri Lankan situation as far as Tamils are concerned. It is not so. (I45)

As another respondent put it, the Eelam Tamils have nothing, but the Tamils of Tamil Nadu have something. They just do not think they have a rightful or even equitable share. Those are entirely different perspectives from which to assess one's position.

I conducted these interviews shortly after the formation of the United Front government in 1996, and there was a great deal of optimism that regional parties were now in power at the center and that a new federal order was imminent. Some of this optimism was not justified, but undeniably, things will never be the same again for regional perspectives in India. Again, this change underlines the emerging single theme of this section: There is not just one way to sing a national anthem.

TAMILS AS A SUBSET OF INDIANS. The apparent reversibility of the relationships indicated by these diagrams makes Version C more interesting than expected. This version represents a subsumed, absorbed Tamil identity. It says, "I am an Indian first."

Primarily actually, I am basically Indian. I speak Tamil. Indian, a Tamil-speaking Indian. (I46)

If this version does indeed illustrate the limiting case of national integration (absorptive assimilation), its merits and drawbacks become pertinent, as does why anyone outside the political center would pick this version as a representation of his or her relationship with the center.

The three versions and the discussions they lead into reinforce the sense that Tamil and Indian identities are equally salient. Loyalty to one does not diminish loyalty to the other. It is only when the two allegiances are presented as contradictory and incompatible that respondents made a choice, and then they made a qualified choice and one that they recognized as involving trade-offs. It becomes clear that if they did not have to choose analytically or politically, they would not experience much in their daily lives that forced that choice upon them. The idea that a person must have one allegiance above all else, and that to a state or a state-nation, begins to look embarrassingly naive, even silly.

When Tamils were asked to choose identities, they picked Tamil, describing it in maternal terms but often linking this identity to a larger Indian one and protesting that the two were not contradictory. The real synthesis, in Madras at least, seems to have been the learned capacity to accommodate as equal two strong affinities in the face of a politics that tries to enforce a synthetic reality where one loyalty alone can prevail. The researcher who poses questions about primary loyalties also runs the risk of forcing respondents to pick an adversarial one. For those interested in conflict prevention and resolution, here is a lesson: Do not ask people to choose when there is no need. They can live with plurality, and so should the powers that be. Searching for what made India a community, or what made any group of individuals a community, I was forced to conclude that individuals simply belong to communities and look for reasons only after the fact.

> Listen, I'll tell you something. . . . This thing that I am an Indian, that is because of a structure, of a need. . . . I am not an Indian. India as India has not always existed. What we call India has had different names at different times. India has never been one. No matter whence you research this history, India has been diverse (*palamaadri*). Even in saying Tamilian, why did Cheran, Cholan and Pandyan fight amongst themselves? They have been Cheran, Cholan and Pandyan, but have they been Tamilian? . . . *This thing that is "Indian" we need it now. India is a country. India should be a country. If that is so, Tamilian as I am, I live in an Indian home. Thus I am an Indian Tamilian. But if you ask me to give up being a Tamilian, and say "India," I cannot accept that. Because the feeling of being Indian, even at this minute, I don't know what it is.* (I75; emphasis mine)

The Pakistani and Sri Lankan Contexts

The Tamilians interviewed in Madras were able to identify with both India and other Tamils. Does their perspective hold true for people in Pakistan and Sri Lanka?

This question of primary allegiance did not feature in the same way in the Sri Lankan interviews. Discussions of history, education, devolution packages, and conflict resolution led to descriptions of the respondents' loyalties and comments on the question of allegiance itself. The following selection of quotations is taken from relevant comments made by Sri Lankan Tamil respondents in response to other questions. In the Pakistani case, where field research was not possible, articles in the *Sind Quarterly*, a journal published in Sind, are the primary resource. These no more constitute a random sample than did the earlier quotations from elite interviews in Madras, but they are used to strengthen the bases of conclusions in the previous section.

The Indian case of Tamil Nadu and the Dravida movement is, in this comparative study, the one in which the ideal of national integration has most closely been achieved. Nevertheless, in the discussion of how they weighted their Tamil and Indian identities, respondents swung back and forth, asserting both. In the other two cases, it was much harder to find either being defined clearly. This difference could be attributed to the universe from which the following views were selected. However, in the Sri Lankan case, I would argue that these results have to do with the nature of the question, and that in itself is a lesson to the scholar and the policymaker. In other words, when I did not force a choice, explications of identity and identity relationships were complex and, in all likelihood, more realistic. Every possible relationship is represented.

> Now there is nothing wrong with [the] slogan Jeeay Sind (Long Live Sind) in itself so long as [it] is placed in the context of a hierarchy of cognate devotional values; Jeeay Islam, Jeeay Pakistan and Jeeay Sind—and in that order. We all want Sind to flourish and prosper if only because it can then make a real contribution to Pakistan's political solidarity, its glory and greatness as a nation. We want Pakistan to flourish because it can thereby make [a] contribution to the cause of Islam. It is only from this viewpoint that our devotion to the values symbolised by various regional cultures of Pakistan and Islam become meaningful. Apart from that mode of regarding our devotion to Sindh, Punjab, Baluchistan or the N.W.F.P. our attitude to them is nothing short of idolatry. (Brohi 1978: 35)

> [19]83 was the peak. Almost all the Tamils were looted, but where can we go? We have to live here. We were born and brought up in this country. We developed our wealth, education, everything in this country. How can we go? . . . I have not changed my passport. I hold a Sri Lankan passport, why? . . . No Sri Lankan likes to change his national identity. You ask anyone. You go to Canada, you go to France. They like to call them as Sri Lankan, because they love this country. . . . The people are very nice, the Sinhalese people. Very helpful. The Sinhalese people did not create the problems. [It is] the political fanatics who made it. (S9)

In the previous two quotations, whereas the distinctions between the larger and the smaller group are spelled out (Sindhis as distinct from Pakistanis, Tamils and Sinhalese as distinct from each other and

Sri Lankans), the larger identification is still given some primacy—far more in the Pakistani quotation than the Sri Lankan, but the difference is explicable in the context of each case and the time at which each view was articulated. In the Pakistani case, 1978 marks the beginning of Islamicization. In the Sri Lankan case, the interview was conducted in 1996, just after the Central Bank bombing and when a great deal of polarization had already occurred.

The following quotation emphasizes the closeness between Sindhi and Pakistani identity, but the Sindhi identity—the local identity—has primacy. Without Sindhis, there would be no Pakistan.

> Sindh is the foundation stone of Pakistan. . . . Sindh has rendered invaluable service, made innumerable sacrifices and gone through the mill for Pakistan. Sindhis have never voted for any ethnic, sectarian, religious or regional group, but always supported the cause of Pakistan. . . . Sindh has contributed more than its due share for Pakistan, and for the people who have settled here. (Tonyo 1991: 32–35)

In contrast to the close relationship described in the previous interview extract, the next extract expresses frustration that two communities do not relate the same way to the larger collective and that the majority challenges the minority's claims to belong to that collective.

> In Sri Lanka, if you compare with other countries, the main fault is that they thought national integration is single ownership. Today there is a clear cleavage between the Tamil community and the Sinhala community because whenever the minority communities speak of the nation they say that it is our town, our right, our Sri Lanka. In Sinhala they say, "Ape rashtra"—This is our land. They say it is their Sri Lanka, then they say the minority always speak of [grievances, but] actually you always exclude the other side. It is the attitude from the very beginning. We have to protect our nation. We have to protect our motherland. Who are those "we"? It is not inclusive, always exclusive. (S81)

A minority in the statewide context and a majority in the regional context, the Sindhis have fought to remain distinct at many levels. Accordingly, they assert what might be considered to be contradictory claims. First, they assert their contribution to the creation of the larger context while resisting assimilation into a standardized national identity. Second, they assert their tradition of inclusion within their ranks of anyone who will assimilate.

> *The very root of all this tragedy consists in the assurances that Pakistan was the homeland of the Muslims in India.* Had it, in even minimum honesty and uprightness of character and human dignity been stated that Pakistan was the homeland of Punjabis, Sindhis, Balochis and Pathans with Bengal as a willing colony, the India Mussalmans would not have been [a] matter of burden, worry and concern to the Sindhis specially. (Mehkri 1994: 9–10; italics in original)

> We have never distinguished between any immigrant in Sindh and the original Sindhi. . . . Anybody permanently settled in Sindh, has his interest linked with those of Sindh, is a Sindhi. Any body born in Sindh or whose parents are genuinely settled in Sindh, who has no eyes fixed on any thing abroad, is a Sindhi, with equal status and rights. It would be dishonest and treacherous to deny these immigrants and their descendants the status of Sindhis, in spite of the unfortunate and pathetic refusal of these people to call themselves Sindhis, which notion also we see being debunked by circumstances and history. (Shah 1988: 14)

This following pithy summary of Sri Lankan politics captures the contingent nature of any identification. Who one is and the relationship that one bears to any other depends ultimately on the context in which one is making that identification. So questions—and policies—that force the issue of identification oversimplify and then overstate each case.

> Politically, the Tamil community feels that they are minorities. They feel politically, they are powerless. But on the other side, the Tamil community has kind of a strength. Culturally . . . our border is not limited within Sri Lanka. If you come to Sinhala community in Sri Lanka, they feel, "Politically we are strong, we have the power, we are majority." But they have a minority complex. Culturally, our community is limited in Sri Lanka. We are minority in the zone. We are minority in the world. . . . So this is a majority community with a minority complex. (S36)

In the following two statements, we see a true polarization that is not evident even in response to the clumsy questions in the Indian case.

The fate of Sindh and its language, Sindhi, is in a crisis. May be, Sindh and Sindhi may disappear for all time. May be, they may survive the war started against them. May be, they may die, but they must die hard.

We Sindhis, we are ashamed to confess, have a weakness for our mother tongue, for our home-land, Sindh, and for our way of life, however humble and simple they may appear to the out-siders. We have survived through centuries.

This Sindhis' struggle for the simple, natural instinct of self-existence and self-preservation may probably take on bitter forms. (Jatoi 1995: 17)

Today I think Sri Lanka is a very politically conscious place. The two major nations—the Sinhala nation and the Tamil nation—is also both gripped by that political fever or fervour. So everything is viewed in that way. And I say that today, the hatred between the two nations, the Sinhalese and the Tamils, though the disparity in population is large, 76% Sinhalese and 12% Tamil, the hatred is at a very, very high level. Never before has there been hatred of this magnitude, and for that reason, I say that though people do talk about a common identity, I think it's just a non-starter. (S11)

The first quotation does not even mention any non-Sindhi group by name; they are merely "out-siders." There is no simpler way to determine identification. The second is very typical of Sri Lankan Tamil discussions of nation and nationality. Three nations (to use the term in its broadest sense) are mentioned—the Tamils, the Sinhalese, Sri Lanka—but when things are bad, the most important relationship is not that between either ethnic group and the state but that between the two ethnic groups.

The Indian case discussion alluded to the possibility of arranging the three Venn diagrams to show the process of alienation. The two sets of quotations that follow show this process. The first set expresses the Sindhi nationalist leader G. M. Syed's views over a period of approximately twenty-five years. The second set is drawn from three sources but illustrates the same process of change. In both cases, the change is growing alienation.

On any impartial consideration of the history of Pakistan and the part played in it by the Province of Sind, it could be easily established that Sind merits a better and fairer treatment than the one she has been getting so far at the hands of the powers that be. It is therefore a high time that this stepmotherly attitude to Sind is reviewed and appropriately changed as early as possible. (Sayed 1984: 8)

Some of us who all the time remained conscious of the national distinctness of the People of Sindh and their significant past history, participated in the movement for Pakistan solely for the purpose of ensuring thereby political independence, economic prosperity and cultural advancement of Sindh. (Syed 1999)

As against Sindhu Desh, Pakistan is an accident of history a freak of nature. Unlike Sindh, Baluchistan, Pakhtoonistan and Punjab, Pakistan is not the product or creation of nature, nor has it any entity comprising one nation, one language, Literature culture or any identity of economic or political interest. (Syed 1999)

Pakistan's rationale hardly improves with this argument. . . . Why should, after all the Sindhis, the Baluchis, and the Pakhtoons accept this position. If the Musalmans of India had necessarily to be moved out of India and settled amongst brotherly Muslim peoples, the entire Muslim brotherhood of the world should have shared the burden. As it is, only the Sindhis, Baluchis and Pakhtoons, and among them too mostly the Sindhis, have borne and are still bearing the brunt of it. These peoples had never subscribed to this principle, nor had they bound themselves by it. It is a false and baseless argument manufactured only to provide an unabashed cover for colonization and exploitation of the homelands of the smaller nationalities in Pakistan. (Syed 1999)

Sindh can exist without Pakistan, but Pakistan cannot exist without Sindh. Pakistan's existence depends on how its ruling Classes treat Sindh. If they don't revise their attitude, and accept the national existence of Sindh and the people and grant them their rights, no power on earth is going to save Pakistan. (Syed 1999)

Sindh is the homeland neither of all Musalmans, nor of Musalmans alone. It is the homeland of Sindhi Musalmans, Sindhi Hindus, Sindhi Christians, Sindhi Sikhs, and Sindhi Parsis. . . . The Musalman migrants from Bharat have no right on Sindh, because the nationalist Sindhis Musalmans do not believe in religiously based nationhood. (Syed 1999)

The Tamils of Ceylon by virtue of their great language, their religions, their separate culture and heritage, their history of independent existence as a separate state over a distinct territory for several centuries . . . and above all by their will to exist as a separate territory, are a nation distinct and apart from the Sinhalese. ("Vadukkodai Resolution" 1976)

The Tamil people of the island of Ceylon (now called Sri Lanka) constitute a distinct nation. They form a social entity, with their own history, traditions, culture, language and traditional homeland. The Tamil people call their nation "Tamil Eelam." (Tamil Eelam home page 1997)

The Ceylon Tamil is one of many hundreds existing today within multi-national states. (Sathananthan 1998)

In short, even from a cursory survey of views in Pakistan and Sri Lanka, it is evident that the Tamils of Madras are not alone in the complexities and contradictions of their answers. Multiple, contingent identifications seem to be the rule rather than the exception, and what varies from case to case is the degree of polarity between the options. This intricacy acts as a buffer because as people move seamlessly from one identification to another, it is easier for them to form coalitions and alliances flexibly as the need arises. There is a definite continuum of increasing alienation, movement along which seems to be accelerated by point-blank, simplistic positing of alternatives. That is, when people are forced to choose one identity, sooner or later they are locked into positions in society from which it is difficult to step out and negotiate.

The Reality of Multiple Allegiances Versus Ideas About the State, Nation, and Citizenship

The old idea that sovereign states must command the undivided allegiance and obedience of their subject-citizens continues to haunt us even as we have come to discount equating nation and state, state and nation. Citizenship in a state need not be vested with any more emotional importance than membership in any other kinship or interest group. As long as citizens have a reason to be loyal and obedient, they will. That reason depends on other things than an artificial hierarchy of loyalties. Multiple loyalties are not rival loyalties until someone asks the question, "What is so-and-so's first loyalty?" The question that might be asked in its stead: "Under what circumstances is this person going to feel obliged to pick one over any other?" and further, "What can states do to prevent these circumstances?"

Those who write on ethnic groups contend uncomfortably with their logical predilection to support the rights of the group, on the one hand, and the inescapable reality and even necessity of the state, on the other.

Equally hard to reconcile are the nationalism of the state and that of the group, expressed sometimes as the conflict between sovereignty and self-determination. The point made here is that the problem lies not in an intrinsic opposition of these sentiments but in our framing of the question. If it is shorn of the dualistic framing of loyalties, scholars, policy-makers, and, most important, citizens need not choose one or the other.

There are three reasons why it is not necessary to use such a frame. First, if the state is intended to serve the purposes of society, and to the extent that it does so, there is no need to place the identity and self-determination of groups and that of the state in mutual opposition. Second, if impulses to organize and act stem from common human needs, self-determination at its best leads to communities of shared interests. Finally, if in our time sovereignty rests not in the state but in the people who constitute it, self-determination should not pose a political problem. By definition, it should always be possible. Even if the premises in the three reasons are rejected as untrue, the questions that arise do not lead necessarily to a dualistic analytical framework where state and society, individual and community, citizenship and alien status, and sovereignty and self-determination are opposed. Immigration, taxation, and extradition laws begin to show that it is possible to accommodate all sorts of variations on this dualistic framework. It is just our analytical modes that have to catch up.

Notes

1. Socialism is less relevant here than secularism because communities are defined also by religious affinity, and the politics of identity in India centers today around the place of various religiously defined communities vis-à-vis the state.

2. The Forty-second Amendment to the Indian constitution was passed during the Emergency. A miniconstitution in its size and scope, it introduced changes that centralized the authority of the state and strengthened the central executive in particular. Most of these changes were reversed after the elections of 1977, which Indira Gandhi lost, but the amended self-definition of the state remains.

3. Bhabani Sen Gupta, conversation, Urbana, Illinois, May 1994. These observations are, however, usually attributed to Rajni Kothari.

4. Draft Constitution and Constituent Assembly Debates, vol. 7, clause 23, 922–923, cited in *The Framing of India's Constitution,* vol. 3 (New Delhi: Indian Institute of Public Administration, 1966), pp. 525–526. The Constituent

Assembly debates (CAD) are also accessible at the Indian Parliament home page (http://alfa.nic.in/debates/vol7pm.htm).

5. This observation is true particularly when it relates to caste, which although not the subject under discussion here, is a very important issue in Indian politics.

6. Alberuni's account of India captured this relationship convincingly (1973). He described Indians as disunited and inward-looking. These qualities were antithetical to the spirit of reason and discovery, and hence Indians were mired in superstition and custom.

7. Several historians say this, and it is fairly explicit in the CAD as well.

8. Translated by Lorna Dewaraja, interview, Colombo, February 19, 1996.

9. The Sanskrit and Pali forms of a word that stands at the core of Hindu and Buddhist worldviews but that is hard to translate into English. In the context of the state, Romila Thapar defines it in her book on Asoka as a "policy of social responsibility" (Thapar 1963: 3). It is more conventionally translated as "righteousness" and is sometimes used to denote "duty" and sometimes to denote "religion," as there is no word for the latter in these languages.

10. To what extent do inclusiveness and nonintervention (and conversely, exclusiveness and intervention) go hand in hand? If they are directly related, does this mean that the state can intervene only as an ethnically defined state?

11. There is a truism among students of Indian history that as the power of the ruler ebbs, his or her titles become more grandiose and pretentious. There is a suggestion of this truism in the 1978 Sri Lankan constitution.

12. The first line of Article 22, which designates Sinhala as the official language, remains. A second clause has been inserted stating that Tamil shall also enjoy this status. This is sometimes interpreted as a grudging concession.

13. Harold J. Laski, *A Grammar of Politics* (London: George Allen & Unwin, 1960), p. 91.

14. One restriction it definitely does place is that she (or even he) cannot be president of Pakistan if she is a non-Muslim. This restriction is consistent through all three constitutions.

15. Article 19 in 1956; Article 18 in 1962.

16. For the purposes of this section, "ethnic" may be read as encompassing ethnicity and religion.

17. "Statehood Is the New Panacea for Backwardness," *Indian Express*, September 19, 1996.

18. Friedrich List, *The National System of Political Economy* (London: 1885), p. 174, quoted in Hobsbawm 1990: 30–31.

19. This earlier view of nationhood partly explains why in 1948 independence was not considered a "viable" option for Kashmir, which, unlike Hyderabad and Junagadh, was not completely surrounded by another state. To some extent, at the level of political scholarship and activism, this view has changed, but states have not changed that much, and so viability arguments persist in discussions of Kashmir and Punjab. A significant difference in each of these cases is visible in the advocacy of the principle of ethnonational self-

determination, a subject that could not have been broached even a few years ago.

20. "In truth, by asking the language question censuses for the first time *forced* everyone to choose not only a nationality, but a linguistic nationality" (Hobsbawm 1990: 100).

21. All my comments and interventions, when quoted in the middle of interview response extracts, are italicized and placed in parentheses.

22. *Indha maanila thaai-ai vananganam* (in Tamil).

3

State Intervention and Integrative Strategies

Once founded, every polity in history has had to face the task of holding together, of maintaining itself in a particular form. The integrative process involves constant negotiation and renegotiation between the polity as a whole (through its agencies) and those who live within its boundaries, by its writ. There is a larger historical movement that forges community at a variety of levels, from the locality to larger kinship networks to communities of faith. Within this larger framework, the polity promotes certain ideas or symbols and undertakes certain projects that intentionally or unintentionally have the consequence of forging a community in its image and of keeping that sense of community alive. Drawing on historical and contemporary examples, in this chapter I explore the range of possible interventions by the state, or integrative strategies. I then examine the effectiveness of state intervention by describing two instances thereof in the South Asian context—political socialization and internal territorial organization.

Integrative Strategies

By integrative strategies, I mean those strategies that have the effect of transforming a populace into a community. This consequence can be intended or coincidental but must be the product of consciously chosen policies.

No matter what its stage of development, every regime or ruling order is characterized by the possession and exercise of power. Power, according to Kenneth Boulding, has three aspects: destruction, production, and integration (Boulding 1989). Destruction may precede production or creation, and this is one way to look at the new polity, which has the power to destroy old legitimacies; win the cooperation and, maybe, the loyalty of constituent peoples; and establish a regime. In our times, the struggle of the Sri Lankan Tamil militants exemplifies this process. Indeed, Machiavelli's advice to conquering princes was to use as much coercion and cruelty as may be necessary to secure the unity and obedience of their new subjects but to do so judiciously in the interests of the state (Machiavelli 1992: 43). Destructive power is also the power to threaten and as such may be used to coerce the populace into cooperation.

Productive power, as Boulding defines it, is economic and also refers to exchange. It is important to the exercise of any power by the state, enabling the state to employ, invest, build, expand, and even threaten. The source of the economic power of the state lies in its ability to tax, borrow, or create money. Taxation is an important facet of building states and nations. The ability of the state to levy and collect taxes depends on whether it is regarded as legitimate. Taxation issues are usually very sensitive, especially in new polities or polities where a minority or foreign elite is dominant. The Boston Tea Party followed the imposition of taxes and duties on the American colonies by the British sovereign. The *jiziya* tax, which only non-Muslim subjects owed in some of the Muslim-ruled kingdoms of South Asia, aroused similar resentment. Grants-in-aid for community development are another exercise of "exchange" power.

Legitimacy is created by integrative power. Integrative power, Boulding says, is "the power to create such relationships as love, respect, friendship, legitimacy, and so on" (1989: 10). As social organization becomes more complex and people are drawn into several groupings, different levels of integration and different identities are juxtaposed. Integrative power is closely related to identity formation. It is associated with communication, learning, and persuasion. From the point of view of this study, its most interesting aspects may be as Boulding states: "Integrative power often rests on the ability to create images of the future and to persuade people that these are valid" (122). Legitimacy is considered by Boulding to be the "core of the integrative system" (113), and its structures are always changing. Legitimacy is determined by the degree of cooperation. Cooperation may be coerced or consensual. A polity is legitimate to the extent that the cooperation that it elicits is consensual rather than coerced. To the extent that the polity is legitimate and integrated, it is a political community.

Reflecting the three kinds of power that states may exercise, strategies whereby political communities are built can also have three faces: destructive, productive, and integrative. Central to the definition used here is that no matter what the nature of the measure itself, if its long-term consequences are integrative, that is, if the regime is transformed into a legitimate political community that can maintain itself, the measure is integrative. For instance, the decision to promote a particular faith and its symbols could have been a choice based on the religious convictions of the elite or based on the perception that the polity needed a binding faith. Either way, if successful, this policy would be likely to integrate the populace into a community of coreligionists. Another instance might be the establishment of an effective law enforcement agency and the codification of laws that could at one extreme become repressive and coercive but could also serve to integrate people into a single political entity.

Robert Axelrod and Robert Keohane (1986) theorize five "circumstantial dimensions" that affect cooperation:

1. mutuality of interests
2. the "shadow of the future"
3. the number of players
4. perceptions of the players
5. institutions

Cooperation theory ultimately says that people cooperate when they perceive cooperation to be in their interests. Thus states that need to elicit cooperation from their citizens need to create those conditions in which citizens will see cooperation as a benefit. What does this mean from the point of view of the polity? What sorts of conditions should it create?

The first thing that the peoples of a new polity would wonder about is how long the polity is likely to last. Stability and the capacity to survive alter the "shadow of the future," to use Robert Axelrod's memorable phrase (1984). If a people believe that the regime has the ability to survive for a long time or that they will live within a regime's jurisdiction for a long time, the incentive for them to cooperate increases. Furthermore, if the polity is large, the question of its ability to survive will also cast a shadow on whether different groups within its borders will feel that it behooves them to cooperate with each other or whether they will disregard its existence, convinced that it is a temporary or ineffectual factor in their lives. If the prevalent perception is that the regime is a transient phenomenon, previous disputes and legitimacies will continue to color the interactions of groups. Perception of the regime as a survivor and as stable depends a good deal on the ability of the regime to communicate its intention to survive and to build institutions that will provide proof of the same. When a regime lays the foundations for an institutionalized polity—through explicit laws and procedures, well-defined offices, and well-briefed functionaries—it offers tangible reason for the populace to believe that it has the intention, if not the ability, to endure.

Institutions have been defined by Samuel Huntington as "stable, valued, recurring patterns of behavior" (Huntington 1968: 12). Institutions are important because they are tangible proof of the regime's existence and ability to survive. They provide a focus for public activity and manifest the public interest (Huntington 1968: 24–32). They provide information and reduce transaction costs within a system (Keohane 1984: 244–247). Institutions and the public interaction with them come to define the common public arena and thus are potential building blocks for a common identity (Anderson 1991: 55–59, 114–116). "The more complex and heterogeneous the society . . . the more the achievement and maintenance of political community become dependent upon the workings of political institutions" (Huntington 1968: 9).

Even if they are convinced that the polity will endure, people will have no reason to cooperate if they do not think that they will receive direct and immediate benefits. It is also possible that in certain circumstances, they may reap whatever benefits there are without having to cooperate. In order to minimize the free-rider problem, the regime can persuade the people either that it is in their interest to cooperate or that it is not in their interest not to cooperate. Either way, the regime needs channels of communication, both to and from the populace, and it needs a system of well-articulated incentives and disincentives.

Channels of communication are vital to the polity. They provide the regime with a medium to reach the populace, and vice versa. Further, even a system of incentives and disincentives needs to be communicated to every level of society. Channels of communication, like safe, well-maintained roads, connect parts of the polity to each other and are therefore a source of productive power. Indeed, in the absence of communication that makes policies and intentions intelligible and acceptable to the ruled, structures can insulate the rulers from the ruled and thus contribute to disintegration.

> The ability to communicate underlies all forms of power. Threats are useless unless they can be communicated to the threatened party. Exchange is impossible unless the exchangers can communicate various offers and bids. Productive power rests to a considerable degree on the ability to communicate within organizations. It may well be that the ultimate dominance of integrative power rests on the fact that integrative behavior creates communications and builds up communication networks that extend far and wide over time and space. (Boulding 1989: 110)

Finally, as Benedict Anderson puts it, "all communities larger than primordial villages of face-to-face contact (and perhaps even these) are imagined" (Anderson 1991: 6). The populace's perceptions of the regime, as well as of each other, can be influenced by an attempt to restate or create anew the ideology or identity of the community. The regime might do this through the use of the mass media, the adoption of particular symbols, and socialization through intervention in schools, among other things.

It follows from the previous discussion that integration may be achieved through institutions, communication, incentives, and ideology. Integrative strategies would then include conscious attempts to create any of these and to foster them.

The policies and actions of the Indian, Pakistani, and Sri Lankan states in the areas of political socialization and unit demarcation are the subject of the next two sections of this chapter. The form, substance, and impact of these interventions will be discussed. In the case of political socialization, I compare what is controversial or problematic about the contents of history and social science textbooks in each country and how these contents are related to particular visions of the polity as a whole. Further, I ask whether there are important differences between "national" and local histories or the histories of different communities within the polity, differences that result in competing visions and mutually contradictory textbooks.

The state's interventions on the question of unit demarcation are more clearly its part in a conversation with its constituent groups, whether or not the latter have a territorial base. In this chapter, I summarize the history of these interventions from the point of view of the unit or group whose place in the whole is being negotiated—Tamil

Nadu, Sind, and Sri Lankan Tamils. This alternative narration permits us to raise questions about the efficacy of the state's part in this conversation. Has the state's contribution to the demarcation dialectic in India, Pakistan, and Sri Lanka promoted or harmed the prospects for integration?

Political Socialization Through History Education

All would agree that the legislator should make the education of the young his chief and foremost concern. In the first place, the constitution of a state will suffer if education is neglected. . . . The citizens of a state should always be educated to suit the constitution of their state. . . . In the second place, every capacity, and every form of art, requires as a condition of its exercise some measure of previous training and some amount of preliminary habituation. Men must therefore be trained and habituated because they can do acts of goodness, as members of a state should do.

—Aristotle 1958: 332

As the state intervenes in the teaching of history, it contributes its story to an arena where there are already many others. Individuals take elements of each and create a narrative in which their lives and the collective experience mesh, collating those elements most consistent with their personal experiences from the stories available. That is to say, for each individual there is a unique recension of the past. When one collates these innumerable individual narratives, one relates a story of the "nation" that may or may not resonate with the state's version of history. Different recollections of the past result in different understandings of the present and visions for the future. Thus any part played by the state in reducing these differences through intervention in the creation of collective memories is a critical ingredient in the integrative process.

State Intervention in Education

Political scientists define socialization as the process whereby societies inculcate their core political values in their young.[1] The five agents of socialization are the family, the school, the peer group, the media, and the state itself. The family and the peer group are largely outside the purview of any but the most totalitarian state, and even then, that control is tenuous. The mass media may be controlled, but that control can easily be undermined by countervailing and underground information campaigns as well as by international media influences. Of all the agents of socialization, the school is the one over which the state has the greatest control. As Richard Merritt points out: "It is possible to reform curricula, to weed out teachers objectionable because of their political taint, to introduce practices such as student government, and even to rewrite textbooks" (1970: 139).

What are the advantages and shortcomings of the state playing a role in school education? The answer depends on how one views the state. If the state is viewed as the incarnation and agent of the general will, then by taking part in the socialization process, the state is merely assuring the continuance of that will and its values. If the state is an agent of a particular class or group, it is likely to reflect the vision and history of that class. Conversely, if its curricula and texts reflect preponderantly the vision and history of that class or group, we might conclude that it is, in fact, an agent of that section of society. If the state with its monopoly over the legitimate use of force is merely a "protection racket," to use Charles Tilly's phrase (1985), it has no place in the education system, which must be self-regulating or socially regulated.

In developing countries, the state is the agent of social change and development. To the extent that it acquires this mandate as a condition of its legitimacy, its intervention in the educational system is logical because social change is partly attitudinal and because values favoring change (and a particular type of change) must be inculcated in the citizenry. Further, if one considers that development includes the eradication of illiteracy as much as that of poverty and disease, the question is, Who, if not the state, is responsible? Massive investment in nonprofit areas such as basic education has been, until recently, primarily the responsibility of the state sector.

More specifically, in South Asia, the tradition is that the state acts as a patron of education. The ruling class (*kshatriya*) protected and supported the priestly class (*brahmin*) in its activities in return for legitimation, for performance in state ritual, and for service as teachers and scholars. Buddhist canon also enjoins the king to support the activities of its monastic class—which might be said to be teaching and socialization. South Asia's Muslim rulers and polities also supported centers of learning, and such support was not always restricted by religion. Kings are known to have established and patronized particular schools and to have been benefactors to scholars and, by extension, their students. In short, in

South Asia, the state has always taken an interest in education, to different degrees of inclusivity. Was it an interest that influenced curriculum design? Not directly, perhaps, but given the importance of patronage and the fact that the curriculum at schools (*madrasas, gurukulas,* or *viharas*) was idiosyncratically reflective of the teacher's worldview, by patronizing one and not another school, the state could determine the prevalent or most powerful teaching of the day.

Is it possible to consider this question of state involvement in education outside the particular context of the South Asian polities being discussed? Is there a particular response that is true across the board? There is not. Perhaps the issue is better served by asking, in the face of the state's ineluctability, how its role might be delimited in this sphere. To countries like those in this study, there is really a continuum of models available. At one end is the model of the United States, where, still reminiscent of de Tocqueville, locally elected school boards determine appointments and curricula, leaving open textbook options. (It is arguable that insofar as the school boards constitute an arm of local government and are elected by political processes laid down by the state, this variation is in fact one of many rather than the limiting case on a continuum.) At the other end is the model of totalitarian states like the former Soviet Union, where the education system served the purposes of the state and none other (Gaworek 1977: 55–74). Even in the Soviet Union, there was some variation. There were some standards, but within their broad parameters, the republics did determine the content of the curriculum. Somewhere in the middle are societies where the school system and extracurricular settings, such as Sunday schools, cohabit with different degrees of consonance. Sri Lanka is actually one of these. In fact, it would appear that the question of whether state intervention is desirable is moot because it is inevitable.

The Centrality of History

All of us have a need to know where we came from. If the nation itself is a modern political form, the need to acknowledge and acquaint others with one's forebears is evident in the use of patronymics and genealogies. The use of the village name as a first or last name in some communities also indicates this need. South Asians, in particular, begin getting acquainted with people by asking, "Where are you from?"—a question that refers to more than place. Today, these simple and informal devices whereby one is placed are supplemented by official, formal ones such as birth certificates and passports. In a sense, one's informal personal history is given an official dimension, and through the categories of the official document—place of birth as opposed to place of origin, permanent address and local address, the use of a father's or a husband's name on women's passports—old structures are formalized and new ones enforced. Indians, for example, have places of birth, domiciles, native places, places where they have ration cards, among others. Sri Lankans carry their place of birth on their national identity cards all their lives, and it sometimes becomes the basis for being passed over or searched at security checkpoints. Until the advent of printing and in the absence of universal literacy, these "origins" were remembered through mnemonics; through the records of courts, clerics, and clerks; and through the narration of family stories. The myths and oral histories that constituted such history education are replaced by formal curricula and schools.

Further, the nation is associated with a historical past. History is everywhere associated with the emergence or creation of a national identity. Most writers on nationalism agree that one of the key characteristics of a nation is a shared history.[2] This commonly remembered past is constructed, imagined (Anderson 1991), or invented (Hobsbawm 1983), as the case may be, and it is understood, in all past periods, to have occurred within the same bounds—geographic and demographic—as the "nation" presently stands (Duara 1996). The authentication of this history is the task of museums, its bounds are defined by maps, and its propagation is facilitated by the use of printing technologies and, now, other media (Anderson 1991). Finally, this association grounds history in a bounded space. History can only be the history of nations (conversely, they who have no history cannot be nations), and this history is the history of definite spaces—the same unit in the past as now.

This idea replicates at the ideational level the narrative of national integration politics that I will reconstruct throughout this work. Nationalism—even (and maybe especially) the nationalism promoted by the state—requires the selection of *one* story; there is no room for a variety of narratives. Self-definition, acquiring a territorial dimension, becomes harder to reconcile to the self-definitions of others in the public arena. A grounded, spatially bounded history works for the ideal-type, single-nation state. In the more typical multination state, the state encounters a multiplicity of narratives and establishes its place in relation to them.

We thus must consider questions about the relationship between "national" and "local" history. A prior question, however, is, What is the "national" history of a multination state? How does one tell such a story so that (1) no one is left out; (2) internecine conflicts, and certainly lesser internal conflicts, conquests, and victories, are downplayed; and (3) the different parts are woven into a seamless structure? Several Indian historians pointed out that they do write a history that is more sophisticated than this. The question is, How many read it? The lowest common denominator of history education is school, and this is for most citizens the only level at which they formally learn history. Given that in this age, that which is formal and printed carries greater authority than any other form of communication, it seems that the school textbook is the place to look for the way in which the potential tension between "national" and "local" histories is resolved. Further, in this region, schooling and textbook and curriculum planning are the preserve of state and state-instituted organizations. Finally, when one raises the question of how one might tell the story of a country, the fact is that one might do a fairly comprehensive job at an advanced level, but at the level of school education this task is much more difficult. School history cannot capture the complexity or the multiplicity of stories that are available.

The act of writing a syllabus, and then, the exigencies of textbook writing involve choosing from the smorgasbord of history and simplifying the dimensions of space and time. What is the basis on which one might demarcate historical periods? If one resolves this issue, one has to select the persons, events, or social processes that will be covered. Choices made in all three instances are dictated by one's perspective and involve losses and trade-offs. Among prominent Indian historians engaged in textbook writing, it is widely believed that a focus on social processes and movements is politically preferable to a focus on persons or events. But as Krishna Kumar (1996) points out, social processes are not necessarily what children grasp most easily. Finally, one has to choose between the local, the regional, the national, and the foreign, that is, where in the world the period will be located. Will the class study the eighteenth century in Europe, India, Tamil Nadu, or Thanjavur? Children relate best to what they can see around them, but what does this observation mean for the idea of India?

History Textbooks as an Instrument of Integration

When the totalitarian state revises the account of history in school textbooks, or when the new nation expands the school system, political elites are attempting to shape and control this process of creating political orientations. (Almond and Powell 1966: 64–65)

In the post-colonial nation-states, the teaching of history has been perceived as a valuable instrument of continuing the nation-building exercise that the struggle for freedom from colonial control had initiated. (Kumar 1996: 25)

Children learn history from many sources—family, religious initiation, popular culture, fiction, everyday rituals, and school. The child encounters dozens of stories and tries to reconcile them. Some of these versions carry greater weight than others. In choosing to look at history textbooks, I am assuming that they are one of the more influential sources. Textbooks, as repositories of historical narratives with official sanction, bear a close relation to the propagation of the state's identity, among other things. Although they compete with other sources of information and although they may not be very good textbooks, now more than ever, they retain—rightly or wrongly—the ring of authority, the promise of truth.

He [the historian] must first recognize, however, that the alarming propensity of partially literate societies to regard oral traditional materials as inferior to written sources has been almost reflexive in its application. Recognition that feedback materials may be co-opted into traditional accounts is essential when working with materials that may claim to be undiluted oral traditions. . . . In his scepticism the investigator must *a priori* assume that any consistency is the result of recourse to printed, written, or para-literate sources or because of deference to "official" accounts. (Henige 1974: 118)

As we see with Sasanka Perera's (1991) work on Sri Lankan schools, when official accounts are reinforced by the teacher's word on the subject, this historical "truth" is invincible in the arena of popular culture or politics. But are history textbooks actually as useful to the cause of national integration as we might suppose? We shall see their potential and their limits in the following accounts of textbooks in India, Pakistan, and Sri Lanka.

The data for these accounts are drawn almost entirely from secondary sources, except in the case of India. In the original research design, the plan was to compare the contents of national and selected provincial secondary school textbooks in India, Pakistan, and Sri Lanka. Unfortunately, the realities of the field context made that task impossible. Visa problems were the first obstacle in accessing primary sources for Pakistan; however, language difficulties would have limited the scope of the comparison there, as they did in Sri Lanka. Because of these major data-collection problems and because of education's importance as an arena of state intervention in the national integration process, the approach to analyzing history textbooks was revised. What follows is meant to be indicative rather than conclusive, and it is hoped that it will inform other research agendas. In the absence of primary data for all three cases, the objective of this section is to identify the main issues surrounding the state's decision to intervene in the political socialization process.

In the Indian case, the objective was to compare the history textbooks used in Tamil Nadu. There, schools operate under four different boards of education—the Tamil Nadu State Board, the Central Board of Secondary Education (CBSE), the Matriculation Board, and the Indian Certificate of Secondary Education (the last is insignificant). For each of these there is a different set of textbooks, and depending on the degree of autonomy enjoyed by the individual schools, they have little option but to use these books. Since the inception of the National Council for Educational Research and Training (NCERT) in 1961, the different boards may still construct different curricula, but there is some normative understanding that NCERT's guidelines will be followed. The books used in the Matriculation Board schools are quite consistent with NCERT guidelines, and CBSE schools use NCERT books. The Tamilnadu Textbook Corporation's books are produced in Tamil and English and as such are the most widely used in the state. The English-language social science texts for classes 6 through 10 prepared by the NCERT and Tamilnadu Textbook Corporation were compared for curricular content—what was included and excluded.

Five sources have been used here for the Pakistani case study, largely as a function of their accessibility. The first is *The Murder of History in Pakistan*, in which K. K. Aziz (1993a) has examined sixty-six textbooks in Urdu and English (published by a variety of textbook boards, all governmental bodies) to show first, how many factual errors they contain and then, how these errors are related to the ideological imperative that governs the books. Although Aziz does not condone the politicization of the curriculum, his primary concern is the inaccuracy of the content. The second source is Aftab Kazi's work—his articles in the *Sind Quarterly* (1991) and his book (1987)—on the theme of education, ethnicity, and nation building. Kazi covers much of the same ground as Aziz, but his interest is in showing the relationship between the content of the books and the prevailing political dispensation, rather than the identification of errors. The third and fourth sources are an article by Ayesha Jalal (1995a) and an essay by Avril Powell (1996). Jalal's article surveys Pakistan studies books and a couple of Indo-Pakistan histories to show that the Islamization agenda has overtaken any scholarly or pedagogical needs. Avril Powell's essay is a comparison of "standard" histories in India and Pakistan. Her interest is in the different ways national identity is reflected therein. Jalal and Powell both allude to the presence of Indian history as the "other" in the history of Pakistan. Powell explicitly compares Indian and Pakistani historiography and shows that in some cases, they are mirror images of each other—the roles of Mughal emperors Akbar and Aurangzeb, for instance. Pervez Amirali Hoodbhoy and Abdul Hameed Nayyar's (1985) essay "Rewriting the History of Pakistan" is an examination of college textbooks. Although these are beyond the purview of this study, Hoodbhoy and Nayyar's essay is relevant because it illustrates the relationship between changes in the official definition of state identity and revisionist historiography and text writing.

There is more writing on mythology, history, historiography, history teaching, and the politics of identity by Sri Lankans writing on Sri Lanka than in the other two cases together (de Silva 1984; Gunawardena 1985: 55–107, 1995; Jeganathan and Ismail 1995; Coomaraswamy 1987: 72–99; Tennekoon 1987: 1–59; Bandaranayake 1985: 1–19; Goonatilake 1985: 21–53; Siriweera 1985: 108–127; Kailasapathy 1985: 161–174; Mathews 1985: 81–87). There are two major studies on textbooks that will form the empirical basis for this section. The first is the early 1980s study *School Text Books and Communal Relations in Sri Lanka,* conducted by Reggie Siriwardena, K. Indrapala, Sunil Bastian, and Sepali Kottegoda (1980) on behalf of the Council for Communal Harmony Through the Media. The second is Sasanka Perera's dissertation, "Teaching and Learning Hatred: The Role of Education and Socialization in Sri Lankan Ethnic Conflict" (1991). The first source is an examination of social studies and religion school texts in Sinhala and Tamil, as well as English readers, published by the Education and Publications Department and used in 1981. The second study is much larger in scope. It looks at textbooks from Sinhala, Tamil, and English medium schools and at language, social studies, and religious studies (particularly Buddhism) texts in particular. Further, it places these in the context of classroom use and draws on classroom observation and interviews with teachers and students in different locations and from both language streams. The two studies mark two points in the history of the Sri Lankan ethnic conflict. The first was undertaken a year or two before the 1983 riots, after which the conflict escalated sharply. The second was undertaken while the Indian Peace-Keeping Force was on the island and the Janata Vimukti Peramuna insurgency was at its height. Both works are driven by the conviction that the state should use the education system to create a tolerant citizenry, and the authors of both find the textbooks they analyze wanting in this sphere. Although my concern here is narrowly with the content of history education, where language and religious studies books impinge on history education, I take cognizance of the authors' analyses.

The Structure of the Educational System

India. Education is a subject on the Concurrent List, which means that both the central and state governments can legislate or act on the subject, but in the event of a conflict, the central law prevails. Two policies govern schooling, at least in principle:

- The 10+2+3 structure, whereby the first ten years are the years of basic schooling and the last three years are spent at the non-professional baccalaureate degree college. The "+2" stage is a part of school in some states and is a replacement for the old pre-university college courses in others.
- The Three-Language Formula was devised in response to the anti-Hindi protests of the 1950s and required the teaching of the regional language, English, and a second Indian language in schools. This formula is honored more in the breach than in the observance. Tamil Nadu is one of the states that does not follow this formula in its schools.

Several boards of education operate in this pluralistic environment. The central government runs a system of schools all over the country that is administered by the Central Board of Secondary Education and the All-India Higher Secondary Board. In addition, in each state, there is a local school board, often further subdivided in the larger states, and there are some variations in the school system—different requirements at the primary and secondary stages, differences in the school calendar, including examinations, and differences, above all, in the language requirements. Finally, there are school boards that are not affiliated with the state or the center. These are sometimes legatees of the colonial certification agencies, such as the Indian School Certificate Examination Board, which offers only the tenth-class examination, and the Matriculation Board, which offers both tenth- and twelfth-class examinations.

Pakistan. As in India, curricula and syllabi are subjects on the Concurrent Legislative List in Pakistan. In practice, however, curriculum development is a centralized affair. The Federal Curriculum Wing (FCW) in the Ministry of Education designs the curriculum, ostensibly in consultation with the provincial bureaus of curriculum. The implementation of the curriculum is left to the provinces (Bregman and Mohammad 1998: 77, Appendix, Chart 4). Textbooks are produced by the National Book Foundation and the Provincial Textbook Boards (Jones 1993: 72), with one textbook being approved in each province for each subject (Bregman and Mohammad 1998:77).

Schooling is divided into four phases. The first five years are spent in primary school, followed by three years in middle school, two years in secondary school, and two years in higher secondary or intermediate school. This schooling may be followed by two or three years at the baccalaureate level. Transitions between stages are examination-dependent, and at the later stages, these examinations are conducted by the Federal Board of Intermediate and Secondary Education and twenty provincial boards (Hoodbhoy 1998: 13). Usually one textbook is approved for the entire province (although with twenty boards, it is clear that more than one textbook is used in each province), and memorizing the textbook becomes the objective of the educational process (Greeney and Hasan 1998: 140). Students learn social studies from classes 3 through 8 and then Pakistan studies in the last two years of secondary school, continuing into college. This curriculum combines history and ideology, as we will see later.

Schools in Pakistan use Urdu, the regional languages, or English as their instructional medium. In the first three years in most schools, students are taught either Urdu (in Punjab and Baluchistan) or the regional language (in the other provinces). English is taught as well, except in Baluchistan. In the fourth and fifth grade, all three are taught (with the previously noted exception). In the sixth grade, Arabic enters the curriculum for three years. In the ninth and tenth grades, the regional language and Urdu are alternated, as are Pakistan studies and the Islamiyat-ethics class (Bregman and Mohammad 1998: Appendix, Chart 5).

Sri Lanka. Sri Lanka is a unitary state, and until the Thirteenth Amendment (1987) to the 1978 constitution, education was a centralized affair. Even after 1987, although the responsibility for primary and secondary schools was devolved to the regions, the power to design the curriculum was retained by the central government (Thirteenth Amendment, Appendix III, 1987; de Silva 1999: 113). The National Institute of Education was established and charged with curriculum development and teacher training. In October 1997, the government proposed further devolution of educational responsibilities to the regions, including curriculum, textbooks, teacher training and the power to establish local universities.

Two policies colluded in Sri Lanka to create a citizenry divided by language. One was the gradual adoption of Swabasha (the policy of education in one's native language) to include more and more levels of the education system; under this policy, the medium of education for students is their native language—Sinhalese students learn in the Sinhala medium and Tamil students in the Tamil; Burgher and Muslim children are given the choice of English, Tamil, or Sinhalese. This process, which began and gathered momentum through the 1950s, began to be reversed with the passage of the 1978 constitution. It stipulated not only that Sinhala and Tamil would be national languages but also that any course offered by a state-aided educational institution in one national language must be offered by that or another institution in the other language (Article 21[2]; de Silva 1999: 125, fn. 7). Second, the policy of free education ensured that the fruits of this segregated education reached everyone. Further, in the 1960s, all the schools were nationalized, including private and parochial schools. In the 1960s, when the linguistic segregation in schools was at its climax, secondary school enrollment rose by 246 percent (de Silva and de Silva 1990: 22). Perera quotes Ministry of Education figures to show that in 1981, out of 9,518 state-run schools, only 57 offered more than one medium of instruction; the remaining schools were linguistically segregated (1991: 51). This segregation, he tells us, is spreading to the university level for a variety of reasons, from the establishment of Buddhist universities to the outbreak of conflict after 1977, which made the University of Jaffna effectively a Tamil university (55–56). On September 16, 1999, the Sri Lankan cabinet decided that from January 2000, Tamil would be taught in all Sinhala-medium schools and Sinhala in all Tamil-medium schools. English would be taught as a link language (United News of India 1999). This measure, accompanied by the devolutionary reform not just of the educational administration but also of curriculum development, has the potential to rewrite the relationship between education and ethnic relations in Sri Lanka. However, it is still too early to assess the implementation and impact of this change.

Since 1977, Sri Lanka too has followed the twelve-year schooling system with five years of primary school from ages five to ten, five years of junior secondary school from ages eleven to fifteen, and finally, two years of senior secondary school from ages sixteen to seventeen (de Silva and de Silva 1990: 23).

The Guidelines for Teaching History

Consistent with the level of governmental intervention in the educational sector in each country at different points in time, history education has reflected official orientations.

India. In India, history is taught as a separate subject within the social studies curriculum from classes 6 through 12. According to NCERT guidelines, some of the objectives of teaching history at this stage are as follows:

> 5. To develop an appreciation of the growth of various components of Indian culture and legitimate pride in the achievements of the Indian people in different periods and in different parts of the country; . . .
> 7. To develop an integrated view of Indian history and civilization and of human civilization as a whole; . . .
> 9. To develop a critical appreciation of the past so that the pupil's personality is free from parochialism, irrational prejudices, bigotry, communalism and every kind of chauvinism and is imbued with a rational, scientific and forward-looking outlook. (*Guidelines and Syllabi for Upper Primary Stage Classes VI–VIII* 1988: 58)

Pakistan. Kazi's work (1987, 1991) and the essay by Hoodbhoy and Nayyar (1985) point to the changes that took place in the history–Pakistan studies curriculum as a consequence of Islamicization. Prior to this, changes in educational policy had affected structure and the medium of education rather than curricular content. Hoodbhoy and Nayyar identify four themes that underlie post-1981 college-level Pakistan studies texts: the "Ideology of Pakistan"; the depiction of Jinnah as an orthodox, religious person who founded a theocratic state; the portrayal of the Muslim clergy as the genuine heroes of the Pakistan movement; and an emphasis on ritualistic Islam that rejects liberal interpretations. Jalal discusses "the twin issues of historic origins and national sacrifice" and the teleological way in which they are narrated, showing how historical content is affected by the ideological concerns of the state (1995a: 78).

Sri Lanka. Since history was replaced by a social studies curriculum in Sri Lanka in the early 1970s, it is hard to say, based on the available sources, what the official guidelines are for history teaching.

A Comparison of Textbook Portrayals of National and Local Histories

Given that in each case different sources form the basis of the analysis, what exactly is analyzed varies a little; in all cases, however, my interest is in a comparison between portrayals of the whole and portrayals of its parts. In the Indian case, I compare how NCERT and Tamil Nadu state board textbooks depict regional histories as they recount what is supposed to be the history of the whole country. In the Pakistani case, the question is, How does each generation of texts deal with the existence of diverse regions in Pakistan? The sources used in the Sri Lankan case provide us with glimpses of how social studies texts narrate Sri Lankan history.

India. The NCERT has very definite views as to the place of local history (NCERT 1988). These are inconsistent on two counts. First, although it believes that children should learn about their immediate environments, it does not favor the teaching of regional history as distinct from national history. Second, whereas it objects to regional histories partly because they are unhistorical, it does not apply this standard to national history. We are told that teaching local history is acceptable in two circumstances—first, when it involves acquainting children with historical and cultural remains in their immediate environment and, second, when the subject is appended to the larger, all-India narrative. The writers of the guidelines also acknowledge the pedagogical value of local history of this sort because it offers opportunities for the student to work on projects independently. However, we are cautioned:

The term [local history] has also been used to mean the history of a region or a State, presenting the region or the State as having a distinct and independent historical identity, traced back to the earliest times. Establishing the historical distinctiveness of a region corresponding to the present political boundaries of a State is often unhistorical and overlooks the historical interconnection of that region with other parts of the country. Introducing this kind of local history at the school stage has the danger of promoting parochialism and regional cultural chauvinism. (NCERT 1988: 59)

From classes 6 (where the children are around ten or eleven) through 10, Indian children study, in this order, ancient India, medieval India, modern India, the medieval and early modern world, and finally, the modern world and Indian cultural history.

The Indian school history syllabus and texts are structured around the idea of a continuous past, extending from ancient to the modern times. . . . It is not as if our elementary school history books do not acknowledge any breaks in history. . . . This style conveys the feeling that "all" the important facts about the past are known to the historian-author of the book, and that the pattern these facts fit in to is a continuous one. . . . The overall treatment of ancient and medieval periods of history appears to impart to the contemporary nation-state a civilizational heritage which is historically continuous. (Kumar 1996: 26)

The Tamil Nadu textbooks conform to the NCERT guidelines and syllabi in terms of the topics they include. They also imitate the sweep of the NCERT books, about which the previous comment is made, but they do so ineffectually. The National Steering Committee on Textbook Evaluation (1994: 44) writes of the Tamilnadu Textbook Corporation's *Social Science 6*, "It is not easy to evaluate this book in terms of any educational objectives." This is true of all the Tamil Nadu textbooks for all levels, replete as they are with pointless assertions, silly questions, and factual errors. In the following paragraphs I point out some of the distinct differences between these textbooks and the NCERT books for the same class. I especially looked for accounts of north-south contact and for indications of where the Tamil country stood vis-à-vis the rest of India. One might expect that the Tamil Nadu books would cover more local history than the NCERT books do, but this is not so.

The NCERT book for class 6 mentions no geographic regions. The south appears for the first time in the sixth chapter, "India from 200 B.C.

to A.D. 30." We are told that "India, South of the Vindhya mountains and the Narmada river, was known in ancient times as Dakshinapatha; now it is called the Deccan. South of the Deccan is the land of the Dravidian speaking people" (NCERT 1994: 71). The Tamil Nadu book, in contrast, reads, "India may be divided into four physical divisions. They are the Himalayan ranges of the north, the Indo-Gangetic plain, the Deccan plateau and the Thamizhagam" (Tamilnadu Textbook Corporation 1995a: 10). Further, "Thamizhagam: It is found to the south of the Deccan Plateau. It contains natural resources. It was ruled by the Cheras, Chola, Pandya and Pallava rulers. These Kings had even naval force. The Yavanas and the Romans established commercial contact with Thamizhagam by the sea-route" (11).

Regarding north-south relations, the NCERT book tells us: "The Satavahana kingdom acted as a bridge between North India and South India. Some of the forests had been cleared and villages established. Roads were built to provide communication throughout the northern Deccan in the Godavari and Krishna valleys. It was no longer unsafe to travel in these paths" (NCERT 1994:74). The Tamil Nadu textbook reads: "The Vindhya mountains separate South India from North India. They prevented close contact between North India and South India" (Tamilnadu Textbook Corporation 1995a: 11).

The Tamil Nadu textbooks go further than the NCERT textbooks in describing the diversity of Indian society.

> Ethnic groups in India: Indians belong to different ethnic groups. The Dravidians were the original inhabitants of India. Later the Aryans who came to India considered India as their homeland. Therefore a race known as the Indo-Aryan race appeared. . . . Due to the fusion of these different races, many new cultures developed. (Tamilnadu Textbook Corporation 1995a: 12)

> Languages: The people of India speak eighteen major languages and eight hundred and thirty other languages. Tamil, Sanskrit, Hindi, Telugu, Kannada and Malayalam are some of the important languages of India. (Tamilnadu Textbook Corporation 1995a: 12)

Having specifically mentioned Dravidians and Dravidian languages (Tamil, Telugu, Kannada, and Malayalam), the textbooks might be expected to distinguish between the history and the political identity of the south, particularly in light of the Dravidanadu movement. However, they lay claim for the south to "true Indianness" by saying,

> In the mediaeval period, North India was divided into many kingdoms. They often fought with one another. In South India, the Cholas conquered many kingdoms. They grew very rich because of trade. They built many beautiful temples. There were saints and Philosophers at this time. Their teaching influenced Indian thought. You should bear this in mind that Indian culture was further developed in South India. (Tamilnadu Textbook Corporation 1995b: 5)

In its description of South Indian history during A.D. 80–1200, the Tamil Nadu class 7 book discusses political history, king by king, in the case of the Cholas, Pandyas, Hoysalas, and Yadavas. However, its "Life of the People" focuses on the Cholas to the exclusion of the others. This exclusion is reflected in the ways that Tamilians narrate their history. Apart from these distinctive touches, the Tamil Nadu book is poorly plagiarized from the NCERT class 7 text, written by Romila Thapar. (The National Steering Committee on Textbook Evaluation [1994: 47] pronounces it "much better than the book for class VI"!) It is poorly plagiarized because it embellishes the Thapar text by asking the unsuspecting eleven-year-old questions such as, "Do you remember Ibrahim Lodi?" and "Do you remember the establishment of Bahmani Kingdoms?" whereas neither have been mentioned before and the eleven-year-old has no personal acquaintance with either medieval reference. The textbook evaluators pronounce the book not suitable to be used as a textbook. The class 10 book, which deals also with Indian cultural history, contains one chapter on the synthesis of Dravidian and Aryan cultures; a one-and-a-half-page chapter, "India—A Cultural Unity in Diversity"; and in the chapter on contemporary challenges, two-and-a-half pages with the sections "Communalism" and "Regionalism and Secessionism." It is noteworthy that in the latter, children are told,

> The reorganisation of the states on linguistic basis in 1956 is considered by many as a grave mistake from the point of national unity and integrity. The reorganisation has set people one against the other on linguistic lines. People of one state do not wish others migrating and settling in their States. The "sons of the soil" theory has taken deep roots. Feelings of secessionism have sprung up in several places.

> People belonging to particular religions have been raising demands to set up sovereign states outside the Indian Union. (Tamilnadu Textbook Corporation 1995c: 157)

In fact, for textbooks in a state whose ruling party once spearheaded a secessionist movement, Tamil Nadu textbooks champion the unity-in-diversity ideal in both their descriptions of the present and the lessons they draw from the past.

> Unity in diversity: There are many differences among the people of India in race, language, religion, customs and culture. But all Indians live together with a sense of unity. All of us live as Indians under the same government, laws and national flag as children of our Mother India. We call this way of life as "Unity in Diversity." (Tamilnadu Textbook Corporation 1995a: 13)

Following paragraph-length descriptions of the Pratihara, Pala, Rashtrakuta, and "Rajput" kingdoms and the mention of Nepal, Kamarupa, Kashmir, and Utkala, we are told, "These kingdoms were always fighting with each other only to establish their strength. All these wars made them weak. When the invaders came to India, they could not defend themselves properly. Don't you understand that 'Unity is strength'?" (Tamilnadu Textbook Corporation 1995b: 13).

This historical education of Tamil Nadu children muddles on, challenging with the abysmally poor quality of its texts the choice of the question "What is the impact of history education on national integration?" We might ask instead, "How can you possibly teach anything, integration or disintegration, with books that are this bad?" Given how poor the books are, it is hard to imagine that even if they should have an integrative or disintegrative agenda, students would be able to grasp that clearly and live by it. Perhaps in the tug-of-war between these agendas, either side rests happy in the other's incompetence.

Pakistan. That national ideology should influence the writing of textbooks is now the accepted view of educationists in Pakistan, says Avril Powell (1996: 194). What this means for historiography and history education is that the entire history of the subcontinent must be retold as if to lead inevitably to the creation of Pakistan in 1947 on the basis of the "Two Nation Theory" (194).

History textbooks in Pakistan are either called "History of Indo-Pakistan" or "History of Pakistan," and each of these indicates a particular choice of topics (Powell 1996: 197). The history of Indo-Pakistan is essentially the history of South Asia. The history of Pakistan, however, is a confusing matter, and each writer interprets it differently to include different geographical areas and historical periods. The history sections of Pakistan studies books about the impact of Islam and the establishment of Pakistan are the primary filters for information.

Kazi looks at textbooks in four historical periods. In the first, 1947–1958, history, civics, and geography are taught separately even though they are part of one curriculum. In Kazi's words, this curriculum "treats the Pakistani nationalities with a 'unity in diversity' perspective" (1991: 52). "Our country Pakistan is like a garden. Its nationalities, Baluch, Bengali, Pathans, Punjabis and Sindhis, are the different flowers of that garden" (Kazi 1987: 81). A larger "national" history is supplemented, he tells us, with accounts of regional histories, "indigenous movements and wars of independence," and even Hindu leaders of the anticolonial struggle such as Gandhi, Nehru, Subhas Chandra Bose, and Rabindranath Tagore. The principal medium of instruction was the local language, and Urdu was introduced only at the secondary level. To Kazi, this curriculum reflects the cultural pluralism and the "centrifugal tendencies" of the elite (1991: 53).

The next period discussed by Kazi is the Ayub Khan–Yahya Khan period, 1958–1971. Following One Unit, history was replaced with a subject called Mu'ashrati Ulum, or social studies, in classes 1 through 8 and by Mutala'a-i-Pakistan, or Pakistan studies, in classes 9 through 12. These new subjects combined elements of history, geography, civics, economics, Islamic studies, and international relations (Aziz 1993a: 2). The new national social studies curriculum was also changed in 1958 so that it described Pakistan not in terms of the diversity of its people but in geographical terms and emphasizing a common faith in Islam (Kazi 1991: 54). Islam was said to have erased all cultural differences between the people of Pakistan.

It is more than a thousand miles' distance between the two parts of Pakistan. Both parts are different from each other in several respects, for example, their geographical location, climate, the inhabitants and their languages. But the inhabitants in both parts of Pakistan are

Muslims. Therefore, under this religious relationship all other differences have been forgotten and all the inhabitants of Pakistan have been united and merged into a nation. (Kazi 1987: 88)

In this period, the focus in the historical narrative moves entirely to the Indo-Gangetic plains. The Pakistan movement is depicted as the consequence of developments in Aligarh and Lucknow, and there is no mention of parallel developments in the regions that actually became Pakistan. This geographical focus is attributed to the growing dominance of Muhajirs in the Pakistani polity in the years after Liaqat Ali Khan. This was also the period in which Urdu came to be taught compulsorily. In the same period, the teaching of the regional language in schools ceased to be compulsory. The coercive nature of the drive toward integration is reflected in these texts, says Kazi (1987).

The third period is really the Bhutto era—1971–1977, after the breakup of Pakistan. Under the new political dispensation, the provincial languages were to be used, in addition to Urdu, as official languages of their respective provinces and therefore came to be used also as media of instruction. Kazi tells us that the texts of this period once more reflect the cultural diversity of Pakistan: "In the state of Pakistan, the Pakistani nationalities enjoy the status of four different brothers" (Kazi 1987: 93).

The communities that make up Pakistan are described in ethnic rather than geographic terms, and religion is seen not just as an abstract idea but in its socioeconomic context (Kazi 1991: 56). Inscrutably, Kazi also says, "The new texts [portray?] Pakistan as an Islamic republic or a Muslim state, rather than the Islamic state, as did the previous administrations" (1991: 56). Earlier exclusions in the historical narrative were marginally amended. Bengali and other indigenous contributions found their way back into the narrative, and the Indo-Gangetic plains ("central Indian provinces") retained their positions as the primary arenas of the Pakistan movement. Hindu leaders of the anticolonial struggle were still excluded from the texts, even those from the regions now a part of Pakistan.

In the last period, which includes the Zia ul-Haq years and the first three thereafter, Pakistan is described by Hoodbhoy and Nayyar (1985) as an Islamic state where the political process is always unstable and lacking in legitimacy. In 1977, Nizam-i-Mustafa, or the policy of Islamicization, was introduced, and the textbooks reflect that change: "What is the meaning of Pakistan? . . . Pakistan was demanded so that the Muslims could live their individual and collective lives according to Islam. Instead of an un-Godly government, they could live their life under the government of God" (Kazi 1987: 97).

The breakup of Pakistan is glossed over and the events leading up to it described so sketchily that students might well conclude that the divisive results of the 1970 elections were singularly responsible for that outcome (Hoodbhoy and Nayyar 1985: 173). Contributions of local leaders to the Pakistan movement are once more excluded. Pakistan is culturally diverse, but no other specific details are provided. Indeed, Kazi quotes a 1982 Pakistan studies textbook as saying, "The seals found in the excavation of Mohenjo-daro are inscribed with writings which have not yet been deciphered by the scholars. These inscriptions tell the story of a 4000 years old [script of] Islamic literature in Pakistan" (Kazi 1991: 58). There is no change in the policy regarding medium of instruction, as Urdu is still compulsory in this period; other languages are not.

Across the four periods, Kazi finds that there is hardly any recounting of regional histories. Local mythology and folklore were covered in the first period and treated as national treasures. The subsequent emphasis on Islam relegated mythology and folklore to the side. On the whole, Kazi finds the textbooks after this early era show intolerance with regard to ethnic and religious differences. As Jalal puts it, "If Hindu India is the enemy without, the proponents of regional autonomy alongside the ungodly secularists are the enemies within" (1995a: 83). The ideology of Pakistan is based on the religious community to the exclusion of all other loyalties, and regional leaders, histories, and autonomy undermine that ideology. In the post-1977 push to promote the ideology of an Islamic Pakistan, the regions are a necessary casualty of textbook revision.

Sri Lanka. This section draws on the discussion of history lessons in social studies textbooks by Siriwardena and others (1980) and Perera (1991). In the early 1970s, history was replaced as a subject by social studies. This move is upheld by Perera as a far-sighted one, since the social studies curriculum acquaints students with a wide range of topics, uses participatory learning techniques, and is taught cumulatively through high school. He says it was very popular among students, as well (1991: 226). In a revision of the curriculum in 1978–1979, some of these appealing features were discontinued. According to Perera, although the social studies books are published in three languages, the advisory committees of editors and writers have usually been Sinhalese, and the translators come from the minority communities. Whereas Siriwardena and Bastian commence their analysis of social studies texts with relief, pronouncing them far less biased than the Sinhala and Buddhism texts, Perera says this lack of bias is only superficial. He analyses the discussion in eight social studies textbooks over the years 1978–1987 in two areas—the concept of *jatiya* (nation, race, ethnicity) and the discussion of general history with reference to ethnic and religious conflict. The difference between Perera's perspective and Siriwardena and Bastian's may partly be attributed to the fact that Perera's research allowed him to observe how these relatively objective texts lose this quality in classroom use.

Teachers from both communities have been educated and trained in segregated environments and, in the absence of proper training, feel an obligation to convey those notions of history and identity that they hold true. As the teachers told Perera, it is their duty. In the Sinhalese medium schools, Perera was told by all the Buddhism teachers that teaching about Sri Lanka's past was an indispensable part of religious education. It would give students an appreciation of the historical role of the polity in preserving the faith. He says, "The texts play a collaborative role in this regard" (1991: 129). Both teachers and students in the Tamil medium schools regarded the history that they must learn by rote for the examinations to be biased, and therefore, the teachers felt obliged to also "show the students reality as it was" (146).

What do the texts themselves convey? A couple of themes are common to the discussion of social studies books in both Bastian and Siriwardena (1980) and Perera (1991), based on the Sinhala version of the books. First, both discuss the confusing use of the word *jatiya* to denote both "race" and "nation." There have been attempts to restrict the word's meaning to "nation" while using another word for "race." What is confusing, say Bastian and Siriwardena (1980: 30–32), is that the textbooks contradict each other from year to year. Perera (1991) also points this out.

More relevant to our concerns here is the cultural and historical information presented about the various communities in Sri Lanka, particularly the Tamils.

> These different races are descendants of different racial groups which came to Sri Lanka at different times. The Aryans, who were the ancestors of the Sinhalese, came here from North India 2500 years

ago. There are two sections of Dravidians. The ancestors of Lankan Tamils settled in this country two or three centuries after the coming of the Aryans. The Indian Tamils are descended from South Indian workers who were brought here by the British to cultivate the up-country estates in the 19th century and from South Indians who came here recently for purposes of trade. (*Nava Samaja Adhyayanaya 6*, translated by Bastian and Siriwardena 1980: 32)

Bastian and Siriwardena note that although they use the word Tamil, the word used in the original is Dravida, which has many other connotations. Dravidian is the name of a group of languages primarily in South India that is said to originate in Tamil, and that term has been appropriated for other purposes. First, Dravidian is used to suggest a racial origin different from Aryan. Second, it is used by the Dravida movement in South India in that sense but to establish a separateness from the political and social formations that are associated with Aryan, Brahmin, northern, and Hindi-speaking India. Employed here to mean Tamil, it draws all those meanings into the study of Sri Lankan history. Thus, passages such as the following contain the potential for conflict: "Apart from the Aryan community, to whom the Sinhalese belong, the largest minority in Lanka are Dravidians" (*Nava Samaja Adhyayanaya 7*, translated by Bastian and Siriwardena 1980: 33).

Continued use of "Dravidian" in the following historical account makes the equation of Sri Lankan Tamil and South Indian in the present context perfectly plausible.

It can be supposed that owing to these continual invasions, the friendship that existed at first between the Dravidians and the Sinhalese broke down, and in time the Dravidians came to be regarded as South Indian invaders. After the Sinhala kingdom was shifted to the southwest, Dravidian power spread in the northern parts of the island about the 13th century. It was from about this time that a Dravidian kingdom came to be established in the Jaffna peninsula. In this way, the South Indian people who came to Lanka for trade and other purposes and as invaders, became permanent inhabitants. (*Nava Samaja Adhyayanaya 7*, translated by Bastian and Siriwardena 1980: 33)

Perera cautions us against attributing the present Sri Lankan conflict entirely to paragraphs such as this, but as he also says, the factual tone of the text lends credibility to it. He discusses in some detail the origin of the idea that the Sinhalese are Aryans (1991: 230–232), and both Perera and Bastian and Siriwardena point out that the information in these paragraphs is not entirely correct and is in some places contradictory.

Nevertheless, these books are considered to be somewhat "professional" (Perera 1991: 234) in their approach. The reference in the ninth-grade textbook to "the migration of Soli, Pandi and Kerala people from South Indian empires" (*Samaja Adyanaya 9,* translated by Perera 1991: 233), as opposed to the invasions of these groups; the acceptance of the existence of an independent Jaffna kingdom; and the discussion in the same text of the mutual influence of the diverse groups in Sri Lanka as well as the obstacles that such divisions could pose to economic development are three examples of such professionalism cited by Perera (1991: 234). However, he does point out that in spite of the fact that some of these books were revised as the ethnic conflict escalated, there is no discussion of the Sri Lankan conflict itself, and the wars to repel invasions of the island are depicted as "race wars" waged by the Sinhalese to overthrow the Tamils (1991: 234).

Although these writers do not find great fault with the social studies textbooks in Sri Lanka, it must be added that their findings are based partly on a comparison with the Sinhala- and Tamil-language textbooks, which both works criticize roundly for their acts of omission and commission. In fact, upon reading these studies, one is led to believe that any positive impact that the social studies curriculum might have would easily be mitigated by the lessons that the language primers contain, to say nothing of the religious studies texts. For example, quoting an article in the *Lanka Guardian* ("Happy Families," May 1, 1979), both Perera (1991) and Siriwardena and others (1980) compare the contents of the beginning readers (1978–1979) in the two languages. In each, a map of Sri Lanka is reported to be accompanied by a verse. In the Sinhala primer, the verse reads as follows:

> Lanka my land
> My beloved land
> Lanka the land of my birth
> This is my land.

In the Tamil primer, the verse is

> We are Tamils
> We are Muslims

We are Sinhalese
Ilankai [Lanka] is our land
We are all people of this land
We are friends.

The Sinhala-language books feature a monocultural Sinhala Buddhist world. Whether or not this is intentional, Bastian and Siriwardena say, "If the school child's only knowledge of Sri Lanka were confined to a reading of these books, he would not even be aware that there were in this country any people other than Sinhalese and Buddhists" (1980: 7). Both studies tell us that the names of the children in these books are primarily and recognizably Sinhalese. Where the lessons might take the opportunity to introduce another culture or the idea of ethnic harmony, they allow that opening to be used in other ways. For instance, although there are some Sinhalese and Tamil festivals that fall on the same day and that have been unifying secular celebrations, attention in the textbooks is paid exclusively to the Sinhalese celebration. "It appears that except in terms of religious preferences, most Sinhalese agree that the monocultural nature of the first three Sinhala readers are not only acceptable but necessary" (Perera 1991: 169).

The earlier Tamil textbooks, approved by the Government Textbooks Committee, began with a religious invocation and an invocation to the Tamil language. K. Indrapala tells us that the third lesson is about Tamils, and it states that Sri Lanka and South India once formed part of a greater Tamil homeland, in which a large part of the subcontinent is included. "In the rest of the book," we are informed, "there is not even a single lesson devoted to Sri Lanka, and indeed the whole book can easily pass as an Indian text-book" (Indrapala 1980: 35). If one considers that children who read this in 1960 would be in their mid to late twenties in 1977, at the time that the militant groups first made their appearance in Tamil politics, we may have a clue to understanding the socialization they brought with them to this historical moment.

Textbooks appearing after the government takeover are markedly different. These are the books in which Tamil children are told that Sri Lanka is their motherland. Like the Sinhala texts, the initial Tamil texts do not feature non-Tamil children, and the setting is identifiably Jaffna. They do show that there are non-Tamil speakers elsewhere in the country and that there are Tamils in Batticaloa and the up-country (whose world features Sinhalese too), and the protagonists are Hindu Tamils. In the third text, there are some lessons that introduce non-Hindu

Tamils and others to the Tamils, but more often than not, Tamil culture is the focus of explanation to non-Tamils.

If one incident has been the battleground for opposing claims to the Sri Lankan past, it is the story of Duttugamenu (Siriweera 1985: 108–127; Obeyesekere 1993: 135–160; Bastian and Siriwardena 1980: 10–17; Perera 1991: 172–179).[3] But other heroes are also evoked in the Sinhala books. Perera tells us that apart from Duttugamenu, there are lessons on Vijayabahu, Parakramabahu I, Gajabahu I, Keppetipola, and Sri Wickrama Rajasinghe. The Tamil origin of the last two is mentioned nowhere. Descriptions of Chola cowardice, South Indian invasions, and the heroism of the above-mentioned heroes in protecting and fighting for Sinhala Buddhism are used to arrive at the standards of behavior to which the students must aspire.

History Education and National Integration: Concluding Observations

Textbook studies in South Asia that attempt to show the relation between textbook content and sociopolitical attitudes falter over two characteristics of the books. First, the textbooks are replete with inaccuracies and other errors. Second, it is difficult to estimate the long-term impact of the books in the lives of the students. In this instance, I began by asking whether history textbooks were an effective means of political socialization.

In the studies of textbooks in all three countries, one comes across complaints regarding quality—accuracy, language, pedagogical devices, production. It seems that far from receiving the attention of the government offices charged with their production, textbooks are churned out with little care. What the National Steering Committee on Textbook Evaluation writes about the class 6 social science textbook in Tamil Nadu applies as well to any of the others: "Lakhs of copies of this book have been printed during the past four or five years and, presumably, students have been obliged to read it. What they would have made of it is beyond imagination" (1994: 47). How does one evaluate the use of history curricula and history textbooks as an integrative tool when they barely meet the criterion of pedagogical effectiveness?

The textbooks from Tamil Nadu also raised unexpected questions. They conform contentwise to the guidelines exemplified by the NCERT books published in New Delhi, making additions rather than departing from recommendations. Few of these additions actually confront the focus of the curriculum on the north, and the additional chapters—for instance, chapters on the Aryan-Dravidian synthesis or the contribution of the Dravidians to Indian culture—are grafted on to the other curriculum. The problem is that in adapting the NCERT books and syllabi, the Tamil Nadu books destroy the carefully assembled narrative and polemical structure of those books. What we have are slapdash collages rather than artful murals, making it impossible to expect that anything, let alone national identity, is taught effectively. Further, two normative questions arise. What message regarding national identity should good-quality textbooks convey, and how can they do so persuasively? Second, and prior, should textbooks convey any such message?

As to the potency of the books, the examination orientation of the education system combined with the traditional stress on learning by rote lends paramount importance to texts. The student must know what is said in the text, and her performance is judged by how faithfully the text is reproduced in an examination. However, it is unlikely that students remember for long what they learn by rote, particularly if they have not understood much of it. Witness: Most of the Indians interviewed could not remember and reconstruct a cogent, complete historical account for their community, region, or India as a whole. As several of them pointed out, their most vivid impressions of the past came from cinema or literature—neither of which they have had to memorize. In contrast, because such history as is taught in Sinhala-language classes in Sri Lankan schools bears such a strong resemblance to the Mahavamsa chronicles, which are part of both the oral and written traditions of the Sinhalese, Sri Lankans are able to remember and relate history with astounding coherence. Yet of the three countries, it is India in which history still has a distinct identity in the curriculum, even as part of social studies. In Sri Lanka, history is no longer taught as a subject, even under the rubric of social studies, and this is the case in Pakistan as well.

The evidence that has been marshaled in the preceding pages allows the following conclusions:

- In India, the Tamil Nadu books are qualitatively unable to compete with the NCERT books, and there has been no effort to do so. In the main, the curriculum and textbooks are the same. Additions to the central agenda are in the introductory chapters that set background, in the odd inclusion of a chapter on

Dravidian culture, and in the occasional comment on an event or personality. The NCERT books and guidelines are guarded about stressing local history and prefer a narrative whose teleology is modern and "national" rather than parochial.

- In Pakistan, each province adopts one social studies book, and they all resolutely overlook regional history, reflecting the centralized curriculum design. Several writers bemoan the mismatch between the curriculum and the textbooks (Bregman and Mohammad 1998: 77; Greeney and Hasan 1998: 140), but we do not have the data to assess the nature or extent of the mismatch.

- In Sri Lanka, the social studies books are held to be less problematic than the language and religion textbooks. Furthermore, these texts are not taught in isolation of events around them— events they barely attempt to address. Finally, it remains to be seen how structural changes might alter the content and impact of the curriculum.

Perhaps it is inevitable that some bias creeps into the historical narrative. If language has the quality of immediately biasing narrative, then how could books be exempt from bias? Any choice of words lends a particular interpretation or perspective to the narrative, quite apart from the bias curriculum design forces—one has to choose what to teach, and it has to be simplified. One must, therefore, decide what it is vital for the child to know, and further, how it must be understood. If, by virtue of using language and by pedagogical imperative, bias cannot be avoided, then should that bias be channeled toward the objective of national integration or any other objective the state determines? This question harks back to the matter of how one views the state and what one regards as its proper place in relation to society and is impossible to answer definitively. If one believes that the state has no business in education, no further discussion is required. If, however, one does accept a certain degree of intervention, then the extent to which the state's agenda influences the school curriculum must logically reflect the extent of the state's intervention. One is caught in a spiral of circular reasoning.

Furthermore, can school textbooks hold their own in the face of other stories and texts? One person in Colombo recalled being told as a schoolboy that he should memorize the textbook but know that it was not correct. Where school textbooks are the new kid on the block as far as sources of historical learning are concerned, what is their relative credibility? Those involved in curriculum design and textbook planning must clearly find a *via media* between the histories current in society and that which best serves the needs of the political system. In the navigation of this *via media*, the relationship between vision and history is important. The vision of the state influences the content of school history curricula and textbooks, and school socialization contributes to (not determines or causes) the creation of a historical memory, to the way the past is remembered and recounted. This memory is in turn reflected in the evolving visions of the collective, which accounts for debates over and changes in school history curricula and textbooks. Even if the present and the past were the only two temporal markers in this sequence, the problem would not be simple. But socialization (and the term *vision*) intrinsically involves a third marker—the future. We socialize citizens today for tomorrow, and therefore, the content of our socialization is not merely a function of what our idea of ourselves is today but what it will or should be. Hence, what we choose to teach today is what we want as a feature of tomorrow's memory.

The textbooks discussed here are so bad that they do not seem capable of inciting conflict or integration. In any event, the only people in these societies preoccupied with textbook content are sections of the educated elite—perhaps because other people have more pressing concerns. Nevertheless, because textbooks can have great incendiary potential, there is still room for us to bring this exercise to fruition.

If the answer to the question of what one might be learning from these books about national identity is that one is lucky to learn anything at all, then the correct question is, What might one teach, if a revision of the curriculum and its textual resources is necessary for pedagogical purposes anyway? The answer depends on what we want our children to learn about the world we want to create for them. As we play this chicken-egg game with our curricula, we pay through the increasing levels of conflict in our societies.

It has been conceded that perhaps both state participation and some bias are inevitable. The exigencies of curriculum design and textbook writing make simplification inevitable, and simplification makes it hard to convey a plural reality. How might this problem be overcome? There are several possibilities, and they are and may be used in conjunction. The first is the easy and most common expedient of having children learn by rote certain word-pictures of this plural reality. The pledges that children learn, the inclusion of children from different communities in the lessons, and the reiteration ad nauseum of certain expressions such as "unity in diversity" fall in this category. More specific to history education, the second possibility is to allow the content of the books to sink to a lowest common denominator, where the narrative so little resembles anyone's vision that only reform is controversial. This alternative would explain the poor quality of history textbooks in India, whose leading professional historians are recognized for their competence. The National Council for Educational Research and Training (NCERT) does attempt to regulate quality and content, but it does not have the power to enforce standards and no one else seems to have the will to do so. Another tactic used by NCERT in India has been to adopt a materialist approach to history, which has the virtue of neutralizing ethnicity and culture. Feudalism, capitalism, industrialization, peasant struggles, and imperialism cut across ethnic categories.[4]

Finally, and ideally, perhaps history could be taught as it is—a motley collection of imperfect recollections with interpretive interjections based on intuitions about the present that calcify into facts about a mythical past. In the South Asian context, where so much oral history and collective remembering blur the lines between history and mythology, a curriculum using this approach, although difficult to design, could be effective. Could history not begin with mythology, introducing students to narrated and therefore varying versions of the same basic plot? This presentation would convey the idea that historical events are remembered differently, making it possible for different perspectives on an event to be represented in both textbooks and in classroom activities. The habit of acknowledging, discussing, considering, and accommodating diverse and contradictory narratives of the past is critical to the construction of a common future.

Unit Demarcation and National Integration

Tracing the state's intervention in the evolving territorial vision of the group is yet another chicken-egg situation. Does state intervention alone cause the self-image of the group to take a territorial form? Does the territorialization of this vision alone and necessarily elicit state intervention? Neither is the case. The narrative is broken up here into three phases—the preterritorial, territorial, and postterritorial phases in the articulation and assertion of a group's identity. Merely a conceptual distinction, this progression is not meant to suggest that the three communities in question—the Indian Tamils, the Sindhis of Pakistan, and the Sri Lankan Tamils—have followed the same path at the same pace or that they have all passed through the three phases.

Indeed, there are important differences in the historical experiences of the three groups. Although the Tamils in India had an understanding of the geographical limits of their culture, the Sindhis were the first of the three groups whose political identity became territorially bounded. Territorial politics have had different outcomes too. For the Indians in the study, it is ancient history. For the Sindhis, the restoration of their province has been followed by other troubles. For the Sri Lankan Tamils, the war is still under way. To speak of a postterritorial phase is most meaningful in the Indian case, where the dialogue has moved to other issues altogether. However, this division permits us to compare the different ways in which the state has intervened from the perspective of these communities. In anticipation of this discussion, the next few paragraphs provide a basic history of the movements for Dravidanadu in southern India, Sindhudesh in Pakistan, and Eelam in Sri Lanka.

The Dravidanadu movement had its origins in a most unlikely source—the rationalist social reform movement led by E. V. Ramasami (Periyar). In turn, the antecedents of this movement lay in the quest for increased representation by prominent landowners, merchants, and professionals who happened to be non-Brahmins. Neither movement was concerned with land or with ethnic identity. If the latter sought to break the Tamil Brahmin monopoly on administrative positions, the former sought to break the Tamil Brahmin stranglehold on social and ritual structures and practice. In 1937, the new Congress ministry in the Madras Presidency introduced the compulsory teaching of Hindi in 125 schools in the district. Periyar's leadership of the anti-Hindi movement transformed the Dravida movement into a cultural nationalist movement (Barnett 1976). Since the anti-Hindi movement was also a movement expressing devotion to Tamil, it underlined intra-Dravidian differences. The Congress had endorsed the idea of ethnolinguistic units in the 1920s, and the identification of anti-Hindi protests with Tamil lent credence to it. The result was a closer identification of Dravidian with Tamil and of Dravida Nadu with the Madras Presidency shorn of its Telugu-, Kannada-, and Malayalam-speaking districts. This ethnoterritorial dimension fortified separatist tendencies in the Dravida movement, and secession entered the agenda in the early 1940s. In the postindependence period, the rhetoric of secession grew stronger, but in expositions of the secessionist argument in Parliament, the movement's new leader, C. N. Annadurai, suggested that this rhetoric was a cover for grievances originating in relative deprivation. Nevertheless, the antisecession amendment was introduced and passed in Parliament in 1962–1963. The Dravida Munnetra Kazhagam (DMK), which had suspended its secessionist demands pending the duration of India's war with China, in a volte-face amended its own constitution and gave up that demand altogether. Almost forty years later, the two major Dravida parties are pillars of the Indian establishment, ever in the forefront of demands for state autonomy even as they participate in the coalitions that have dominated cabinet formation in New Delhi.[5]

By virtue of the fact that Sind as a whole was annexed and appended to the Bombay Presidency, the territorial scope of the Sindhi identity was never in question. However, whereas the form and shape of Sind were not contentious, its appearance and disappearance as a distinct entity on political maps was. The history of the Sindhudesh demand is in that sense a history of the struggle to separate Sind from the larger political formation in which it was merged at any point in time. Between 1847 and 1935, the goal of the Sindhi nationalists was to separate Sind from the Bombay Presidency (Rajagopalan 1999, 2000). In 1935, this goal was achieved, and the legislators of this new province were among the first to vote to join Pakistan at the time of Partition in 1947. In the first years after Partition, Sind received large numbers of refugees from what had become India. The demographic balance in Karachi, Sind's commercial and political center, was thereby altered. In addition, Karachi had been made the federal capital, its administrative buildings had been taken over by the federal government, and Urdu had replaced Sindhi in the school system. So after less than twenty years of having their own province, Sindhis experienced their loss of space to a larger collective all over again—except this time the process occurred in stages. The process came to a head with the imposition of One Unit in 1956. Again, Sind's identity as a province was submerged in that of a new unit, West Pakistan. The focus of Sindhi nationalism was once again separation—this time from Pakistan itself. Counterfactual conjecturing might suggest why the Sindhi secessionist movement did not succeed as did the Bengali, or why this movement did not become the primary determinant of events in Sind after 1971. However, what is important is that notwithstanding the earlier protests of Sindhi leaders such as G. M. Syed when Sind as a province was restored, the restoration seemed to happen as a function of the constitutional restructuring that followed the secession of East Pakistan. Sindhi regained its state patronage, and in this phase, Sindhi politicians were prominent both in local and national politics. Insofar as the struggle to get a separate province is concerned, the territorial phase of Sindhi nationalism should have ended at this time. However, by then, those who had moved to Sind (and particularly Karachi) at the time of Partition (the Muhajirs) outnumbered Sindhis in the city. Their need for a place for themselves in the context of Pakistan and their choice of Karachi as that city came into conflict with the goals of Sindhi nationalists. So in the past three decades, the territorial agenda of Sindhi nationalists has shifted from the restoration of their separate status to an internal turf battle with the Muhajirs over the future of Karachi.

Sri Lankan Tamils were the last of the three groups in this study to envision their identity in territorial terms. Although it is now common to speak of the north and east of the island as Tamil areas, in the precolonial period political borders were fluid, and in the colonial period Tamils moved to other parts of the island. Preindependence Tamil politics dealt largely with issues of representation in a majoritarian polity. With the introduction of the federal idea into that politics came the territorial element. The migration of Sinhalese settlers to the areas traditionally associated with a concentration of the Tamil population added another plank to this territorial claim—internal colonialism. As language and educational issues complicated ethnic relations, proposals for federating units in the north and east were replaced by the demand for an independent Tamil nation on the island—Eelam. Starting later than the other two communities, Sri Lankan Tamils who demand their own state do so in a climate of increasing violence and, therefore, extremely high stakes on either side. The investment and losses on both sides ensure that this secessionist demand will not meet the fate of the others. Legislation and external war are not going to facilitate a voluntary abandonment of the demand, as in the Dravidanadu case. The protracted war over Eelam makes the Sindhi nationalist struggle look as though it has been resolved—not merely distracted.

The Preterritorial Phase

The preterritorial phase in the evolution of a group's identity is simply the entire time before questions of land, belonging to land, and wanting a particular piece of land enter its political profile. The pre-Westphalia period in Europe and the precolonial period in other parts of the world may be said to be more or less preterritorial. This is not to say that people did not care where they lived, that polities lacked a land base or aspirations for land, or that the idea of geographical bounds for identity was completely lacking. What it means is merely that the territorial cutoff points that now tell us where one state ends and another begins and, by extension, where one ethnic community's homeland ends and another's begins were neither as definitively demarcated nor so contentious in the detail. Thus although Sind has been known as such for centuries and although armies and travelers have gone to Sind all that time, Sind was simply the land around the Indus delta, beyond the Hindu Kush foothills on one approach and the Thar desert on another. The people in that area came to speak a similar language. They owed allegiance to more than one religious or political authority. In other words, Sind in its preterritorial phase was a geographical idea that came to bound common cultural markers but had no political salience. The following pages identify and describe events and changes in the preterritorial phase that lent a territorial cast to the political identity of the Sindhis, Indian Tamils, and Sri Lankan Tamils.

Sind. Outside Europe, it is safe to say that the notion of territorially bounded nations and states followed the establishment of colonial boundaries (Anderson 1991). Thus, of our three cases, Sind was the first to exit the preterritorial phase. The annexation of Sind defined its limits, even though it was appended to the Bombay Presidency in 1847. Even the merger did not completely erase those limits, since Sind was administered as a "nonregulation" province within the presidency. The loose network of allegiances to feudal chiefs and *pirs* that had defined the old political arrangements in the area were replaced by a coherent administrative structure that gave value to belonging and having control within the unit. Thus began the territorial phase in Sindhi politics.

Tamils in India. In the case of India's Tamils, the preterritorial phase was longer. A succession of pan-Indian or supraregional powers had made incursions into the deep south after the thirteenth century— Allaudin Khilji's troops, the Vijayanagara empire, the Mughals and the Marathas. New dynastic houses were founded as a result, some of whom were descendents of those deputed to administer these new lands, for example, the Nayakas of Madurai, the Marathas of Thanjavur, and the Nawabs of Arcot. When the three Carnatic wars were fought between 1746 and 1763, the Nawabs of Arcot held revenue rights for three important regions in Tamil country—the northern areas around Arcot, Madurai, and Thanjavur. By 1801, the British had established their power in the area through a variety of means, but the important point is that their territorial gains followed the subjugation of particular dynastic houses rather than a conquest of a place called Tamil Nadu or Thamizhagam. Furthermore, the Madras Presidency, established that year, was composed of the Nizam's largely Telugu-speaking districts, Tipu Sultan's Kannadiga subjects in Mysore, and Tipu's Malayalam-speaking Malabar holdings. Thus, unlike in the case of Sind, colonization alone was not sufficient to territorialize Tamil identity in India.

The spread of English education and the growth of new professional opportunities both reinforced and altered old social patterns. The Brahmins continued to do two things that they had always done—support the dominant regime and seek the educational opportunities that would get them jobs in that regime. Thus they were the first to enter English schools and the first to enter the ranks of the colonial administration. At the same time, outside the sphere of the administration, a new professional and commercial elite was emerging, and its caste origins were mixed. The natural antagonism between an administrative elite and a professional elite of lawyers and those in trade was exacerbated by their caste differences. Opposition to what appeared to be a Brahmin monopoly over administration and its political and other perquisites, plus a determination to end that monopoly, brought together the founders of the Madras Non-Brahmin Association in 1909. This association metamorphosed ultimately into the South Indian Liberal Federation in 1916, which later came to be known as the Justice Party. At this stage, there was nothing ethnic or territorial or even anticolonial about this movement. Indeed, given the class composition of its leadership (prominent landowners and merchants), it was more like an interest group or lobby.

Between 1920 and 1935, the Justice Party contested elections to the Madras legislature, and its platform remained the betterment of the non-Brahmin community vis-à-vis the Brahmins. During this period, two things happened. On the one hand, a deteriorating relationship between landowning classes and untouchables in the rural areas and conversions from the latter community to Islam meant that the Justice Party's base among the untouchable and Muslim communities eroded. On the other hand, restive with the domination of the Congress and its agenda by upper-caste leaders, E. V. Ramasami (EVR, or Periyar) led several others out of the party to start the Self-Respect Movement, which aimed to ameliorate the conditions in which the lower castes were forced to live. A natural affinity of interests made this movement the successor to the Justice Party, which was in decline. Even at this point, there was nothing natural or inevitable about this movement acquiring ethnoterritorial overtones.

That push over the edge might well have been provided by two policies favored by the main rival of the Justice Party—the Congress. In the 1920s, the Congress had begun to favor linguistic provinces and, consequently, had reorganized its provincial wings to reflect the linguistic provinces that might be formed. As a result, the Madras Pradesh Congress Committee was broken up into four Pradesh Congress committees representing Madras, Kerala, Andhra, and Karnataka. What was left of Madras as a result of this division was essentially Tamil country. Second, when the Congress won the elections to the Madras provincial assemblies in 1937, one of the first acts of the new ministry was to introduce the compulsory teaching of Hindi in 125 schools. The experience of EVR and his followers seemed to identify the categories of Aryan, Brahmin, and Hindi with the Congress, on the one hand, and Dravidian, non-Brahmin, and Tamil, on the other. This equation and EVR's leadership of the anti-Hindi movement established him as the leader of Tamil speakers at large. Thus, a movement that had hitherto been about rights for the depressed classes now acquired ethnolinguistic overtones. The ethnic mix of the Justice Party leadership did not continue into the second generation, reinforcing this transformation.

Interestingly, the Pakistan Resolution precedes the Dravida Nadu Resolution by only a couple of months. When the Pakistan Resolution was passed, the Madras Congress Legislature Party passed a resolution supporting it, albeit revoking it a few months later (Rajayyan 1982: 380; see also Gandhi 1997: 225, 234–240, 243–244). The fact that the Congress could support the Pakistan Resolution and not the depressed classes' rights or the idea of a Dravida identity incensed EVR and others even more. It convinced them that if the British were to transfer power to the Congress, that move would not constitute liberation for them. It would merely replace a relatively neutral set of rulers with an elite made up of Brahmins and Banias who were responsible for the oppressive social structure of caste. The idea of secession gained currency in the Justice Party with the growing intensity of the anti-Hindi movement and its rhetoric. India would, in its vision, be a commonwealth or confederation of two federations in north and south India, each made up of autonomous linguistic or culturally based states (Laputan Flapper 1959: 52).

Although, as Sumathi Ramaswamy (1997: 63–65) points out, for the Dravida movement, the devotion to Tamil that led to the anti-Hindi agitation and later the demand for a separate Tamil Nadu were theoretically antithetical, inevitably that movement did come to express itself in the idiom of Tamil nationalism before long. The antithesis stemmed from the fact that the definition of Dravidian created a category of which Tamil was only one subset. The early Dravidian movement drew its leadership, as we have seen, from non-Brahmin professionals of different linguistic communities. However, many Brahmins (and indeed non-Indians) were among those who showed what Ramaswamy calls devotion to Tamil (Thamizhpatru). Another way to look at this matter is as S. V. Rajadurai and V. Geetha do: "When the Tamils sought to give expression to their historical identity in the context of modernity, it emerged as an aspect of a larger 'Dravidian' consciousness" (1996: 555). The fact that people in the non-Tamil regions of Madras were more focused on the question of linguistic self-determination than on their common Dravidian antecedents placed limits on the feasibility of a Dravidian identity or homeland.

C. N. Annadurai (1985) lists the sequence of secession events in the political vocabulary of the Dravida movement: In July 1940, a secession committee was formed at the Dravidanadu Secession Conference held in Kanchipuram; in August 1940, the Tiruvarur Provincial Conference resolved that Dravidanadu should be a separate state (*thani-naadu*); in August 1944, at the Salem Provincial Conference, the Justice Party was renamed Dravidar Kazhagam and that Dravidanadu should be a separate state was written into the party's constitution;[6] finally, Dravidanadu Secession Day was celebrated on July 1, 1947 (Annadurai 1985: 9–10). Thus the Dravida movement formally entered its territorial phase.

When one looks at the evolution of the idea of this community, there is no obvious moment that it crystallizes in one or another form. People first envision themselves in some fashion—in this case, on the basis of caste read also as race—but, having done so, search for a territorial base. That base seems to wend its way into that vision at some point, subsequently acquiring the aura of fact. The anti-Hindi agitation of 1938–1939 made that conjunction plausible in this case, with the

Justice Party choosing to frame its protest in Hindi versus Tamil (as opposed to the other languages spoken by Dravidians) terms.

Sri Lankan Tamils. As in other parts of South Asia, dynastic polities with definite core areas and fluid peripheries characterized Sri Lankan history. This was true of the kingdoms that were supplanted by European colonial rule. The British brought the entire island under their jurisdiction and then, between 1845 and 1889, subdivided the unitary colonial state into nine provinces. Although the territorial principle was thereafter ensconced in the administration, it did not enter the politics of Ceylon until the 1920s.

In 1912, the introduction of elections had two consequences. First and simply, competition developed among the Sri Lankan elite. Second and profoundly, Sri Lankan politics became more and more territorially bound. Writing about colonial constitutions, Martin Wight held, "The existence of an electorate presupposes political unity in the broad sense—a feeling of community, a common consciousness" (Wight 1952: 25). But as he goes on to point out, because it is sometimes hard to carve out territorial units in a plural society, the first unit of representation is communal, creating several parallel electorates. These electorates "crystallize and perpetuate" (28) differences among the communities. Wight optimistically held that the "measure of political progress" lies in transforming these communal constituencies into territorial ones (28–29). But here we are faced with a conundrum that Sri Lanka's experience illustrates: When the communities so represented live largely in different regions, as they do in Sri Lanka, communal representation reinforces the differences among the regions. So a switch to any other basis of electoral demarcation comes too late.

When the Donoughmore Commission introduced population-based territorial constituencies, which functioned in addition to the communal electorates, in 1931, the populous southwestern quadrant of the island acquired a majority of the new constituencies and seats. This new configuration reinforced the political and economic influence of this region, and because communal electorates were not abolished, ethnic separateness was also reinforced (de Silva 1993d: 101). Furthermore, one of the federalizing features that the Donoughmore commissioners suggested to diminish the preeminence of the southwest also employed ethnic categories: The commission encouraged legislators to acquaint themselves with the views of *various ethnic groups*, holding, to that end, sessions of the legislature in Kandy and Jaffna

(Wilson 1988: 15). "Because we were never integrated, never brought to realise that we are all from the same country. But we felt that we are living in the same country but we are different people. Because to the British we were different" (S7).

The Donoughmore Commission report facilitated two political developments that are relevant to the territorialization of Sri Lankan Tamil identity. First, the idea of provincial councils—or some form of federalism with the provinces as the federating units or units of devolution—gained currency. S.W.R.D. Bandaranaike had been an advocate of this idea since 1926, and in 1949, the Federal Party was established with the objective of establishing a federal Sri Lanka. Second, the majoritarian elements in the Donoughmore report led to the Tamil demand for fifty-fifty representation in the legislature. There is agreement among most scholars and analysts that this report marks the beginning of communal politics in Sri Lanka. Tamil politicians began to see their role in balance-of-power terms vis-à-vis the Sinhalese politicians. With majoritarian democracy reinforced by the Soulbury Constitution in 1948, there was no turning back on these issues. Territoriality had entered the communal politics of Sri Lanka.

Conclusions. The preterritorial phase is ended in all three cases by actions or policies of the state and its agents. In the Sindhi case, the annexation and administration of Sind as Sind caused mobilization around the idea of the separation of Sind, the first Sindhi nationalist mobilization. In the Indian Tamilian case, the introduction of Hindi in the Madras Presidency schools and the prospect of transfer of power to the Congress tipped the scales in favor of Dravidanadu. In the Sri Lankan Tamil case, the deployment of territorial solutions to governance problems and the creation of communal electorates seem to have combined to force the issue.

The Territorial Phase

By the territorial phase of a group's political history, I mean the phase in which territory becomes an integral marker of the group's identity and territorial demands and claims enter the political agenda of the group. Given the argument of this work that in this phase battles over land are in fact battles over identity, territorial issues also appear in the interaction between the group and other groups and between the group and the state. Thus, this phase marks an escalation in the negotiation of both state identity and the place of the group within the state; words and symbols become "grounded" in clearly marked tracts of land. In other words, this is the point at which the group starts clamoring for territorial resolutions to its grievances. Theoretically, what is sought could range from the renaming of a street or locality to secession, depending on the size and dispersion of the group's population. In two out of these three cases, the territorial phase began with a demand for autonomy at the level of provinces and escalated to the demand for a separate nation-state. Only in the Indian case was secession the first demand made. The following discussion covers those demands and the responses they were met with. Again, I will endeavor to trace the role of state intervention in shaping the course of events.

Sind. The territorial phase in the history of Sindhi politics may be divided into three campaigns. The first commenced almost at the time of the annexation and was the campaign to separate Sind from the Bombay Presidency, to which it was appended. The second campaign was a repeat performance except that this time the state in question was Pakistan and the merger, the One Unit system that prevailed between 1955 and 1972. The third is less a campaign than an embattled response to the claims made by the Muhajirs, whose numerical advantage in Karachi jeopardizes the position of Sindhis in their own province. I will focus on the interaction between the state action (first colonial, then Pakistani) and the Sindhi political leadership.

From the time of its annexation in 1843 until it was merged with the Bombay Presidency in 1847, Sind was administered by Charles Napier who assumed its governorship. After 1847, Sind became a non-regulation province, and the commissioner of Sind enjoyed greater autonomy than any of the other provincial authorities. Although Sindhis complained about the neglect of their province by the Bombay authorities, even such development as took place had important demographic, commercial, and political consequences. This development had four important dimensions—infrastructural investments, incentives for entrepreneurship and experimentation, the introduction of British-style educational institutions that were state-aided and standard throughout the province, and finally, the development of Karachi. Slow and grudging as this development was, the Hindu mercantile class grew in wealth and influence, and immigration into Sind, especially from other parts of the Bombay Presidency, brought in Jews, Christians, Bohras, and Ismailis and other trading communities (Khuhro 1978:

14–19, 52). The resentment felt by the local elite at their loss of socio-economic status and their diminished political influence in the corridors of power, now in Bombay, was directed at both the Hindu Sindhi commercial class and the newcomers.

As this class began to organize with a view to creating educational opportunities for its people, the separation of Sind from Bombay naturally was at the center of its political platform (see Rajagopalan 2000). The All-India Muslim Educational Conference in Karachi in 1907, the Indian National Congress's session in Karachi in 1913, the meeting of the Sind branch of the Central Muhammadan Association in 1917, and the Aligarh session of the All-India Muslim League in 1925 all raised the question of separation with increasing passion. The last of these passed a resolution that stated:

> That, whereas, there is no ground, ethnological, geographical or otherwise, for the inclusion of Sindh with the presidency of Bombay and whereas past experience has shown that such inclusion is in the highest degree determental [*sic*] to the best interest of the people of Sindh and the development of that part of India, the All-India Muslim League is of the opinion that Sindh should be separated from Bombay and constituted into a separate province. (Ahmad 1970: 84, in Khan 1993: 3)

However, receiving contradictory advice on the question from the Nehru report, which favored separation, and the Bombay Provincial Committee, which did not, the Simon Commission report recommended that such separation be delayed pending a review of the financial and administrative implications thereof. Between 1928, when the Simon Commission came to India, and 1935, the movement for a separate Sind gained momentum. By May 1930, even Shahnawaz Bhutto, who had earlier opposed the idea in his capacity as president of the Bombay Provincial Committee, was convinced enough to organize a meeting of *nawabs, sardars, zamindars,* and other traditional elite groups of lower Sind in Hyderabad in support of the idea. The First Round Table Conference (1930) appointed a committee to look into the financial consequences to Sind of separation. The Second Round Table Conference (1931) recommended a conference of Sindhi leaders to see how Sind could make up the financial losses incurred by its separation. This conference was held in Karachi (1932), and it proposed that the central government finance the deficit annually to the tune of 82 lakhs of rupees for fifteen years.[7] In 1932, the Sindh Azad Conference met twice, deciding at its August meeting to observe Separation Day all over Sind on September 16, 1932. In spite of opposition from Hindus, this was a successful call. A joint parliamentary select committee met in 1932 to study the question of separation, and it found in favor. This finding was duly stated in a white paper published in April 1933. The demand for separation was finally conceded in the Government of India Act of 1935.

Division over the separation of Sind seems to have loosely coincided with communal lines (Tahir 1990: 179). Although the early leadership of the movement was made up of Hindus and Muslims, that composition began to change partly because of the Khilafat movement (179–181) and partly because, having formed a majority in the Bombay Presidency, Hindus did not wish to be reduced to a minority in Sind. Conversely, the idea of a separate Sind gained currency among Muslims, and especially the Muslim League leaders, because having one Muslim-majority province would strengthen their case against a united India. The Congress, which was dominated by the privileged in the pre-Gandhian phase, would for the most part have favored the subsumption of Sind. Thus it was that the struggle for Sind found its natural outlet in the Pakistan movement.

Indeed, the impression one is left with, reading accounts of the arguments for the separation of Sind, is that for Sindhi politicians, working with the Muslim League was a means and the Pakistan movement held out to them the promise of autonomy. Khuhro states,

> The important fact to remember is that for most serious and even idealistic politicians All India issues were never of the first importance, they were primarily working for their provincial objectives—of bettering the conditions of the people of the province, some fighting local battles against Hindus, bureaucracy, and some interested in power and its trappings, but all at a provincial level. (1992: 56–57)

Notwithstanding the proliferation of political parties in the province (Khan 1993; Khuhro 1992: 48–49), at the Karachi session of the Muslim League in 1938, Sindhi politicians joined the League, hoping that it would yield for them and their province the desired results. Mobilization around the issue of regional autonomy facilitated mobilization around the idea of Pakistan. All evidence suggests that the vision of Pakistan prevalent at the time was one in which Sind would have enjoyed autonomy. The Pakistan Resolution (1940) stated:

> Resolved that it is the considered view of this session of the All-India Muslim League that no constitutional plan would be workable in this country or acceptable to the Muslims unless it is designed on the following basic principles, viz., that geographically contiguous units are demarcated into regions which should be so constituted, with such territorial re-adjustments as may be necessary, that the areas in which the Muslims are numerically in a majority as in the North-Western and Eastern zones of India, should be grouped to constitute Independent States in which the constituent units shall be autonomous and sovereign.

This passage continues to be interpreted by regionalists all over the country as evidence that Pakistan was visualized as a confederation of sovereign units. Writing about Pakistani constitutional history, Abrar Hasan says that Jinnah would have favored a confederation of autonomous, sovereign units because "he would not have liked in Pakistan what he did not like elsewhere" (1985: 46). Responding to the Cripps Mission proposals, Maulana Hasrat Mohani is said to have felt that "the Muslim League could not but reject the proposals of the British Cabinet, because they could only lead to the establishment of a single Dominion or two or more dominions possibly including a Pakistan Dominion, whereas the object of the Muslims of India was to establish completely independent zonal states whose constituent units should also be autonomous and sovereign" (Hasan 1985: 46).[8] The crux of the argument that Pakistan has been a travesty of the vision in this resolution lies in the use of "Independent States," rather than "Independent State" (Azam 1990: 105–113). Further, the resolution says that these states shall be autonomous and sovereign. Azam rejects the idea that this language constituted the promise of a confederation or any such loose arrangement. He quotes Jinnah as saying, "The theory of Pakistan guarantees that federating units of the national government would have all the provincial autonomy that you will find in the constitutions of the United States of America, Canada, and Australia" (Azam 1990: 108–109). Azam himself concludes that "States" and the other terms, "*units, areas, regions and zones,* implied the federating units and nothing else" (1990: 109).

In an essay that sets out to examine precisely this question of the impact of the Pakistan Resolution on ethnonational groups in Pakistan,

Mohammad Waseem (1990: 514–530) writes that the ambiguity of the resolution raises the basic question of whether its vision is that of one Muslim state or of several Muslim states.[9] In order to resolve this question, Waseem delves into the history of proposals for a distinct Muslim political unit. He quotes Iqbal as saying that in order to retain maximum control at the center, the British "shifted the experience of democracy from the Centre to the Provinces" (Waseem 1990: 516). The movement toward Pakistan began with attempts to use this shift to the advantage of the Muslims with autonomous Muslim-majority provinces within a federation. Several variations on this arrangement were proposed. Sikandar Hayat Khan suggested "a loose federation of blocs of provinces along with a weak centre, whereby the Punjab was expected to dominate the whole Northwestern India" (Waseem 1990: 516). Units within each bloc would be autonomous. The Sind Muslim League took this proposal a step further. "In 1938, it passed a resolution in favour of a separate federation of the four Northwestern Muslim provinces, Muslim Indian states and areas inhabited by a majority of Muslims" (Waseem 1990: 517). This idea, of course, resembles the idea of Pakistan further evolved into other forms. Khaliquzzaman proposed that three or four federations be established in India, which would be coordinated by a central body: a confederation of federations, as it were. Two of these federations would be Muslim. So it was that the call for Pakistan and the call for greater provincial autonomy drew support from the same ranks and were, therefore, opposed by the Congress. This controversy underscores again the close relationship between territory and identity that has been discussed elsewhere in this work.

The second time that Sindhis organized to assert their territorial distinctiveness, they were responding to two very familiar developments—the influx into their province, particularly into Karachi, of outsiders (in this case, Partition refugees from India) and a two-step loss of control over their space with Karachi becoming the federal capital in 1948 and the promulgation of One Unit in 1955. Hyder Baksh Jatoi wrote in 1957 that Karachi had historically been a part of Sind, but with its separation from Sind in 1948, the imposition of One Unit in 1955, and the abolition of Sindhi as a medium of examination in Karachi University in 1957, it seemed as though Sindhi was being eliminated altogether. "When the name 'Sind' goes from the map of Pakistan, logically, Sindhi language should also disappear. That must be the vision and ideal of the powers that be, in our Islamic Republic of Pakistan" (Jatoi 1995: 42–43).

The Establishment of West Pakistan Act in 1955 merged the provinces of West Pakistan into one province, further divided into ten divisions with Lahore as the provincial capital. This merger—called One Unit—formed the basis of the 1956 Pakistan constitution. It served the purpose of bringing parity between the western and eastern wings of Pakistan, neutralizing East Pakistan's demographic advantage. From the point of view of West Pakistan's minorities, however, it meant a further loss of autonomy; the only winner was the central government, which had arrogated to itself powers similar to those the colonial government had enjoyed. The 1962 constitution retained the centralized federal structure with One Unit.

The campaign against One Unit marks the second high point of mobilization around a territorially based Sindhi identity, the first being the movement to separate Sind from Bombay. In Sind, non-Sindhis had benefited most from One Unit. Now that Sindhis were in a minority in the provincial legislature, they could do nothing to prevent the flow of jobs and land away from their community. Sindhis and the non-Sindhi bureaucracy were unable to communicate with each other. In 1957, the Anti–One Unit Resolution was passed in the West Pakistan Assembly (Shah 1983: 10). Under G. M. Syed, a new Sindhi nationalist movement arose, drawing support from young Sindhi intellectuals (Malik 1993). Syed had entered politics during the Khilafat movement and participated in the campaign to separate Sind from Bombay. Although once an ardent supporter of the Pakistan movement, having introduced the Pakistan Resolution in the Sind legislature, Syed parted ways with the League and then was imprisoned for his opposition to President Ayub Khan. In 1953, he founded the Sind Awami Mahaz, a four-party nativist coalition based in Sind. One of its components was the Sind Hari Committee, a communist movement whose leader, Hyder Baksh Jatoi, coined the slogan that came to be associated with the movement: "Jeeye Sind" (Long live Sind). By the late 1960s, Syed's alienation was complete, and he became the advocate of an independent Sindhudesh. Other leaders who had been part of this movement included Mumtaz Ali Bhutto and Rasul Baksh Palejo, who later broke away from the Mahaz in 1967 and founded a Sindhi movement based on Maoist principles.

Why were Sindhi nationalists more amenable in this round to the idea of secession? Although many of the issues were the same, two important differences remained. When the first campaign for separation was gathering force, secession from a colonial state against which an independence movement was growing made little sense. Instead, that bent of Sindhi nationalism joined in the movement for Pakistan. The second difference was that given the promise of the Pakistan Resolution and the evidence of events in East Pakistan, the sense of betrayal by the national state was greater.

In the 1960s, East Pakistan was in turmoil. In March 1967, the Pakistan Democratic Movement was founded by a coalition of four political parties, including Mujibur Rahman's Awami League. They had a six-point agenda (Jahan 1972: 167–168):

1. Establishment of a federation on the basis of the Lahore Resolution.
2. Restriction of the powers of the federal government to defense and foreign affairs.
3. The use of two separate but freely convertible currencies, or a common currency unit in the two wings, with constitutional provisions to prevent the flight of capital from East Pakistan to West Pakistan.
4. Restriction of the power to levy taxes to the units, which would then give the federal government a portion of the taxes they collected.
5. Two separate foreign exchange accounts and the right to enter into trade agreements and arrangements for each wing.
6. The creation of a militia or a paramilitary force for East Pakistan.

Zulfikar Ali Bhutto's Pakistan People's Party (PPP) and the Sindhi nationalist groups opposed the six-point scheme, which would have guaranteed the same autonomy to other provinces as the Bengalis were claiming. The scheme "clearly proved that Sind had already missed the bus so far as securing the requisite confirmation and guarantee for its autonomy was concerned" (Joyo 1985: 17). Indeed, subsequent experience in North-West Frontier Province (NWFP) and Baluchistan showed that in spite of the PPP having a provincial base, upon assumption of power, it had scant regard for provincial governments. The politicians of Sind (and other provinces of West Pakistan) lost out on several counts as a result of this event. First, by not supporting the East Pakistani demands for autonomy, they exposed the inconsistency of their positions. Second, the role of India in the Bangladesh secession made it possible for subsequent regimes (including that of Bhutto) to use that bogey at every hint of dissent and opposition. Third, as Partition tilted the arguments in the Indian Constituent Assembly in favor of a strong center, so did the separation of Bangladesh build the case for the Pakistani state to be more rather than less centralized. Finally, in the aftermath of war, Bhutto's government was enormously popular, causing other Sindhi politicians and their organizations to be sidelined.

Sayid Ghulam Mustafa Shah, the founding editor of *Sind Quarterly,* whose pages were devoted to the cause of Sind, variously defined, points out that the province was brought into the national mainstream for the first time in its history by the election of Bhutto (Shah 1978: 3). Once Bhutto was in power, however, he systematically severed the PPP's ties to its mass support base and brought both party and state under a centralized chain of command that revolved around his personality (Hussain and Hussain 1993: 122). Even so, Shah contends that it was only with the rise of the PPP that Sind began to enjoy the benefits of being represented in the federal capital. He argues that what Sind needed was to be represented by the same party as Punjab and that because other rulers of Pakistan feared the mobilization of Sind, they were especially repressive in that province.

Nevertheless, the Sindhi separatist movement suffered a setback in 1970 when Zulfikar Ali Bhutto's Pakistan People's Party swept past it in the elections. This victory created a long-standing rift between Syed and Bhutto, which led the former to ally himself in the years to come with General Zia ul-Haq. The odd alliance is also explained thus: Syed believed Zia's regime's policies would destroy Pakistan and pave the way for the realization of his dream, and Zia needed an ally who would not join the Movement for the Restoration of Democracy (MRD) in 1983. A number of Sindhi organizations formed a coalition in 1988, the Sindh National Alliance, which again lost the election. "The overwhelming Sindhi support for the PPP both in 1970 and 1988 seems to suggest that Sindhis share a strong commitment to Pakistan" (Malik 1993: 61). In 1972, the Jeeye Sindh Mahaz demanded provincial autonomy (as opposed to secession), adoption of Sindh as a national and official language, one-fourth share in civil and military services, and repatriation of all lost land to Sindhis. Charting a different course from the Jeeye Sindh Mahaz, in the late seventies, Palejo was associated with the Sindh Awami Tehreek, which was later part of the MRD. In 1986, this party was merged into the Awami National Party, founded by Khan Abdul Wali Khan. Mumtaz Ali Bhutto founded the Sindh-Baluch-Pushtun Front.

The 1973 constitution restored a federal structure wherein residual powers rested with the now-restored provincial units. The constitution specified the Federal List and the Concurrent List. Although residuary powers lay with the units, there was no provincial list. The federal government continued to retain the power to topple provincial governments and impose federal rule—a power that it did exercise.

By all reckoning, the end of One Unit should have signaled the transition of Sindhi politics out of the territorial phase, but the continuing predominance of Muhajirs in Karachi and their growing nativism precluded that. Instead, the third struggle of Sindhi territorial politics started at this time.

The restoration of Sindhi's place and patronage in the province's educational system and administration, which followed the restoration of the province, gave the Muhajirs cause to protest. Furthermore, relations between the Muhajirs and other communities in Karachi deteriorated in the face of continued migration into the city. Since Partition, Waseem (1997) identifies one wave of migration in the 1960s by up-country Punjabis and Pathans, a second in the 1970s by rural Sindhis when Karachi reverted to being the capital of Sind, and a third in 1979 by Afghan refugees when the Soviets occupied Afghanistan. Karachi became the exit point for refugees and dissidents from Iran as well as a center for the illicit trade in drugs and arms (Hussain and Hussain 1993: 6). Some of these traders inevitably found local buyers for their goods. Finally, in 1983, supported by many provincial parties, including some leading Sindhi organizations, the Movement for the Restoration of Democracy (MRD) began in Sind. As with most mass uprisings, it acquired a momentum of its own. In rural and small-town Sind, it lasted four months, during which there were violent confrontations between the rioters and the security forces. The old alliance between politicians and criminals now came to be glorified in the name of the movement as it attacked symbols of state power (Hussain and Hussain 1993: 46). This outburst seems to have alerted the Muhajir community to the latent nationalism of the Sindhis. Whereas the Muhajirs and the Sindhis both resented Punjabi domination, the Sindhis also resented Muhajir domination of Karachi.[10]

The Muhajirs, in contrast, had gained nothing from the dissolution of One Unit, as theirs was not an ethnoterritorial identity. As Sind was the province of the Sindhi, and Sindhis began to reclaim some of the jobs and opportunities that they had lost to the Muhajirs, in 1984, Altaf Hussain founded the Muhajir Qaumi Movement (MQM)—a transformation of what had begun as the All Pakistan Muhajir Students Organization on the campus of Karachi University. The MQM followed the Muhajir Suba (Province) or Karachi Suba movements, but its separatism took the form of demands for quotas and for recognition as a distinct ethnic group. It also demanded that Muhajirs be recognized as the fifth nationality in Pakistan. Between 1986 and 1988, there were riots in Karachi, Quetta, and Hyderabad between Muhajirs and Pathans, some of whom were from Afghanistan. These violent altercations affirmed the Muhajirs in their identity, but more crucially, they brought the army into Karachi and gave the federal government an opportunity to interfere in Sind. Since then, Sind has been polarized with rural Sind supporting the PPP and Karachi and Hyderabad supporting the MQM.

Most pertinent to the larger discussion here is the question of how Muhajirs relate their identity to the city that is their territorial base. It is important to know that all the immigrants from India at the moment of Partition in 1947 did not settle in Sind. A very large proportion settled in Punjab. At this time, for obvious reasons, they had no territorial base. The difference was that whereas they assimilated to the local setting in Punjab, they did not in Sind. The Muhajirs in Sind were settled around Karachi, and Karachi's already cosmopolitan population became more mixed when that city became the federal capital and was detached from Sind. This meant that the denizens of Karachi did not need to learn Sindhi or to assimilate. The early rulers of Pakistan were largely from this community, and they were the ones who favored the One Unit arrangement. In this early period, Pakistan itself was the province of the Muhajir, and therefore, there was no need for the community to find itself a territorial home. In the years that followed, inasmuch as Muhajirs played an important role in Pakistan, they dominated affairs in its capital. With the creation of Bangladesh and the restoration of the old provinces in a federal structure, this situation changed. Suddenly, when Sindhis began to reclaim their province after 1971, everyone had a home except the Muhajirs.

Nativism is one kind of territorial vision. It stops short of partition, but two of its core ideas often fuel separatist or secessionist visions. The first idea is that of preventing further immigration into an area; the second, recognizing the claims of a group on the basis of prior arrival. The MQM makes both these demands. So do the Sindhis, whose initial grievances might also have passed for nativism. The third campaign of Sindhi nationalism is neither flourishing nor finished.

Dravidanadu. Unlike the Sindhis in their three campaigns, Tamils in India went straight from nonterritorial politics to secession and just as quickly gave up secession for an activist role in maintaining India's federal nature.

On August 15, 1947, India became independent. E. V. Ramasami declared it a day of mourning, whereas Annadurai welcomed independence. This event highlighted the parting of ways between them, and the Dravidar Kazhagam split in 1949. Annadurai and his followers formed the Dravida Munnetra Kazhagam (DMK), and Ramasami continued to lead the Dravidar Kazhagam.

In the first years after independence, the Congress enjoyed great popularity and electoral success, forming governments in many states, including Madras. This popularity was based on its role in the independence movement as well as the promise of development held out by Nehru's modernizing vision and the five-year plans. In addition, Nehru's political style engaged regional leaders who were able to cultivate independent power bases. However, three things furthered the cause of the Dravida parties. The first was C. Rajagopalachari's educational reforms, which stipulated that students should spend half the day learning the traditional occupation of their parents and which would perpetuate the caste system. Second, there was the perception that in the distribution of central largesse, the south was neglected, or as the Dravida leaders put it: "Vadakku vaazhgiradu, therkku theiygiradu" (The north flourishes, the south languishes). Third, in 1956, the linguistic reorganization of states reduced Madras to its Tamil-speaking areas, and the question of renaming Madras Tamil Nadu became an important one.

In the aftermath of Partition, afraid to make room for any potentially disintegrative features, the Constituent Assembly set up a highly centralized state that was not very different from British India. Nevertheless, the linguistic reorganization of states was the culmination of a process that had begun in 1905–1906 with the partition of Bengal. During the colonial period, the Congress had supported linguistic self-determination, and the agitation for the separation of Andhra Pradesh from Madras was a product of that support. In other cases, such as the demands for Sind and Dravidanadu, ethnolinguistic identity was asserted as a more intense articulation of previous alienation, and linguistic self-determination took the form of secession or separatism.

What were the reasons for the Dravida demand for secession? It is now commonly held that the demand for secession was an outcome of the view that no progress was possible for non-Brahmins in a Brahmin-

and Bania-dominated India. The solution was to leave the union. Asked why the Dravida movement had chosen to secede after centuries of coexistence, Annadurai told the story of two brothers who lived in harmony, devoted to each other (Annadurai 1961: 17–18, translation mine). The younger brother did all the work. He attended to the business affairs of the family, thinking, "Let my elder brother enjoy our wealth. His happiness is mine." The older thought, "My younger brother deals with everything. Where is the need for me to do anything?" However, when they both had grandchildren, the younger brother began to feel sorrow and anger—resentment. He worried that the property would not be divided equally among their grandchildren. So their property was partitioned. After the partition however, their relationship was amicable and loving again. The older brother sent his younger brother the pick of his produce, and the younger would send his brother the choicest of sweets made in his house.

The 1949 split had occurred over two issues—Periyar's stand on Indian independence, and the role of the Dravida Kazhagam (DK). The DK remained a social reform movement and stayed out of politics. The DMK entered mainstream politics, contesting elections for the first time in 1957 and winning a small number of seats in the state assembly. In 1959, the DMK captured the Madras city government, and in 1962, Annadurai was elected to the Rajya Sabha, the upper house of the Indian Parliament. The year 1963 marks a watershed in the history of the Dravida movement. In the course of this year, two issues were to be raised in the Rajya Sabha that the DMK leader eloquently opposed. The first was the question of the Official Languages Bill. The second was the introduction of the Sixteenth Amendment to the constitution, otherwise known as the antisecession amendment.[11]

The following time line (Table 3.1) shows that the two issues came up practically simultaneously and that as the debates over one unfolded and overlapped into the other, the core arguments began to look identical. It seems, in retrospect, that the arguments for secession and separatism could not have been better staged by idealogues at a DMK convention.

The Indian constitution provided for the use of English as an official language for the first fifteen years after the commencement of the constitution. In anticipation of the expiration of that date, there were protests in the non-Hindi areas, particularly in Madras State (Tamil Nadu) against the "imposition" of Hindi. In April 1963, Nehru assured parliamentarians from the south that the switchover from English and

Table 3.1   **Events Surrounding the Passage of the Antisecessionist and Official Languages Bills**

Date	Constitutional (16th) Amendment Bill	Official Languages Bill	Other Events
1-21-63	Introduction of bill in the Lok Sabha		
1-22-63	Debated in Lok Sabha		
1-25-63	Debated in Rajya Sabha		
4-22-63		Nehru's assurance to MPs	
4-27-63		Passed in Lok Sabha	
5-2-63	Passed in Lok Sabha	Debate in Rajya Sabha	
5-3-63			Bhupesh Gupta introduced a bill in the Rajya Sabha to rename Madras as Tamil Nadu; it was defeated.
5-9-63	Passed in Rajya Sabha		
10-5-63	Presidential assent		

Hindi to Hindi would not be made without the consent of non-Hindi speakers. The Official Languages Bill essentially maintained this position. Opposition to the bill seems, from newspaper reports of the time, to have centered around the proposed use of "may" for "shall" in the context of English continuing to be used in addition to Hindi for official purposes in the union and in Parliament. The DMK members of Parliament (MPs) maintained that as "may" could legally be interpreted as "may not," it was not guarantee enough that non-Hindi speakers would be consulted. Nehru's response was that "may" had the meaning of "shall" in this case. If that were true, the DMK wanted to know, what was the problem with using "shall"? ("Assurance on Hindi" 1963).[12] The debate over this issue remains one of the most eloquent exchanges on the question of language policy in India. Annadurai spoke at length, arguing that this policy debate was important precisely because it was the concern of a minority (*The Hindu,* May 3, 1963). He argued that in a federal government, it made no sense to insist on one common language. He pleaded for the indefinite continuation of the status quo and said that English was simply the most convenient language and "distributes advantages and disadvantages even" ("Imposition of Hindi" 1963). The bill did pass, and the DMK, as it had warned, launched an agitation of considerable proportion. Tapping into the fears and pride of the Tamil masses, the DMK was able to draw on previous anti-Hindi campaigns to carry its effort. In response to Kamaraj's questioning of a secessionist party's concern with the union's official language, Annadurai is reported to have said, "I have filed a partition suit; I cannot allow the property to be sold away" ("Anti-Hindi Campaign" 1963).

Take a look at this picture: Annadurai comes to the Rajya Sabha in 1962, the antisecession bill is introduced at the beginning of 1963, and a motion to rename Madras is rejected and the Official Languages Bill passes in spite of the DMK's protests in Parliament and public opinion in the south. It simply does not make sense that this should be the moment when the DMK gives up its demand for secession. This is the central puzzle of this section.

In order to solve it, we have to step back to 1962. In October 1962, the border dispute between India and China erupted into hostilities, leading to an upsurge of patriotism. The DMK response is best illustrated in two actions. In October 1962, it suspended its demand for Dravida Nadu pending the duration of the war. Further, the party mobilized its cadres to collect a large sum of money to aid the war effort.

Editorials and articles in the DMK's periodicals show an interesting change at this time. From the weekly expositions on the neglect of the south and the need for a separate state, the focus of the articles was now on the need for sacrifice for the nation. Issues of *Dravida Nadu* in the period between October 1962 and March 1963 are a useful example. Whereas the earlier first-page poems in this paper were secessionist in theme and tone, they were now replaced by poems of a different tone.[13] The poems and editorials of this period exhorted the supporters of the party to give of themselves and their possessions generously and to help the national government repulse the Chinese aggressor.[14] The style of the editorials changed as the war wore on, from essays to headline lists to staccato exhortations, mostly ending, *"Vetri Namadhe!"* (Victory is ours!). Variations of this mood in the writing continued well into the new year.

The justification for backing off from secessionist demands was that without the nation, there could be no secession. Annadurai called the secessionist agitation off, exhorting the party cadres to support the war effort.[15]

Anna was in Vellore Jail at this time when the war came. When the war came, what Anna said was that we will give up Dravida Nadu secession. It is important to save the state. There is a threat to our sovereignty (*muzhu-sottantirattukku*) and we must act as one. He gives an example for this: only if there is a house can you change the roof-tiles; likewise, only if there is a state (*naadu*) can we ask what we want of it. So we must save the state. Immediately the government released him. (I74)

In the Rajya Sabha, Annadurai reiterated that the DMK would suspend all agitational activity: "I enter the name of the DMK in the roll call of honour that is being now formulated for the safety, for the dignity and future of this country, this nation" (Annadurai 1975b: 139).

Around this time, the National Integration Council was set up, and in accordance with one of its recommendations the antisecession amendment was introduced in Parliament. Although the DMK had suspended secessionist activity because of the war, Annadurai spoke forcefully in the Rajya Sabha against this amendment. His opposition was on two grounds: First, he asserted the right to self-determination and called on the Congress's own support of the principle, and second, he asked the government to try to understand the grievances that led to the demand for a separate state.

In interviews conducted in summer 1996, most politically active respondents said in no uncertain terms that the demand for Dravida Nadu was always symbolic. Marguerite Ross Barnett mentions a meeting in 1960, attended by Muthuvel Karunanidhi, V. R. Nedunchezhian, E.V.K. Sampath, V. P. Raman, and K. Mathiazhagan, at which it was decided that the Dravida Nadu demand should be abandoned (Barnett 1976: 109–110). When Annadurai heard of this, he is said to have "pointed out that since the party cadres had been developed on the separation demand, the party could not simply drop this demand and maintain credibility in the eyes of the lower-echelon leadership." But in principle it was agreed that ultimately the demand would be dropped. This agreement seems to lend credence to the assertion by non-DMK respondents that the demand was never a serious one.

In November 1963, the DMK constitution was amended and the demand for Dravida Nadu was replaced by a proposal to set up a Dravida union within the framework of the Indian constitution and with the maximum possible autonomy. The DMK has been faithful to this principle over the decades. It has actively participated in many regional opposition and non-Congress groupings and is always in the forefront for the demand for greater rights, powers, and resources for the states—even though it has not spoken of a Dravida union for several years.

Sri Lankan Tamils. Communal differences in Sri Lanka were exacerbated in the postindependence period by changes in citizenship laws and language policy, resettlement programs in the hitherto Tamil-dominated dry regions, and changes in educational standards whereby not merely the political efficacy and access but also the simple economic survival of the Tamils was diminished and threatened. Efforts to heal the growing breach, such as the Bandaranaike-Chelvanayakam Pact in 1957 and the Senanayake-Chelvanayakam Pact in 1965, played with territorial restructuring (as a precursor of political devolution) as a solution to the problem. The first experimented with regions as the unit of devolution, creating a single administrative unit in the north and two or more in the east. The region's jurisdiction would extend to infrastructure, development, social services, and "colonization," as the resettlement programs have come to be known, and Tamil was to be the language of administration in these regions. But what constituted a region and a region's relation to the provinces were not clear. The Senanayake-Chelvanayakam Pact downgraded the unit of devolution to the district, which compromised the opponents of devolution as well as the proponents of federalism. For the latter, in addition to a smaller resource base and less decisionmaking autonomy from the center, the division of regions or provinces demarcated by the ethnic identity of their populations into districts was tantamount to a strategy of divide and rule. For the former, devolution was tantamount to federalism, which was in turn equated with secession. In these circumstances, it was to be expected that territorial claims would finally enter the political agenda of the Tamils.

By the early 1970s, several factors combined to abet the growth of militancy among young Sri Lankans from both major ethnic groups. These included the policy of modifying university entrance standards in order to redress what was seen as the disproportionate academic advantages of students from some districts, including Jaffna, Colombo, and Kandy; the liberalization of the Sri Lankan economy; and finally, the consequences of two decades of mutually segregated education in Sinhala and Tamil. Moreover, the 1972 and 1978 constitutions in Sri Lanka reflected the degree to which Sri Lanka's social and political climate had changed. These two constitutions transformed the secular and liberal Ceylon of the 1948 Soulbury Constitution into a Sri Lanka where Buddhism has the foremost place and Tamil's place as the second official language has been hard won. The first outbreak of violence was the 1971 Janata Vimukti Peramuna insurrection in the south.

In 1974, the Federal Party and sections of the Tamil Congress and the Ceylon Workers Congress combined to form the Tamil United Front. With the adoption of the Vaddukodai Resolution in 1976, it renamed itself the Tamil United Liberation Front (TULF). It was thereby resolved that

> by virtue of their great language, their religion, their separate culture and heritage, their history of independent existence as a separate state over a distinct territory for several centuries till they were conquered by the armed might of the European invaders, and above all by their will to exist as a separate entity ruling themselves in their own territory, [the Tamils] are a nation distinct and apart from the Sinhalese.
>
> Whereas throughout the centuries from the dawn of history, the Sinhalese and Tamil nations have divided between them the possession of Ceylon, the Sinhalese inhabiting the interior parts of the country in its southern and western parts from the river Walawe to that of Chilaw and the Tamils possessing the northern and eastern districts . . . Tamil Eelam shall consist of the Northern and Eastern Provinces.

In a world of sovereign nation-states, the demand for secession from an existing state marks a degree of alienation that is hard to remedy. The youth wing of the TULF had reorganized as the Liberation Tigers of Tamil Eelam (LTTE). Walking a fine line between banditry and political militancy, the Tigers targeted centers of economic and political importance in the Jaffna area. Hostility between the communities grew. The activities of the Sri Lankan army in the north alienated the local people and won the Tigers their support. Communal riots in 1977 worsened the situation so that the 1978 constitution's efforts to provide minority rights were unacceptable to the TULF, and expatriate Tamils began to fund the Tamil militants, who could therefore get better arms and training. In 1983, LTTE ambushed an army convoy, an action that led to the worst anti-Tamil riots in Sri Lankan history. The riots polarized Sri Lankan society in an unprecedented way. In 1993, a retrospective on the riots concluded: "Though there were numerous acts of heroism by individual Sinhalese, there is no doubt that the main Tamil narrative of the events of July 1983 was based on the belief that the government and the Sinhalese tolerated July 1983 so as to 'teach Tamils a lesson'" (Coomaraswamy 1993: 25–26). Worse still, what Coomaraswamy called "the failure of moral outrage" suggested that the Sinhalese and the government considered the riots legitimate.

Between the mid-1960s and the mid-1980s, there was a certain amount of administrative decentralization in Sri Lanka, related mostly to development objectives. There was no corresponding devolution of power. After the 1983 riots, the influence of the Tamil militant groups increased and the TULF's demands escalated. The rhetoric of a "traditional Tamil homeland" in the north and the east took root. Concretely, the TULF at this point demanded provincial councils that would be linked now by regional councils. In such a scheme, the Northern and Eastern provinces would be linked to form a unit where the Tamils would be the dominant majority. As the demands escalated, so did intransigence on either side, and the All-Party Congress that met between 1983 and 1986 could not resolve the question.

The provincial councils scheme was revived in a modified form in 1986, this time modeled on the Indian quasi-federal system but within the framework of a unitary state. According to K. M. de Silva, the Indians suggested that the Eastern Province might be divided into three parts, the Tamil parts linked by a corridor. They further suggested "the excision of the Sinhalese parliamentary electorate (Amparai) of the Batticaloa district of the Eastern province so that the Tamil component of the latter would reach a level of parity with other ethnic groups there" (de Silva 1993d: 118).

The Indo–Sri Lankan Accord of July 1987 stipulated that the Sri Lankan government would reinstate the provincial councils. The Northern and the Eastern provinces were to be merged subject to a referendum held in the Eastern Province within a year. The Provincial Councils Bill and the Thirteenth Amendment to the constitution were passed in 1987, and in spite of the inevitable protests, the North-Eastern Province was created in 1988. The Provincial Councils (Pradeshiya Sabhas) Act detailed the procedure to be followed in the councils, the Provincial Public Service, sources of finance for the councils, and interim provisions for uniting more than one province into an administrative unit. The Thirteenth Amendment specified the place of the province in the power structure of the state.

The Indo–Sri Lankan Accord did not solve matters. If anything, it complicated them. The Indian Peace-Keeping Force, which was stationed in Sri Lanka to supervise the disarmament of the militant groups, ended up fighting the LTTE, which reneged on its initial signature to the accord. In the years that followed, strange political alliances were made that isolated the Indians altogether; they pulled out in 1989.

In August 1994, the People's Alliance coalition, led by Chandrika Bandaranaike Kumaratunga, won the elections on a platform of peace. The LTTE ignored the new government's invitation to talks. In August 1995, the government tabled a set of devolution proposals for debate, following them up in a few months with a watered-down version. A military campaign that was launched in November 1995 provided the backdrop to the devolution debate. If repeated military campaigns in the north have eroded confidence in the government's sincerity, incidents like the bombing of the Central Bank in Colombo in 1996, the Temple of the Tooth in Kandy in 1998, and the spate of bombings and assassinations in 1999 that have targeted Sinhalese and Tamil politicians leave no doubt as to the LTTE's intention to fight to the last Tiger. When the fieldwork for this project was conducted in 1996, one person characterized the devolution debate as a "dialogue of the deaf." Attempts to work out a political solution have focused on creating a consensus among the mainstream parties, which seek to balance the exigencies of electoral politics in a majoritarian democracy with the appealing mantle of the peacemaker. The LTTE at one end and the influential Buddhist clergy at the other hold this fragile consensus hostage. The fate of the new constitutional proposals presented to Parliament in August 2000 (discussed in Chapter 2) hangs in the balance.

Of all the contentious issues surrounding devolution, the unit of devolution is the most contentious on three counts. The first is the question of *what* shall constitute the unit of devolution. As we have seen, in the decades after independence, region, province, and district, merged and separate, have been discussed as the appropriate unit of devolution. "The concept of a region lacked clarity because it was at once larger than a province, and smaller than a province" (de Silva 1993d: 105). Although the idea of devolution to provinces was first espoused by S.W.R.D. Bandaranaike, when the Tamils took it up, it seemed excessive to the Sinhalese leadership. Devolution to districts was never likely to be real devolution of power, because their limited resource base would ensure their dependence on the center, which would then be able to play segments of an ethnic population off against each other. Furthermore, in a climate where Tamils were asking for a separate state, districts were clearly not an adequate response. This issue was forced by the Indo–Sri Lankan Accord, which selected provinces as the unit of devolution.

The second count on which the unit of devolution is contentious is whether creation of a new unit or level of government meant changing the basic nature of the Sri Lankan unitary state. The strongest opposition to devolution stems from this source. Although the origin of this unitary state can be traced to colonial times, the idea of the entire island being ruled from one center is arguably part and parcel of the Sinhalese nationalist mythology. This begs the question, To whom does this state belong? Faced with an option between federalism and partition of the island, one can make the case that the former is preferable. Among those who speak for the rights and claims of the majority in Sri Lanka, federalism is the same as secession—either because it undermines the single central sovereign or because it may permit the creation of local fiefdoms.

The most contentious dimension of this issue is the basis of unit demarcation. The Tamil demand for devolution assumes that the unit of devolution will be coterminous with the traditional homeland that Tamils claim. There are two problems with this assumption. To start with, the historical bases of their claim are specious. Moreover, the category of *Tamil* in this claim is also contested. Although Tamils treat the Tamil-speaking Muslims as a part of the Sri Lankan Tamil community, the Muslims do not accept this inclusion. It is also cited by the more conservative among the Sinhalese as a reason to oppose devolution to the degree demanded by the Tamils.

At the time of writing, the Sri Lankan Tamils seem to be stuck in this phase, and the prospects for conflict resolution appear dim. The 2000 constitution proposes to deal with the unit-of-devolution issue by providing for a referendum ten years after its promulgation that will determine whether the northern and eastern regions will be merged. As positions seem to have hardened on either side to the point of irremediable intransigence, what appears like excess to one side is too little, too late to the other. One can hardly speculate as to how and when this group will enter the postterritorial phase of its political evolution.

Conclusions. Although it is tempting to portray the range of possible territorial demands as though there were a natural sequence of escalation, the three cases studied here suggest that in fact, this is not so. In the Sind case, the essential demand is separation, and when the question of independence is raised, it does not appear to be an escalation as much as a response to particular circumstances within the state. Deescalation from secession is not linear either in the Sind case, as the struggle in the third campaign is a struggle against another group's territorial claims. In the Indian case, the movement is from nonterritorial to secessionist and then to power-sharing demands. There is no gradual mounting of territorial demands. Finally, the Sri Lankan case illustrates to perfection how the absence of synchronism can exacerbate the most predictable patterns of escalation.

Therefore, it is probably more valid to ask what triggers territorialization and then escalation than to assume a natural upward spiral. In the Sind case, in the first two campaigns, territorial mobilization was a response to state action. In the last, however, it is a response to nativist demands made by migrants, which are in turn partly a response to Sindhis reclaiming control of their province. In the Indian Tamilian case, territorialization is as much a response to the actions of rivals in power (the Congress in 1936–1938) and in the political arena (the Congress Party as well as those whose quest for linguistic self-determination broke up the Madras state). In the 1960s, however, both the continuing resistance to Hindi (a nonterritorial issue) and the abandonment of demands for secession (a territorial issue) were responses in large part to state action. In Sri Lanka, state actions and policies are patently the trigger at every stage—either by omission or commission—so much so that this story is narrated dialectically by Sri Lankans from every corner of the debate. The state, therefore, although not the only actor on the scene, appears to play an important part in this process.

The Postterritorial Phase

Groups enter the postterritorial phase of their history when their territorial demands cease to be central to their political agenda. Other issues of representation and power may remain, but none of them are territorial. The territorial claims have been either met or dropped or have simply become irrelevant. Of the three groups studied here, only the Indian Tamils are truly in this phase. Although secession does not appear to be part of the Sindhi agenda any more, outstanding grievances against the Muhajirs and unresolved conflicts over and in Karachi block the Sindhis' exit from the territorial phase. Equally deadlocked is the Sri Lankan situation. The last to make territorial claims, Sri Lankan Tamil militants appear to be poised to fight to the last. This section draws essentially on the Indian experience. The lessons that this case holds for the others will provide a segue to consideration of the state's intervention in this arena.

Sind. The continuing violence in Karachi over the past decade has led to an army presence in the city. Support for the army and for the Islamabad government are as contentious as any other issue. Constantly shifting alliances define the fluidity of the situation. The years of round-robin governments since Zia's death in 1988 have only complicated matters. The Sindh National Alliance, which comprises a large and varied set of parties and movements, and the MQM are the local players. The PPP bridges the local and federal, providing, too, a common target or a rationale for other alliances. The Muslim League is yet another national player with whom the MQM at least might and does ally. In the face of Muhajir mobilization, Sindhi nationalists are neither able to move beyond this phase of their own political history nor able to bring it to fruition.

The politics and performance of the Sindhi nationalist movement have in common with the militant Tamil movements of Sri Lanka that neither is accompanied or preceded by a movement to reform the community itself. As a result, the Sindhis have been unable to use their grievances to any concrete purpose. Petulantly, they have protested their fate, and shortsightedly, they have worked with the state when they might have gained the most from opposing it. The result is that they are faced today with two wars, both old, both acrimonious. The first is with the Punjabi-dominated state and the second is with "outsiders" in Sind. It is almost as if, faced with the futility of the larger struggle against the state and its forces, the Sindhis have settled for nativist squabbles, ranging themselves on one side or another. If Sind's opportunities have been squandered by leaders who chose to play politics, its hopes must lie there too—that the exigencies of politics will one day bring about a redefinition of who is an insider and who is not, permitting a reconsideration of the larger, more fundamental issues of democracy and power sharing in Pakistan.

Sri Lankan Tamils. Intensifying violence, intransigence, and alienation appear to trap Sri Lanka in the territorial phase. Moving asynchronously, the Tigers, the Sri Lankan government, the opposition, and different sections of the public are conciliatory or belligerent, willing to negotiate or not at varying times. It is hard to imagine any change in the present situation.

Tamils in India. The DMK swept to power in 1967 in the fourth general elections, winning 138 out of 234 seats, and followed through on its earlier agenda in two notable ways. First, it renamed Madras state as Tamil Nadu in 1968. This demand had been raised at the time of States Reorganization. K. Rajayyan reports, and his book is the only source to do so, that in 1957, K. Kamaraj agreed to adopt the name Tamil Nadu, but he also retained the name Madras (Rajayyan 1982: 398). The DMK, however, wanted the state to be called only Tamil Nadu, a proposal that, as we saw earlier, was outvoted in 1963.

In 1969, the DMK set up the Rajamannar Committee to examine the questions of state autonomy and center-state relations and to make recommendations toward a more equitable balance. In the meanwhile, the central government had appointed the Administrative Reforms Commission (1966). The three-member Rajamannar Committee submitted a report in 1971 in which it endorsed the position of the DMK that the constitution should be amended so as to secure the states' maximum autonomy. It was not, however, an empty partisan enterprise. Indeed, the committee anticipated the efforts of the Sarkaria Commission by over a decade and conducted a thorough investigation. The committee's chief recommendations included:

1. An Inter-State Council comprising chief ministers of all the states, with the prime minister as the chair, which would cover areas of Union jurisdiction that affect the states. This council would be consulted before the passage of all relevant bills and its decisions would be binding.
2. The replacement of the Planning Commission by a statutory body of technocrats who would advise a state planning apparatus.
3. A permanent Finance Commission to ensure a greater share of the tax revenue for the states.
4. The transfer of several subjects on the Union and Concurrent Lists to the State List.
5. Reform in the appointment procedures and role of the governor.
6. The high courts should be the highest court of appeal for all matters falling within the jurisdiction of the state.

Following the tabling of this resolution, the Tamil Nadu Assembly passed a resolution on state autonomy exhorting the central government to accept the committee's recommendations. Prime Minister Gandhi's reply was to point out that the Administrative Reforms

Commission had covered much of the same ground (*Sarkaria Commission Report* 1988: 715). When the Commission on Centre-State Relations (which came to be known as the Sarkaria Commission) was set up by the central government in 1983, the Tamil Nadu state government and a host of regional parties from the state, mostly offshoots of the Dravida movement, wrote in to reinforce the federalist bent that has become part and parcel of Tamil responses to the idea of India.

The Gandhi era was one of increasing central interference in state affairs. In Congress states, the intervention was through the decisions of the party High Command, in Delhi; in non-Congress states, one of the most popular intervention mechanisms was Article 356, or the "president's rule," which was also used in dubious circumstances in the case of Tamil Nadu in 1976 and 1992 (Ahmed 1994).[16] The office of the governor was used as a lever to meddle in the day-to-day affairs of the state government. Accordingly, the Dravida parties in general, and the DMK in particular, were forced (and able) to position themselves as the vanguard in the struggle for state autonomy. Resistance during the Emergency, support for non-Congress political efforts (including participation in the United Front central government in 1996), promotion of consultation and cooperation between regional parties (particularly in the south), and active participation in investigations such as the Sarkaria Commission are the forms this leadership has taken.

The Janata Party interregnum, 1977–1979, showed the same fine disregard for center-state relations as the Congress Party had. Congress-led state governments were dismissed as soon as the Janata Party settled into office. At the end of this period, when the Congress was returned to power with an absolute majority, non-Congress governments were dismissed. This time, however, Indira Gandhi's government was operating in a different environment. The Assam agitation and the Punjab crisis were not dealt with through constitutional amendments, unlike the relatively quiet, constitutional Dravida struggle. Both of them, but especially Punjab, are believed widely to be the creation of Gandhi's politics in those areas. But the old ways continued in the south. In 1982, Indira Gandhi dismissed the very popular elected Telugu Desam government in Andhra Pradesh. That action renewed southern interest in working together for relative autonomy. The chief ministers of the four southern states and Pondicherry met in Bangalore in March 1983 to discuss center-state, primarily financial, issues. In order to preempt anything that they might initiate, the central government set up the Sarkaria Commission to inquire into center-state relations. Later, other non-

Congress chief ministers joined in these meetings, including Farooq Abdullah, the chief minister of Jammu and Kashmir.

The Sarkaria Commission conducted its inquiry over a four-year period. The longest depositions to the commission came from Tamil Nadu and Punjab. Although the commission found in favor of a strong center, it advocated "cooperative federalism." The one idea that it adopted from the Rajamannar Committee was that of the Inter-State Council. On the contentious questions of president's rule and the role of the governor, the commission advocated the adoption of conventions of fuller and open communication that would prevent the misuse of these provisions.

In the 1980s, the Dravida parties underwent another split with actor-politician M. G. Ramachandran forming the breakaway All-Indian Anna Dravida Munnetra Kazhagam (AIADMK). The AIADMK and DMK have alternately been in power at the state level with the Congress now reduced to the status of a balancer. In 1996, the Tamil Nadu State Congress partly split over the issue of which Dravida party to support, and the stronger faction formed the Tamil Maanila Congress (Tamil Regional Congress), whose name itself indicates a shift away from the Congress's hallmark of an all-India image. In an interesting twist, which excited the imaginations of people interviewed in Madras, the DMK became a partner in the 1996–1998 United Front government; its members held three portfolios, including the important industries portfolio. The DMK had come full circle from the days when it had built its support base, declaring, "Vadakku vazhgirardu, therkku theiygiradu" (The north flourishes, the south languishes). The Dravida parties are now acquiring the importance that kingmakers enjoy in any situation where the choice of the king is less than obvious. The Bharatiya Janata Party–led coalition that replaced them in 1998 was dependent on the support of the Anna DMK for its survival and was brought down by its withdrawal of support. The 1999 decision by the DMK to support the coalition must be read as the ultimate turnabout for a party whose members and supporters in 1996 had said categorically to this researcher that for a rationalist movement like the DMK, secularism was a nonnegotiable tenet.

Tamil Nadu politics in the 1980s was marked by the Eelam factor. All evidence indicates that at the outset, the Indian and Tamil Nadu governments went out of their way to train, aid, and shelter Sri Lankan Tamil militants. Since the 1983 Colombo riots, the flood of refugees into Tamil Nadu has been constant with erratic ebb and rise. In 1990, the militant and refugee presence in Tamil Nadu caused expense, for sure, but the reversal of popular support for the Tigers resulted from inflation caused by the inflow of cash through the militants, the deteriorating law and order situation, and the assassination of Rajiv Gandhi. The Dravida parties, which had found common cause with their Sri Lankan Tamil brethren, have been forced in the main to backtrack on that support. There are still marginal groups, such as the Marumalarchi DMK, that support the militant drive to Eelam, but at this point, they do not enjoy much support. The question as to whether the Tamil Nadu public has any interest in seceding to form a Tamil union with the Eelam Tamils—a possibility that worries many Sri Lankans—yielded the following typical response:

> The reasons for the Eelam Tamils to have their own country don't apply to the Tamils of India . . . because the Tamils of India don't need a separate country. Because the kind of oppression of Tamils here or whatever sufferings the Tamils have had to undergo under their Hindi heartland bosses are not similar to the sufferings of the Eelam Tamils under the Sinhalese flag. . . . It is not a difference of degree. (145)

In the 1990s, as coalitions in the Indian political system shifted and changed at many levels, there was equal uncertainty and excitement about the future. In 1996, the DMK returned to power after a space of seven years. Madras, the capital of Tamil Nadu, was renamed Chennai, an act reminiscent of an older zeal to promote Tamil and Tamilness. From the Chennai standpoint, the participation of the Dravida parties in the central government is the harbinger of a million possibilities for restructuring the political system. The changes that are sweeping the Indian polity in terms of the class and caste composition of the power elite were presaged in Tamil Nadu. The "Tamil Naduization" of Indian politics would suggest that the integration of Tamil Nadu into the Indian national mainstream is complete—that is, until further notice.

Understanding the postterritorial phase. Although only one of our three cases really offers evidence regarding this phase, several ideas emerge for our consideration.

What happened to the demands that were being made? The only territorial changes that have occurred since the end of the secessionist agitation are the renaming of the state and cities within Tamil Nadu/Madras.

However, notwithstanding the resistance of the center in the 1950s to renaming, it has become a commonplace political device, and the political map of India at the beginning of the 2000s shows entirely different place names than it did even forty years ago. It appears that the DMK's territorial demands have become so irrelevant as to mark the margins of the Dravida movement today. The repeated dismissal of the question as settled and uninteresting during interviews in 1996, as well as the tendency of breakaway groups to seize the headlines by announcing their intention to secede, illustrates this irrelevance. Instead, the DMK and the AIADMK are far more interested in maximizing their (and Tamil Nadu's) share of the political and economic spoils.

This change of strategy reflects their entry into the mainstream of Indian politics. They are not rebels, mavericks, or insurgents anymore. After more than thirty years in power, the Dravida leadership furnishes some of the more experienced administrators and elder statesmen in an Indian political playing field that appears to admit more players by the day. The issues that they cut their political teeth on—reservations, language policy, state autonomy, and even secession—are articulated today in more violent forms and face far more inept state responses than the DMK did. Consolidation of their hold over Tamil Nadu and their growing influence in New Delhi increase their stakes in integration and make secession less attractive.

This is not to say that there are no outstanding issues in the postterritorial phase. The DMK and its brethren still seek to redress the existing distribution of authority and resources within the Indian state in their favor. States' rights and autonomy and a greater share of the resources of the Indian state are what they seek (see Bukowski and Rajagopalan 2000). To this end, they have been in the forefront, organizing opposition and regional conclaves and caucuses. Also, the Dravida parties have staunchly opposed the tendency of successive central governments to abuse the emergency provisions of the Indian constitution to destabilize state governments. In other words, restricting the central government's ability to intervene and interfere in the affairs of the states is a key issue of this phase. Finally, in order to ensure both outcomes, they seek an enhanced role at the center—as kingmakers or as part of the government.

Concluding Notes on Unit Demarcation

What can we say about state intervention in unit demarcation? First, it appears that in all three phases, the state is central but hardly the sole actor. Groups respond also to the actions of political rivals and to the demands of other groups or are spurred on by demands or events in other parts of the country and abroad. Nevertheless, insofar as decisions about territorial organization are the state's to arbitrate and enforce, the state becomes implicated in the politics of territorial claims even when they arise in response to nonstate factors.

That qualifier aside, in all three cases, state actions have precipitated territorialization (and further escalation) most of the time. The colonial state and the merger of Sind, the Pakistani state and One Unit, the Sindhi provincial government and its pro-Sindhi policies, language policy in the Indian and Sri Lankan cases, and the reorganization of states in the Indian case are all instances of state intervention that prompt or escalate territorial demands.

Failure of the state to intervene or respond does not help either. Perceived and real neglect by the state in all three cases, including the failure of the state to comprehend and address nativist concerns about migrants and settlers in the Sindhi and Sri Lankan Tamil cases, the failure of the Indian state to reassure the Indian Tamils on the language issue or to correctly understand what Annadurai kept calling the "reasons for secession," and the abject failure of successive Sri Lankan governments to address real Tamil concerns, also ratcheted the stakes in the negotiation between the state and the group to the point where territorial claims were inevitable or nonnegotiable. Thus the state errs both by intervening and by not responding. The task of a study such as this one must be to trace the middle ground between these two contradictory findings and suggest some yardstick for our understanding and for policymakers.

What is abundantly clear, even as we hold the state largely culpable in this matter, is that in the Indian case, three state-related factors are also responsible for the transition to the postterritorial phase. First, a threat to the state posed by the war with China forged a working unity within the regional and central leadership. Second, Nehru's early reassurances, even if not entirely successful, at least showed that the center was listening to what was arguably the main grievance of the DMK at that point. Finally, the introduction of a constitutional amendment that placed restrictions on the advocacy of secession was inordinately effective. Assessing its prospects for continued political activity as dim in that climate, the DMK accordingly amended its own constitution. The fact that the DMK's struggle was not armed and that the state also did not resort to arms made this solution feasible. In other words, if action and inaction by the state can exacerbate matters, responsiveness and restraint on the part of the state facilitate resolution—in this case, movement toward negotiation of nonterritorial issues with the group.

State Intervention and
Integrative Strategies: Conclusion

In the first section of this chapter, integrative strategies were defined as any measures consciously undertaken to create institutions, channels of communication, incentives, or ideology. The two arenas of state intervention that were then discussed—political socialization and unit demarcation—both have integrative potential. Political socialization most obviously is a means of communicating and teaching ideology. It also creates common terms of reference for people within a polity and thus facilitates communication among different sections of the population on the one hand and between them and the state on the other. Unit demarcation is potentially integrative in three ways. First, any existing territorial arrangement and the political equations therein embedded are among the most basic institutional features of any polity. Second, any such arrangement is necessarily a system of incentives and disincentives by virtue of embodying a particular distribution of power and authority. Finally, as I have argued in both preceding chapters, territorial structure is state identity writ across the physical landscape of the state.

Thus by choosing to intervene in these two arenas, the state may be presumed to have chosen to intervene in the integrative process. Indeed, in both cases, the rhetoric and rationale of national integration have colored the decisionmaking process. School pledges, textbook chapters on the integrity of the nation and the oneness of its people, refusals or concessions regarding changes in units for national security reasons or to guard against "fissiparous tendencies" are all instances of such intervention.

That said, what conclusions may be drawn about the question of state intervention in national integration? To answer this question, let us first recapitulate the findings of the two preceding sections.

In the section on political socialization, it was held that a state role in the educational system is inevitable. Examining the experience and track record of India, Pakistan, and Sri Lanka in socializing their citizens through history education, it was found that the poor quality of the books and their dubious pedagogical impact made it hard to assess their utility in the context of national integration. Clumsy attempts to convey the nature and identity of the polity were common to textbooks in all three countries, however, making the intent of the government-run educational establishment clear. In the circumstances, we are left asking, If state intervention is inevitable and if it is bound to be ideological, what elements would maximize the integrative potential of the curriculum?

Based on critical studies of existing textbooks and curricula, we might suggest the following:

1. The curriculum should begin with what is recent and familiar to students and then address more remote issues.
2. When history is taught as part of a social studies curriculum, it should take cognizance of important current events.
3. Rather than presenting one simplified history, the curriculum should integrate local and national histories.
4. Where there is unwillingness to give up the single narrative model, perhaps historiographical approaches that minimize identity differences would serve the ends of integration better.
5. Ideally, the fallibility of any single version of history should be conveyed through the teaching of the curriculum. That is, students should be taught that because people remember events in different ways, multiple recollections and perspectives are acceptable.

Chapter 4 of this book suggests principles that might accentuate the integrative aspects of state intervention in general. Several of these bear a resemblance to the previously listed suggestions.

On the question of unit demarcation, we see more clearly that the state is damned if it does and damned if it doesn't. The list of reasons groups suddenly demand territorial restitution or more extreme changes includes state action as well as state inaction. Furthermore, the state seems to have the capacity not just to escalate but also to deescalate conflict. This dilemma, again, makes our task complicated. It is important to identify the parameters of state action—how much is too much, how little is too little, and other combinations in between. This question of degree is addressed in Chapter 4.

Notes

1. Some scholarly works that have contributed to the study of political socialization include Almond and Coleman 1960, Greenstein 1968, Pye and Verba 1965, and Sigel 1970.

2. The classic definition of Ernest Renan comes to mind: "A nation is a soul, a spiritual principle. Only two things, actually, constitute this soul, this spiritual principle. . . . One is the possession in common of a rich legacy of remembrances. . . . The nation, even as the individual, is the end product of a long period of work, sacrifice and devotion. The worship of ancestors is understandably justifiable, since our ancestors have made us what we are. A heroic past, of great men, of glory (I mean the genuine kind), that is the social principle on which the national idea rests. To have common glories in the past, a common will in the present; to have accomplished great things together, to wish to do so again, that is the essential condition for being a nation" (Renan 1882, in Hutchison and Smith 1994: 17).

3. The name Duttugamenu is spelled differently by various authors.

4. Recently, central and state governments that are dominated by the Bharatiya Janata Party have attempted to review and revise history curricula. It is in fact the materialist-nationalist tug-of-war over historiography and history textbooks that has been controversial in India, whereas in Sri Lanka, the issue of ethnic images and historiography is critical; central-regional concerns are raised in the Pakistan section. Thus Indian history textbooks are less offensive when we consider them from the particular perspective of this study but would likely fail to meet other political standards (Rudolph and Rudolph 1982).

5. Although once marginal segments such as the Pattali Makkal Katchi and the Marumalarchi DMK are gaining strength on the ground and in the legislatures, they have not yet overtaken the old guard. However, Suryanarayan (2000) points out that there is a renewal of support in Tamil Nadu for the Sri Lankan Tamil militants, and these are the parties that are most vehement in propagating the cause of Eelam.

6. The debate over the party's new name was also a debate over how central the territorial vision was to its political mission: "One of the earliest debates was whether it should be called Dravida Kazhagam or Dravidar Kazhagam. The moment it is Dravidar Kazhagam . . . Dravida is the region. You make it region specific. Dravidar means people. Periyar feels we can't be geography specific. We can't reduce ourselves to a nation-state imagination which has been determined by a territory. Not a territorial imagination, it's a people-centric imagination. So he shifts to Dravidar Kazhagam and he defines Dravidar as people who do not respect *Sanatana Dharma*. People who have the ability to overcome the divisions imposed by the *Sanatana Dharma* imagination which divides people as Brahmin and Sudra, are all Dravidas. And therefore it becomes Dravidar Kazhagam" (I1). (*Sanatana dharma* is one of the words Hindus use to describe their religious beliefs and practices. *Sanatana* means "old" or "traditional," and in this context, a *sanatana dharma* follower would be a person who accepted the existence and continuance of caste.)

7. Much of this passage is drawn from Tahir (1990: 175–203).

8. It is not clear in the text whether the Maulana said or wrote this in so many words or whether this was the opinion he was known to have.

9. See particularly Waseem (1990: 515–520) for this section.

10. "We would like to close by quoting A. K. Brohi in his deposition before the Military Tribunal set up to try Shaikh Mujibur Rehman for treason. Addressing the Military Tribunal he said, 'Gentleman it appears during the last nearly quarter of a century or so in Pakistan we have been so thoroughly obscessed [*sic*] with the talk and the ideas of treason and loyalty. It appears the Frontier Province has produced three or three and a half traitors, the Baluchistan has to its share about two or two and a quarters traitors, and so Sind can claim about two or two and three quarters of traitors, and East Pakistan has about three or three and a half traitors. It appears Punjab alone has produced no traitors. Don't you think what a fine and fortunate thing it would be for Pakistan, if the Punjab also had a couple of traitors to its credit. If they were in that case I can assure you this country would be such a haven of peace, good-will freedom and democracy to live in'" (Shah 1984: 5).

11. This amendment pertained to Article 19 of the constitution, the fundamental right to freedom, and imposed a restriction on secessionist propaganda and activity.

12. As it carried, the bill uses both "may" and "shall" in different contexts: "The English language *may* . . . continue to be used in addition to Hindi" everywhere it was being used officially by the union government and for parliamentary business. English "*shall* be used for purposes of communication between the Union and a State which has not adopted Hindi as its official language." Communication in Hindi between a state that has adopted Hindi and one that has not "*shall* be accompanied by an English translation" (Government of India 1963, clause 3, emphases mine).

13. Examples of the earlier poems are Kavi. Ka. Akilan, "Viduthalai Petriduvom" (We will get freedom), *Dravida Nadu,* September 9, 1962; Kavignar 'Sura,' "Arappuratchi" (Moral revolution), *Dravida Nadu,* September 16, 1962; Cho. Ra. Ezhilan, "Thandalai Ettru Viduthalai Kaannbom" (We will accept punishment and see freedom), *Dravida Nadu,* September 23, 1962; Na. Ali, "Vetri Muzhakkuvom" (We will declare victory), *Dravida Nadu,* September 30, 1962. Examples of the later poems are Ee. Udayavinan, "Viduthalai Kannvizhikkum" (Freedom will stare us in the eye), *Dravida Nadu,* October 28, 1962; Sura, "Ellai Kaappom" (We will protect the frontier), *Dravida Nadu,* November 4, 1962; Pulavar Aran, "Naattai Kaappom" (We will protect the country), *Dravida Nadu,* November 11, 1962.

14. A rally held in Madras on December 2, 1962, to raise funds for the war effort is always cited as proof of the DMK's underlying patriotism. At this rally alone, the party raised more than Rs 35,000 for the war fund.

A sample of the editorial headlines: "Vaari Vazhangugal" (Give generously), *Dravida Nadu,* November 4, 1962; "Namadhu Pani" (Our task), *Dravida Nadu, November* 11, 1962; "Ilaignar Padaiye! Ezhu!" (Youth force! Arise!), *Dravida Nadu,* November 18, 1962; "Ungal Pangu" (Your share), *Dravida Nadu,* November 25, 1962; "Uloothanai Virattiduvom!" (We will drive out the deceiver!), *Dravida Nadu,* December 23, 1962.

15. Annadurai called off the agitation when he was released from prison on October 2, 1962. He had been arrested along with others in an agitation over rising prices.

16. The other instance was in 1980, when the nine state governments were dismissed by the returning Congress (I) government.

4

Building Communities
out of States: Two Principles

How do you build a political community? The identity-integration tussle between three substate communities and the Indian, Pakistani, and Sri Lankan states provides the setting for our consideration of this question. Political socialization through history education and the politics of unit demarcation are two areas in which groups encounter the state's definition of its identity and its place and in which these definitions are contested and negotiated.

The state socializes children through the teaching of state-approved history curricula in schools. These children remember their collective pasts on the basis of this history and others (oral histories, mythologies, cinematic histories). Out of this memory comes a vision of the community in which they would like to live. The seeds of dissonance between the state's idea of itself and the ideas of substate groups in that society are sown here. The dissonance is compounded when these visions lead, as visions do, to demands for territorial actualization. That is, differences between a group's definition of itself and the state, on the one hand, and the state's definition of itself and the group within, on the other hand, have the greatest potential for conflict when the group seeks to found a homeland or any other kind of territorial enclave.

This study has insights for three political problems—integration, conflict prevention and management, and postconflict peacebuilding. Integration is sometimes the prior problem and, in this book, is the central consideration. State-led integration is a process requiring a vision that is expressed concretely in constitutional provisions and internal power structures. This expression is then taken into the political arena, where citizens are socialized and their contrary demands and visions are accommodated and reconciled. Integration involves the reconciliation of dissonance between the vision of the state and those of its constituent parts. This political conversation takes place in the context of the state's ability to use force to achieve its ends—an ability with integrative and divisive consequences. The success of the state's intervention is contingent upon its ability to discern its limits and to do neither more nor less than is necessary to reach its goal.

If reconciliation is the first principle that should govern integration efforts, then the Indian management of the Dravidian secessionist demand, contrasted with the Sindhi and Sri Lankan Tamil cases, suggests that accommodation should be the second. The term *accommodation* is a rubric for three other principles. First, it is not enough for the state to accommodate only when the costs of not doing so are too high. What is being advocated is early accommodation, which is both cheaper and more effective than other offerings when difference becomes conflict. Furthermore, it appears as though timing is crucial in another way. The stage of the conflict and the leadership and level of mobilization are also important. The cases studied here suggest that conflict is most likely prevented at the stage before rival visions acquire a territorial agenda. This study suggests two possible points of intervention—at the stage of socialization and when identity is given constitutional expression. The second principle of accommodation is the acceptance of multiple loyalties. Finally, integrative success is also marked by flexibility and the willingness to yield on certain demands.

In the pages that follow, the two principles of reconciliation and accommodation are discussed, and it is argued that if state intervention in national integration is a given, these principles must guide that intervention.

Reconciliation

The problem of integration does not arise so much because society comprises different cultural, religious, and socioeconomic groups but because they cannot agree on a common vision or definition of the collective to which they belong. There are differences between the way the state envisions itself and the way in which its constituents define themselves. The visions of the constituents are more or less incompatible with each other. All of these visions are constantly shifting in response to each other and other factors. Were these to be reconciled, an "internal" reconciliation would still be necessary because of the changes that occur in each vision without corresponding changes in its territorial embodiment—the land it occupies or the land it claims. Even as these visions adjust to each other, they change, and thus continual reconciliation is needed.

Reconciling the Self-Definitions of the State and Its Parts

The first and most basic reconciliation that state and civil society seek is that between the state's vision of itself and the self-definition of the parts. As we have seen, the state views itself one way as a whole entity, and that view leads it automatically to define its units in a particular way. The whole, the state in our case, envisions itself and its parts, articulates that vision in the constitution, and embodies that vision in the internal structure of the state. Likewise, the part—group or region—entertains a self-definition that is compatible with one particular definition of the state-of-the-whole. The vision of the part, group, or region within the state as embodied in territorial terms manifests different degrees of its acquiescence to or rejection of the state's vision by seeking autonomy, separation, secession, or sovereignty. Visions of the whole and visions of the parts are mutually derivative. Thus reconciling them involves reconciling (1) the vision of the whole, (2) the whole's vision of the part, (3) the part's vision of itself, and (4) the part's vision of the whole.

When Sri Lanka became independent in 1948, the elites, Sinhalese and Tamil, to whom power was transferred, shared notions of representative democracy and a democratic state. This shared vision has frayed over the past fifty years. It was in the debates over the nature and detail of representation, even before independence, however, that the seeds of two ethnically separate visions began to germinate. The Sinhalese, as the majority in a majoritarian democracy, found agents in the Bandaranaike government to express their will. The Tamils responded with a renewed articulation of a Tamil self-definition. Battles over education and employment spilled over to issues of decentralized development. The Tamil vision found its embodiment in the idea of a Tamil homeland in the north. This embodiment was authenticated in historical terms. For several years, the Tamil and Sinhalese visions seemed to be competing for actualization.

In the 1990s, two more voices were heard in this contest. The first is the voice of the People's Alliance government, acting on behalf of the Sri Lankan state, in the attempt to achieve a reconciliation. Although one might say that the reconciliation sought is one between the Sinhalese and the Tamils, it is also—and that is why it is used as an example here—a reconciliation between the Tamils and a state that has come to reflect the Sinhalese vision to the exclusion of others. The People's Alliance government represented a new willingness of that state to work toward this reconciliation of state and group self-visions.

The second voice in the conflict is that of the Sri Lankan Muslim, raised specifically to contest the embodiment of the Tamil vision in a homeland that includes Sri Lanka's Northern *and* Eastern provinces. The emergence of the Muslim voice takes us to the next type of reconciliation.

Reconciling the Mutually Incompatible Visions of the Constituents

Each part of a state has its own vision and the subsequent embodiment thereof. Where the visions of the parts are not compatible, their embodiment will also be contentious. As long as a state's parts assert these contentious visions, a reconciliation between any one part and the state is almost counterproductive because it resolves only part of the problem of national integration. Worse, such a reconciliation may compound the problem by making the state appear partisan. Thus the state must play arbiter and agent in the achievement of rapprochement among the parts' visions of themselves, and of one another, in their vision of the whole. This is the second reconciliation that facilitates national integration.

As we saw in the Sri Lankan case, the government's attempt to find a solution to the ongoing crisis involves first a reconciliation between a state apparatus with a Sinhalese cast and the Tamil vision. The reconciliation is impeded by a Sinhalese vision that will not quit and a Muslim vision that is fighting for space. The Sinhalese vision contests the vision of the Sri Lankan state as multiethnic and possibly federal. The Muslim vision contests the embodiment of the Tamil vision. Therefore, a reconciliation between the self-definitions of the state and its parts must be accompanied by a reconciliation among the visions of the parts.

We also see the same need in the case of Sind. The contest over Karachi is a contest between a vision of Sindhi nationality embodied in the province of Sind, including Karachi, on the one hand, and the search for an embodiment of the Muhajir vision—or the search by the Muhajir community for a home of its own in Pakistan. The need to be territorially moored is in evidence yet again. In this case, actualization of the Muhajir vision is possible only through a diminution of the way in which the Sindhi vision is embodied. The reconciliation between the Sindhis and the Pakistani state is a product of functional integration to some extent, but it is also a product of Muhajir challenges to Sindhi nationalist claims.

But the process of national integration cannot be achieved even if the first two reconciliations are complete. Visions change, and the process is ongoing.

Reconciling Shifting Visions with Their Relatively Static Territorial Embodiments

Visions of the state or of any collective are like pieces in a kaleidoscope. They shift as you gaze, and they shift as they are articulated. There may be a time lag between the ever-shifting vision and its embodiment as identification with a territory. Actualizing the vision— that is, gaining a territory—and altering the vision are slow processes, since such actualization and alteration both require reconciliations among groups and between them and the state. The third reconciliation is that between the shifting vision and its relatively static embodiment.

The Dravida movement's history is an illustration of the dynamism of visions. The movement began as a social reform movement; membership in the community was determined by caste origin. To name the community, the linguistic term Tamil was adopted. The rhetoric of the movement imbued this linguistic term with racial connotations. In 1938, when Hindi was introduced in the schools of the Madras Presidency, the community responded as a linguistic bloc. The anti-Hindi agitation was founded on behalf of Tamil, even though Dravidians spoke at least four languages. From this identification with Tamil came the beginnings of the territorial embodiment of the community's vision, an embodiment that ultimately confined the movement to speakers of one of its four languages.

The vision and the agenda of the Dravida movement have changed several times, but its embodiment has remained the same. As long as the movement maintained a rhetorical position that was Dravidian, the growth of the demand for a linguistically determined Andhra Pradesh

Figure 4.1   From Vision to Territorial Actualization

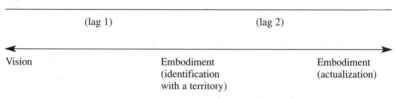

undermined this position. By 1960, the vision had become not so much Dravidanadu (a homeland for all the Dravida peoples) as Thani Thamizhnadu (a separate Tamil homeland). In the 1980s, in the support extended to the Tamil militants in Sri Lanka, there was some notion of an overarching community, but it did not extend to territoriality. There was no talk of a united Tamil country, notwithstanding the fears of the Sinhalese in Sri Lanka. The territorial base, the embodiment of the Tamil vision in India, will not shift so fast as to accommodate minor changes in the periphery of its political elite. Therefore, it did not matter that in fact there was no change in the geographical extent of Tamil Nadu. Had the changed vision of the Tamil community entailed also a changed territorial vision, backtracking from the support extended to the Tigers would have been harder. (Imagine the horrors of the Sri Lankan war repeated on the other side of the Palk Straits!)

Embodiment of a vision occurs in two stages: first as identification with a territory, and then, when that identification is actualized through the recognition of territorial demands. There is a lag between each pair of these stages (see Figure 4.1) that holds not only the seeds of conflict but also the opportunity to prevent conflict.

The time between identification and actualization of a vision's embodiment, as communities face impediments to their preferred territorial arrangements, is most likely to be contentious. Thus the best opportunity to prevent conflict lies prior to the identification of a vision with a particular territory. The reconciliation effort might begin here and would not be very different from the reconciliation between the state's and groups' identities (i.e., the first of the four reconciliations). In other words, if reconciliation were achieved between the differing visions of the state and substate groups (the first and second reconciliations), the need to contend with territorial claims and counterclaims would not arise.

Reconciling Visions That Change Asynchronously

Every vision is subject to shifts and changes, and each changes at a different pace. Each shift evokes ripples of change in other visions, and the changes do not happen synchronously.

In the absence of ongoing reconciliation among these changing visions, other types of reconciliation are harder to achieve because people are not ready at the same time for negotiation, or for conflict. This situation prevails today in Sri Lanka. There are three major players in this conflict—the state, the Sinhalese, and the Tamils—and one minor player, the Muslims. These four have never been ready at the same time to negotiate and compromise. Further, in the case of the Tamils, there has been the issue of representative leadership. Who is to speak on their behalf, and in what circumstances can an agreement be reached? Similarly, in India in 1963, the antisecession amendment was passed to address the secessionist propaganda of the Mizos and the Tamils. Today, other entities that were relatively acquiescent in 1963 are threatening the survival of the state in its present form, notably the Kashmiri and Bodo militants. National integration is, in the most difficult instance, the reconciliation of multiple shifts at varying rhythms.

As we have seen, given the circumstances in which the polity operates, the different kinds of reconciliations are neither sequential nor finite. The process of communities envisioning themselves and then embodying that vision is ongoing, and both vision and embodiment are liable to change. Moreover, every entity has a vision, and every vision changes at a different pace. Can states, as the political actors with the greatest interest in integration, ever hope to gain control of the situation? Probably not. Nevertheless, as visions proliferate and evolve, are territorially embodied and actualized, states are forced to respond and act in the interest of their own survival.

The Importance of Accommodation

Divested of the many digressions and subplots, the integration story is really a very simple one with an almost commonsensical moral: If integration is to be lasting and sustainable, states should be a facilitating agent in an arena of many other agents, and the process should be one of reconciling multiple visions at different levels. That said, the case studies suggest a very simple principle—accommodation. There are three applications of this principle: acceptance of multiple loyalties, flexibility in response to demands from within, and a willingness to consider demands while they are still minor.

Acceptance of Multiple, Simultaneous Loyalties

The assumption that people can have only one primary political loyalty is wrong. People have and are comfortable with several equal loyalties, and they are not mutually exclusive. These loyalties do not compete until someone forces the question of which one is primary. As discussed in Chapter 2 of this book, during interviews conducted in Madras in summer 1996, I asked a series of questions intended to elicit respondents' perceptions of their place in the larger Indian context. When I did not ask them to choose, they alternated between identities they regarded as primary. When asked to choose, they picked one or the other, sometimes inconsistently. It was clear that almost all respondents were uncomfortable having to choose between being Indian and being Tamil. A couple of them made a point of saying they were both and proud of both. The same complexity was seen with regard to the Pakistan and Sri Lanka cases.

What does this complexity mean for the purposes of policymaking? Within the state, the citizen may have different categories of official belonging—being a citizen, holding a passport, being registered to vote in a particular place or entitled to food and fuel rations in a particular place, having a particular domicile or an identity card that records place of birth and place of residence. Officially, it does not really matter whether a citizen feels civic loyalty, family pride, or ethnic solidarity. Each document is issued in the confidence that the citizen has only one identification. If the state does not explicitly ask for a declaration of *primary* identification, the issue remains unproblematic on both sides.

The important lesson for policymaking is the avoidance of situations where the citizen must choose between her many identifications and allegiances. She may, for example, be asked for purposes of affirmative action how she identifies herself, but to extend that request to a choice between those identifications would be detrimental. To predetermine a set of choices by one reading of the citizen's identity (such as those with Tamil fathers attending Tamil medium schools in Sri Lanka) is to force a choice upon the citizen. By taking away her right to choose, the state presumes the citizen's primary identification. Identity cards that indicate ethnicity force private identification into public scrutiny. If the citizen is treated differently on the basis of that identification, such documents become divisive insofar as they impose a hierarchy of preferences on identity. Differential taxation and differential legal systems also require citizens to declare themselves in very public ways and are therefore to be avoided.

I am suggesting that the choice of identity occurs at a variety of levels and is more insidious at some levels than others. On a day-to-day basis, our choices to be one thing or another have no political import. When we write on forms and declarations, optionally or compulsorily, how we identify by religion, language, race, and other criteria, our choices are a little more public, but because we can sometimes choose not to answer or to change our responses, because the information is usually restricted to a few, and because benefits may accrue to us based on our responses, our participation is not politically divisive. Choosing among schools and choosing a set of personal and taxation laws are more public acts. The state and all the citizen's personal and social milieu comes to know of her choices, which are included in public records and have public consequences.

People infer others' choices and preferences in certain contexts. Take the case of cricket matches in South Asia. Whereas some attribute great integrating qualities to cricket, cricket has also served to spotlight divisions in societies. The idea that Indian Muslims identify with Islam and Pakistan rather than India finds its crudest and most overt public expression in the allegation that they support the Pakistani cricket team and not the predominantly Hindu Indian team. Likewise, Sri Lankan Tamils are said to support the Indian team rather than the predominantly Sinhalese Sri Lankan team. How does one alter the social milieu so that these choices are not expected and no choice can therefore be branded the wrong choice? Such a change requires an ideological legerdemain that the state may be incapable of and that it is incumbent on well-meaning forces in civil society to put into effect.

Flexibility

The willingness of any political system to recast itself is the hallmark of political success. Not bending is preparing to break, as was suggested a moment ago. It is easy to assume that at the end of a process (any process), there will be an outcome and that it will be permanent. Thus at the end of nationalism, there is the state. At the end of political development, there is the stable state. And at the end of democratization, there is the democratic state or society. The terms that one generation negotiates and sets are supposed to hold for all time. If we place such a high value on final outcomes, any process that subjects us to inconvenience must lead, almost righteously, to an outcome that will never again change.

In the current devolution debate in Sri Lanka, what is being discussed is a state federal in form and unitary in letter. The British set up a unitary state in Sri Lanka to serve their own ends, and today, this colonial creation has taken on a quality of permanence that Sri Lankans, particularly Sinhalese, regard as vital to their continued survival as an ethnic group. That unitary government is not possible in this day and age has been conceded by the Sri Lankan government in two kinds of decentralizing processes it has undertaken since the 1970s. It has undertaken the first, decentralizing development administration, more or less voluntarily. The process of devolution, or power sharing, has been forced upon it by political events. Why, then, the hesitation in calling the state a federal state? The moderate Tamils will settle for nothing less, the Sinhalese will not give on this point, and the state is rendered inflexible by its own need for legitimation by the *sangha*.

India has serendipitously found a way to deal with subnational aspirations that it grossly undervalues. The Indian Union is made up of two kinds of units—centrally administered territories and states. The states are larger and have more resources and autonomy than the centrally administered, or union, territories. Over the past fifty years, when faced with regional demands, the center, or the union, employs one of four strategies: name changing, reorganization, upgrading a unit to statehood, and carving out autonomous or new states. The central government also has the expedient in the case of Kashmir, Mizoram, and others of conferring "special status," which allows a greater degree of autonomy for those states. Although the states of India purportedly underwent linguistic reorganization in the 1950s and 1960s, there is nothing uniform about the basis or form of unit demarcation within the Indian Union. However, history is likely to endorse the accidental wisdom of an ad hoc approach in dealing with what Nehru called "fissiparous tendencies."

The point is that to search for unchanging truths and unassailable positions is a false quest. Things must change, and there is no point in resisting that change. It is better to create the mechanisms for change than to stand against it because one believes oneself to possess some great truth.

Early Accommodation

"Yield and overcome." These words from the *Tao Te Ching* could have found no better illustration than the experience of South Asia in dealing with ethnic discontent. Giving a little now is better than giving a lot later. And the giving must be shown in actions and not just words. It seems to be true across the board that the earlier the accommodation is made, the lower the cost and the greater the benefit. States stand firm, stand tall, and finally are broken by the winds of discontent that blow around them.

The contrast between the Indian government's response to the Dravidanadu demand and to Kashmiri nationalism illustrates the benefit of early accommodation. In the case of the Dravida secessionist movement, the central government's assurances that Hindi would not be imposed on non-Hindi speakers came early enough so that, coupled with the advent of the 1962 war with China, the DMK decided to drop its demand for a separate state. The antisecession amendment made it necessary for the DMK to back down, but early accommodation made the volte-face possible. In Kashmir in 1989, another rigged election proved conclusively that the central government's commitment to Kashmir was more window dressing than anything else. Without entering into the usual debates about Kashmir, let me make this simple argument: If Kashmir was to be integrated through the political process, that process should have been more accommodating. Would it not have been less costly to have a disagreeable opposition leader rule Kashmir than to do what Congress governments at the center repeatedly did, that is, topple the state government or rig the election?

The same can be seen by juxtaposing the Pakistani response to Bengali demands with the way the center has dealt with Sind. When the Bengalis in Pakistan asked that their language be recognized and that their position as the single largest community within the state be reflected in the political apparatus, the state did not see fit to gracefully accommodate these demands. Nevertheless, in 1971, with Indian assistance, East Pakistan broke away to form Bangladesh. In the Sindhi case, many events affected the outcome. One, the creation of Bangladesh, left a more manageable Pakistani state, and in the aftermath of the 1971 war, some changes were initiated in the power shar-

ing between the center and the provinces. Further, that the leader initiating these changes, Zulfikar Ali Bhutto, was a Sindhi landowner did
not hurt. The resistance to General Zia's takeover of government was
led by Benazir Bhutto out of Sind. The Movement for the Restoration
of Democracy reinforced Sind's entry into the national mainstream.
Over the years, to Sindhis, it is not the state that has threatened them
but the Muhajirs, who have settled and transformed Karachi into a non-
Sindhi city. That, however, is a different battle.

Although the renewal of interest in studying the state is important
and useful, all too often, the work of political scientists valorizes the
need to fortify the position of the state and the state apparatus. The
political development and modernization literature is particularly prone
to assuming that states, by definition correct in their ideologies, policies, and practices, must be maintained, institutionalized, stabilized.
However, states are all too often wrong. Academics and policymakers
alike had better ask, "How do we get states to correct themselves when
they are wrong?" or "How do we build states with self-correcting
mechanisms?" rather than "How do states remain strong in the face of
opposition?" When strength is equated with the ability to enforce and
sustain the status quo, the imperatives of resistance and control rather
than avenues of accommodation preoccupy the elite. However, in order
to be strong, states must yield. One might narrate South Asian history
to show that both repressive and accommodative polities existed, but it
is the latter (those of Asoka and Akbar, most famously) that underwrote
important periods of syncretism and integration. When regimes used
coercion to gain cooperation (for instance, during Aurangzeb's rule),
the resultant social contracts barely survived the decline of those
regimes. The task at hand is to alter the political game and attendant
political culture to recognize that fact.

Building Nations out of the
States of South Asia

Reconciliation and accommodation do not constitute a magic formula
for integrative success. Indeed, as I have argued elsewhere in the book,
perfect integrative success is a chimera. However, in this process without end, reconciliation and, accommodation facilitate peaceful meta-
morphoses of the polity and, quite possibly, peaceful transitions out of
violence. At the end of the day, intransigence fosters alienation, and the

use of force creates festering hostilities before, during, and after the conflict. What might appear as huge compromises (allowing two scripts rather than imposing one) are ultimately nothing compared to dealing with the question of partitioning the state, for instance. Without entering into the argument of whether it is important for a state to survive, I hope to have shown that no state can survive when its policies are neither conciliatory nor accommodating. In South Asia and elsewhere, the key to forming a political community that includes, without effacing, the nations and peoples bounded by state borders lies not in masterfully welding them into a national citizenry but in accepting that there can be no everlasting integration in any one form, that every order must instantly be renegotiated, and that the state's role is ultimately the management of change so that it is peaceful.

Acronyms

ACDIS	(University of Illinois at Urbana-Champaign's Program in) Arms Control, Disarmament and International Security
AIADMK	All-Indian Anna Dravida Munnetra Kazhagam
CAD	Constituent Assembly debates
CBSE	Central Board of Secondary Education (Tamil Nadu)
DK	Dravida Kazhagam
DMK	Dravida Munnetra Kazhagam
FCW	Federal Curriculum Wing (Pakistan)
LTTE	Liberation Tigers of Tamil Eelam
MQM	Muhajir Qaumi Movement
MP	member of Parliament
MRD	Movement for the Restoration of Democracy
NCERT	National Council for Educational Research and Training (Tamil Nadu)
NWFP	North-West Frontier Province
PA	People's Alliance
PAKSTAN	Punjab, North-West Frontier Province, Kashmir, Sind, and Baluchistan
PPP	Pakistan People's Party
TULF	Tamil United Liberation Front
UP	Uttar Pradesh

Bibliography

Abeyasinghe, T.B.H. 1995. "The Kingdom of Kandy: Foundations and Foreign Relations to 1638." In *The University of Peradeniya, The History of Ceylon.* Volume 2. Edited by K. M. de Silva. Peradeniya: University of Peradeniya.

Abeysekera, Charles, and Newton Gunasinghe, eds. 1987. *Facets of Ethnicity in Sri Lanka.* Colombo: Social Scientists Association.

Agnew, John, ed. 1997. *Political Geography: A Reader.* London: Arnold.

Ahmad, Jamil-ud-Din, ed. 1970. *Historic Documents of the Muslim Freedom Movement.* Lahore: Publishers United.

Ahmed, Bashiruddin. 1979. "Process of Integration." *Seminar* 240 (August): 12–17.

Ahmed, Feroz. 1985. "Pakistan's Problems of National Integration." In *Islam, Politics and the State: The Pakistan Experience.* Edited by Asghar Khan. London: Zed Books.

———. 1988. "Ethnicity and Politics: The Rise of Muhajir Separatism." *South Asia Bulletin* 8: 33–45.

Ahmed, Rashmee Z. 1994. "Court in the Act." *The Independent.* March 20.

Aitken, E. H. 1907. *Gazetteer of the Province of Sindh.*

Akilan, Kavi. Ka. 1962. "Viduthalai Petriduvom" (We will get freedom). *Dravida Nadu.* September 9.

Alavi, Hamza. 1992. "The Politics of Ethnicity in Pakistan." In *Regional Imbalances and the National Question in Pakistan.* Edited by S. Akbar Zaidi. Lahore: Vanguard.

Alberuni. 1973. *Alberuni's Indica : A Record of the Cultural History of South Asia About A.D. 1030.* Abridged and annotated by Ahmad Hasan Dani. Islamabad: University of Islamabad Press.

Ali, Na. 1962. "Vetri Muzhakkuvom" (We will declare victory). *Dravida Nadu.* September 30.

Allen, Douglas, ed. 1993. *Religion and Political Conflict in South Asia: India, Pakistan, and Sri Lanka.* Delhi: Oxford University Press.

Almond, Gabriel A., and G. B. Powell. 1966. *Comparative Politics: A Developmental Approach*. Indian edition. Boston: Little, Brown.

Almond, Gabriel, and James Coleman. 1960. *The Politics of the Developing Areas*. Princeton: Princeton University Press.

Altekar, A. S. 1958. *State and Government in Ancient India*. Delhi: Motilal Banarsidass.

Altekar, G. S. 1987. *Studies on Valmiki's Ramayana*. Poona: Bhandarkar's Oriental Research Institute.

Amarasekara, Gunadasa. 1991. "Time to Look Within." The Third Senaka Bibile Oration, Colombo, September 26.

Amin, Shahid, and Dipesh Chakrabarty, eds. 1996. *Subaltern Studies IX: Writings on South Asian History and Society*. Delhi: Oxford University Press.

Anderson, Benedict. 1991. *Imagined Communities*. Second edition. London and New York: Verso.

Anderson, James. 1988. "Nationalist Ideology and Territory." In *Nationalism, Self-determination and Political Geography*. Edited by R. J. Johnston, David B. Knight, and Eleanore Kofman. London: Croom Helm.

Annadurai, C. N. 1961. *Inpath Dravidam*. Madras: Tamil Nadu Puttaka Nilayam.

———. 1975a. "An Appeal to Conscience." In *Anna Speaks: At the Rajya Sabha 1962–66*. Edited by S. Ramachandran. New Delhi: Orient Longman.

———. 1975b. "Let Us March as One People." In *Anna Speaks: At the Rajya Sabha 1962–66*. Edited by S. Ramachandran. New Delhi: Orient Longman.

———. 1975c. "Secession and Sovereignty." In *Anna Speaks: At the Rajya Sabha 1962–66*. Edited by S. Ramachandran. New Delhi: Orient Longman.

———. 1985. *Ilatchiya Varalaaru*. Fourth edition. Madras: Maruti Press.

Ansari, Sarah F. D. 1992. *Sufi Saints and State Power: The Pirs of Sind, 1843–1947*. Cambridge: Cambridge University Press.

"Anti-Hindi Campaign." 1963. *The Hindu*. June 11.

"Anti-Secession Bill Passed." 1963. *The Hindu*. May 3.

Appadorai, A. 1987. *Indian Political Thinking in the Twentieth Century: An Introductory Survey*. Second edition. New Delhi: South Asian.

Aran, Pulavar. 1962. "Naattai Kaappom" (We will protect the country). *Dravida Nadu*. November 11.

Aristotle. 1958. *The Politics of Aristotle*. Edited and translated by Ernest Barker. London: Oxford University Press.

Ariyadasa, D., and E.S.W. Perera. 1969. "Text Books." In *Education in Ceylon (from the Sixth Century B.C. to the Present Day): A Centenary Volume*. Ministry of Education and Cultural Affairs, Ceylon. Colombo: Government Press.

Arnold, David, and Peter Robb, eds. 1993. *Institutions and Ideologies. A SOAS South Asia Reader.* Surrey: Curzon Press.

Arooran, K. Nambi. 1980. *Tamil Renaissance and Dravidian Nationalism, 1905–1944.* Madurai: Koodal.

"Assurance on Hindi." 1963. *The Hindu.* April 22.

Austin, Granville. 1972. *The Indian Constitution: Cornerstone of a Nation.* Bombay: Oxford University Press.

Axelrod, Robert. 1984. *The Evolution of Cooperation.* New York: Basic Books.

Axelrod, Robert, and Robert O. Keohane. 1986. "Achieving Cooperation Under Anarchy: Strategies and Institutions." In *Cooperation Under Anarchy.* Edited by Kenneth A. Oye. Princeton: Princeton University Press.

Azam, Ikram. 1974. *Pakistan's Security and National Integration.* Rawalpindi: London Book Company.

Azam, Kousar J. 1981. *Political Aspects of National Integration.* Meerut and New Delhi: Meenakshi.

Azam, Raja Ikram. 1990. "From 'States' to 'State': The Semantics and Philosophy of Pakistan Resolution." In *Pakistan Resolution Revisited.* Edited by Kaneez F. Yusuf, M. Saleem Akhtar, and S. Razi Wasti. Islamabad: National Institute of Historical and Cultural Research.

Aziz, K. K. 1987. *A History of the Idea of Pakistan.* Volumes 1–4. Lahore: Vanguard.

———, ed. 1992. *Prelude to Pakistan 1930–40, Documents and Readings Illustrating the Growth of the Idea of Pakistan.* Volumes 1–2. Lahore: Vanguard.

———. 1993a. *The Murder of History in Pakistan.* Lahore: Vanguard.

———. 1993b. *The Pakistani Historian: Pride and Prejudice in the Writing of History.* Lahore: Vanguard.

Bachelard, Gaston. 1964. *The Poetics of Space.* Translated by Maria Jolas. New York: Orion Press.

Bakshi, Rajni. 1995. "What Does It Mean to Be Indian Today?" *Humanscape* (August).

Balachandran, P. K. 1992. "Interview of the Week: K. N. Govindacharya." *Sunday Observer* (Bombay). November 29.

Banaszak, Lee Ann, and Eric Plutzer. 1993. "Contextual Determinants of Feminist Attitudes: National and Subnational Influences in Western Europe." *American Political Science Review* 87: 147–157.

Bandaranayake, Senake. 1985. "The People of Sri Lanka: The National Question and Some Problems of History and Ethnicity." *Ethnicity and Social Change in Sri Lanka.* Colombo: Social Scientists Association.

Banerjee, Anil Chandra, ed. 1961. *Indian Constitutional Documents, 1757–1947.* Third edition. Calcutta: A. Mukherjee.

Barnett, Marguerite Ross. 1976. *The Politics of Cultural Nationalism in South India.* Princeton: Princeton University Press.

Barrows, Walter. 1976. *Grassroots Politics in an African State*. New York and
    London: Africana.
Barth, Fredrik. 1970. "Introduction." In *Ethnic Groups and Boundaries*. Edited
    by Fredrik Barth. Boston: Little, Brown.
Basham, A. L. 1959. *The Wonder That Was India*. New York: Grove Press.
————, ed. 1975. *A Cultural History of India*. Oxford: Clarendon Press.
Bastian, Sunil. 1987. "Plantation Labour in a Changing Context." In *Facets of
    Ethnicity in Sri Lanka*. Edited by Charles Abeysekera and Newton
    Gunasinghe. Colombo: Social Scientists Association.
————. 1990. "Political Economy of Ethnic Violence in Sri Lanka: The July
    1983 Riots." In *Mirrors of Violence: Communities, Riots and Survivors in
    South Asia*. Edited by Veena Das. Delhi: Oxford University Press.
Bastian, Sunil, and Reggie Siriwardena. 1980. "Sinhala Text-Books." In
    School Text Books and Communal Relations in Sri Lanka. Edited by
    Reggie Siriwardena, K. Indrapala, Sunil Bastian, and Sepali Kottegoda.
    Colombo: Council for Communal Harmony Through the Media.
Basu, Bharati. 1986. *National Integration and Education*. Hyderabad: Basu.
Basu, Durga Das. 1969. *Constitutional Documents*. Calcutta: S. C. Sarkar.
————. 1982. *Introduction to the Constitution of India*. Ninth edition. New
    Delhi: Prentice-Hall of India.
Baumann, Gerd. 1987. *National Integration and Local Integrity: The Miri of
    the Nuba Mountains in the Sudan*. Oxford: Oxford University Press.
Berger, Peter L., and Thomas Luckmann. 1966. *The Social Construction of
    Reality: A Treatise in the Sociology of Knowledge*. New York: Anchor
    Books/Doubleday.
Bhattacharya, Neeladri. 1991. "Myth, History and the Politics of
    Ramjanmabhumi." In *Anatomy of a Confrontation: The Babri Masjid–
    Ram Janmabhumi Issue*. Edited by Sarvepalli Gopal. New Delhi: Penguin
    India.
Bill, James A., and Robert L. Hardgrave Jr. 1981. *Comparative Politics: The
    Quest for Theory*. Boston: University Press of America.
Binder, Leonard. 1971. "Crises of Political Development." In *Crises and
    Sequences in Political Development*. Edited by Leonard Binder, James S.
    Coleman, Joseph LaPalombara, Lucian W. Pye, Sidney Verba, and Myron
    Weiner. Princeton: Princeton University Press.
Binder, Leonard, James S. Coleman, Joseph LaPalombara, Lucian W. Pye,
    Sidney Verba, and Myron Weiner, eds. 1971. *Crises and Sequences in
    Political Development*. Princeton: Princeton University Press.
Blaustein, Albert P., and Gisbert H. Flanz, eds. 1975. *Constitutions of the
    Countries of the World: Cumulative Supplement*. Dobbs Ferry, NY:
    Oceana.
Borneman, John. 1992. *Belonging in the Two Berlins*. Cambridge: Cambridge
    University Press.
Bose, Sumantra. 1994. *States, Nations, Sovereignty: Sri Lanka, India and the
    Tamil Eelam Movement*. New Delhi: Sage.

Boulding, Kenneth E. 1989. *Three Faces of Power.* Newbury Park, CA: Sage.

Brass, Paul. 1985. *Ethnic Groups and the State.* Kent: Croom Helm.

———. 1991a. "Ethnic Groups and the State." In *Ethnicity and Nationalism.* New Delhi: Sage.

———. 1991b. *Ethnicity and Nationalism: Theory and Comparison.* New Delhi: Sage.

———. 1997. *Theft of an Idol: Text and Context in the Representation of Collective Violence.* Princeton: Princeton University Press.

Bregman, Jacob, and Nadeem Mohammad. 1998. "Primary and Secondary Education—Structural Issues." In *Education and the State: Fifty Years of Pakistan.* Edited by Pervez Hoodbhoy. Karachi: Oxford University Press.

Breuilly, John. 1993. *Nationalism and the State.* Second edition. Manchester: Manchester University Press.

Brohi, A. K. 1978. "The Soul of Sind." *Sind Quarterly* 6, no. 2.

Brown, David. 1989. "Ethnic Revival: Perspectives on State and Society." *Third World Quarterly* 10, no. 4: 1–17.

Brown, Judith M. 1985. *Modern India: The Origins of an Asian Democracy.* Oxford: Oxford University Press.

Brown, Michael E., ed. 1993. *Ethnic Conflict and International Security.* Princeton: Princeton University Press.

Buch, M. N. 1992. "Moles Eating into the Vitals of Indian Society." *The Independent.* October 22.

Bukowski, Jeanie J. 1997. "Governance Reconsidered: The Redistribution of Authority in the European Arena." Ph.D. diss., University of Illinois at Urbana-Champaign.

Bukowski, Jeanie J., and Swarna Rajagopalan, eds. 2000. *Re-distribution of Authority: A Cross-Regional Perspective.* Westport, CT: Praeger.

Burg, Steven L., and Michael L. Berbaum. 1989. "Community, Integration, and Stability in Multinational Yugoslavia." *American Political Science Review* 83: 535–554.

Burger, Angela S. 1992. "Changing Civil-Military Relations in Sri Lanka." *Asian Survey* 32, no. 8: 744–756.

Buzan, Barry. 1991. *People, States and Fear.* Second edition. Boulder: Lynne Rienner.

The Cambridge History of India, Volume I: Ancient India. 1937. New York: Macmillan.

The Cambridge History of India, Volume IV: The Mughal Period. 1937. New York: Macmillan.

Caporaso, James A., ed. 1989. *The Elusive State: International and Comparative Perspectives.* Newbury Park, CA: Sage.

Carnoy, Martin. 1984. *The State and Political Theory.* Princeton: Princeton University Press.

Chan, Steve. 1990. "State-Making and State-Breaking: The Origins and Paradoxes of the Contemporary Taiwanese State." In *Changes in the*

State: Causes and Consequences. Edited by Edward S. Greenburg and Thomas F. Mayer. Newbury Park, CA: Sage.

Chandra, Bipin, Mridula Mukherjee, Aditya Mukherjee, K. N. Panikkar, and Sucheta Mahajan. 1989. *India's Struggle for Independence.* New Delhi: Penguin.

Chandraprema, C. A. 1991. *Sri Lanka: The Years of Terror: The JVP Insurrection, 1987–1989.* Colombo: Lake House.

Chandrashekar, S. 1995. *Colonialism, Conflict and Nationalism, South India: 1857–1947.* New Delhi: Wishwa Prakashan.

Chano, Saheb Khan. 1984. "Sind Finances in 1843–1847 and Its Annexation to Bombay." *Sindhological Studies* (Summer): 56–66.

Chatterjee, Partha. 1982. *Nationalist Thought and the Colonial World: A Derivative Discourse?* Delhi: Oxford University Press.

————. 1994. *The Nation and Its Fragments.* Delhi: Oxford University Press.

————, ed. 1997. *State and Politics in India.* Delhi: Oxford University Press.

Chellam, Ve. Thi. 1995. *Thamizhagam Varalaarum Panpaadum.* Madras: Manivacakkam Pathipakkam.

Chopra, P. N., ed. 1988. *The Gazetteer of India, Volume Two: History and Culture.* New Delhi: Publications Division, Government of India.

Choudhury, G. W. 1967. *Documents and Speeches on the Constitution of Pakistan.* Dacca: Green Book House.

Choudhury, Savitri. 1992. "A United States of India?" *Times of India.* January 26.

Clay, Jason. 1989. "Epilogue: The Ethnic Future of Nations." *Third World Quarterly* 10, no. 4: 223–233.

Clifford, James, and George E. Marcus, eds. 1986. *Writing Culture: The Poetics and Politics of Ethnography.* Berkeley and Los Angeles: University of California Press.

Coleman, James A. 1971. "The Development Syndrome: Differentiation-Equality-Capacity." In *Crises and Sequences in Political Development.* Edited by Leonard Binder, James S. Coleman, Joseph LaPalombara, Lucian W. Pye, Sidney Verba, and Myron Weiner. Princeton: Princeton University Press.

Coleman, James S., ed. 1965. *Education and Political Development.* Princeton: Princeton University Press.

"Communal Divides." 1990. *Seminar* 374 (October).

Connor, Walker. 1994a. "A Nation Is a Nation, Is a State, Is an Ethnic Group, Is a … ." In *Ethnonationalism: The Quest for Understanding.* Princeton: Princeton University Press.

————. 1994b. *Ethnonationalism: The Quest for Understanding.* Princeton: Princeton University Press.

Constitution of India. 1993. Comments by P. M. Bakshi. Delhi: Universal Book Traders.

Constitution of the Islamic Republic of Pakistan (as modified up to the 4th January 1977). 1977. Government of Pakistan Ministry of Law and Parliamentary Affairs, Law Division. Karachi: Manager of Publications.

Coomaraswamy, Radhika. 1987. "Myths Without Conscience: Tamil and Sinhalese Nationalist Writings of the 1980s." In *Facets of Ethnicity in Sri Lanka*. Edited by Charles Abeysekera and Newton Gunasinghe. Colombo: Social Scientists Association.

———. 1993. "July 1983 Retrospective: A Summary of the Proceedings." *Thatched Patio* 6, no. 4.

———. 1994. "Chelvanayakam, Wilson and Tamil Politics. Review Essay." *Thatched Patio* 7, no. 1: 40–48.

———. N.d. *Sri Lanka's Ethnic Conflict: Mythology, Power and Politics*. Colombo: International Centre for Ethnic Studies.

———. N.d. *The Abdication of Politics: Nationalism and the New International Economic Order*. Colombo: International Centre for Ethnic Studies.

Coser, L. A. 1956. *The Function of Social Conflict*. New York: Free Press.

Crook, Nigel. 1996. "The Control and Expansion of Knowledge: An Introduction." In *The Transmission of Knowledge in South Asia: Essays on Education, Religion, History and Politics*. Edited by Nigel Crook. Delhi: Oxford University Press.

Czempiel, Ernst-Otto, and James N. Rosenau. 1989. *Global Changes and Theoretical Challenges*. Lexington, MA: Lexington Books.

Dalton, Dennis. 1982. "The Concepts of Politics and Power in India's Ideological Tradition." In *The States of South Asia: Problems of National Integration*. Edited by A. Jeyaratnam Wilson and Dennis Dalton. Honolulu: University of Hawaii Press.

Das, Arvind N. 1995. "Rulers and the Ruled." *Telegraph*. January 5.

Dash, Keshab Chandra, ed. 1992. *Social Justice and Its Ancient Indian Base*. Delhi: Pratibha.

David, Kumar, and Santasilan Kadirgamar, eds. 1989. *Ethnicity: Identity, Conflict and Crisis*. Hong Kong: ARENA.

De, Urmila. 1992. "Matters of Convention." *Telegraph*. April 21.

de Silva, C. R. 1974. "Weightage in University Admissions." *Modern Ceylon Studies* 5, no. 2: 151–176.

———. 1982. "The Sinhalese-Tamil Rift in Sri Lanka." In *The States of South Asia: Problems of National Integration*. Edited by A. Jeyaratnam Wilson and Dennis Dalton. Honolulu: University of Hawaii Press.

———. 1984. "Ethnicity, Prejudice and the Writing of History." G. C. Mendis Memorial Lecture.

———. 1987. *Sri Lanka: A History*. Delhi: Vikas.

———. 1999. "The Role of Education in Ameliorating Political Violence in Sri Lanka." In *Creating Peace in Sri Lanka: Civil War and Reconciliation*.

Edited by Robert I. Rotberg. Washington, DC: Brookings Institution Press.

de Silva, Chandra Richard, and Daya de Silva. 1990. *Education in Sri Lanka, 1948–1988.* New Delhi: Navrang.

de Silva, Daya, and C. R. de Silva. 1992. *Sri Lanka Since Independence: A Reference Guide to the Literature.* New Delhi: Navrang.

de Silva, H. L. 1992. "The Indo–Sri Lanka Agreement (1987) in the Perspective of Inter-State Relations." *Ethnic Studies Report* (International Centre for Ethnic Studies) 10, no. 2.

de Silva, K. M., ed. 1973. *History of Ceylon.* Peradeniya: University of Ceylon.

———. 1985. *Nationalism and the State in Sri Lanka.* Colombo: International Centre for Ethnic Studies.

———. 1993a. "Ethnicity, Language and Politics: The Making of Sri Lanka's Official Language Act No. 33 of 1956." *Ethnic Studies Report* (International Centre for Ethnic Studies, Kandy) 11, no. 1.

———. 1993b. "Regionalism and Decentralization of Power." In *Sri Lanka: Problems of Governance.* New Delhi: Konark.

———, ed. 1993c. *Sri Lanka : A Survey.* London: C. Hurst.

———, ed. 1993d. *Sri Lanka: Problems of Governance.* Delhi: Konark.

———. 1995. *The "Traditional Homelands" of the Tamils.* Kandy: International Centre for Ethnic Studies.

de Silva, K. M., and R. J. May, eds. 1991. *Internationalization of Ethnic Conflict.* London: Pinter.

de Silva, K. M., and S.W.R. de A. Samarasinghe, eds. 1993. *Peace Accords and Ethnic Conflict.* London: Pinter.

de Silva, Padmasiri. 1987. "The Concept of Equality in the Theravada Buddhist Tradition." In *Equality and the Religious Traditions of Asia.* Edited by R. Siriwardena. London: Pinter.

Debates, India (Dominion) Constituent Assembly, Delhi. Available and accessed at URL <<http://alfa.nic.in/debates/debates.htm>>.

Dennis, Jack, ed. 1973. *Socialization to Politics: A Reader.* New York: John Wiley.

Deutsch, Karl W. 1961. "Social Mobilization and Political Development." *American Political Science Review* 55: 493–511.

———. 1966. *Nationalism and Social Communication.* Second edition. Cambridge: Massachusetts Institute of Technology Press.

Deutsch, Karl W., et al. 1957. *Political Community and the North Atlantic Area.* Princeton: Princeton University Press.

Devahuti, ed. 1980. *Bias in Indian Historiography.* Delhi: D. K. Publications.

DH News Service. 1998. "Govt. Creates 3 New States, Grants Statehood to Delhi." *Deccan Herald.* June 30.

Dharma, P. C. 1989. *The Ramayana Polity.* Bombay: Bharatiya Vidya Bhavan.

Dharmapala, Anagarika. 1965. "History of an Ancient Civilization." In *Return to Righteousness: A Collection of Speeches, Essays and Letters of the*

Anagarika Dharmapala. Edited by Ananda Guruge. Ceylon: Government Press. First published as a booklet in Los Angeles, 1902.

Dhas, D. J. Sathia. 1993. "Diluting Dravidian Dogmas." *Indian Express.* January 1.

Diamond, Larry, and Marc F. Plattner, eds. 1994. *Nationalism, Ethnic Conflict, and Democracy.* Baltimore, MD: Johns Hopkins University Press.

Dijkink, Gertjan. 1996. *National Identity and Geopolitical Visions: Maps of Pride and Pain.* London and New York: Routledge.

"DMK Declared a State Party." 1958. *Homeland* 1, no. 34 (March 9).

"DMK to Strive for New Union in South." 1963. *The Hindu.* November 4.

"The DMK's Dilemma." 1963. *The Hindu.* August 9.

Doyle, Michael. 1983. "Kant, Liberal Legacies, and Foreign Affairs." *Philosophy & Public Affairs* 12: 205–235.

———. 1986. "Liberalism and World Politics." *American Political Science Review* 80: 1151–1169.

Drake, Christine. 1989. *National Integration in Indonesia: Patterns and Policies.* Honolulu: University of Hawaii Press.

Drekmeier, Charles. 1962. *Kingship and Community in Early India.* Stanford: Stanford University Press.

Duara, Prasenjit. 1996. *Rescuing History from the Nation.* Chicago: University of Chicago Press.

Duchacek, Ivo. 1970. *Comparative Federalism: The Territorial Dimension of Politics.* New York: Holt, Rinehart and Winston.

Education in Ceylon (from the Sixth Century B.C. to the Present Day): A Centenary Volume. 1969. Ministry of Education and Cultural Affairs, Ceylon. Colombo: Government Press.

Eisenstadt, S. N. 1973. *Tradition, Change, and Modernity.* New York: Wiley.

Elazar, Daniel. 1987. *Exploring Federalism.* Tuscaloosa: University of Alabama Press.

Encyclopaedia Brittanica Online. http://www.eb.com.

Enloe, Cynthia H. 1986. *Ethnic Conflict and Political Development.* Lanham, MD: University Press of America.

Evans, Peter B., Dietrich Rueschemeyer, and Theda Skocpol. 1985. *Bringing the State Back In.* Cambridge: Cambridge University Press.

Ezhilan, Cho. Ra. 1962. "Thandalai Ettru Viduthalai Kaannbom" (We will accept punishment and see freedom). *Dravida Nadu.* September 9.

Ferguson, John. 1978. *War and Peace in the World's Religions.* New York: Oxford University Press.

Fernando, J. Basil. 1991. *Modernization vs Militarization: Ethnic Conflict and Labour in Sri Lanka.* Hong Kong: Asia Monitor Resource Center.

Fernando, Tissa, and Robert N. Kearney. 1979. *Modern Sri Lanka: A Society in Transition.* Syracuse: Maxwell School of Citizenship and Public Affairs.

Fox, Richard, ed. 1991. *Recapturing Anthropology: Working in the Present.* Santa Fe, NM: School of American Research Press.

The Framing of India's Constitution. 1966. Volume 3. New Delhi: Indian Institute of Public Administration.

Frankel, Francine R., and M.S.A. Rao. 1990. *Dominance and State Power in Modern India, Decline of a Social Order.* Volume 2. Oxford: Oxford University Press.

Frankenberg, Ruth. 1993. *White Women, Race Matters.* Minneapolis: University of Minnesota Press.

Frankenberg, Ruth, and Lata Mani. 1993. "Crosscurrents, Crosstalk: Race, Postcoloniality and the Politics of Location." *Cultural Studies* 7, no. 2.

Frykenberg, Robert Eric. 1996. *History and Belief: The Foundations of Historical Understanding.* Grand Rapids, MI: Eerdmans.

Galtung, Johan. 1968. "A Structural Theory of Integration." *Journal of Peace Research* 5: 4.

Gandhi, Mohandas Karamchand. 1991. "Independence and Decentralization." In *The Essential Writings of Mahatma Gandhi.* Edited by Raghavan Iyer. Delhi: Oxford University Press. First published as "Independence" in *Harijan*, July 28, 1946.

Gandhi, Rajmohan. 1997. *Rajaji: A Life.* New Delhi: Penguin India.

Gangal, S. C. 1993. "Dominance of the Centre." *Indian Express.* April 23.

Garcia-Ramon, Maria Dolors, and Joan Nogue-Font. 1994. "Nationalism and Geography in Catalonia." In *Geography and National Identity.* Edited by David Hooson. Oxford: Blackwell.

Gaworek, N. H. 1977. "Education, Ideology, and Politics: History in Soviet Primary and Secondary Schools." *History Teacher* 11: 1.

The Gazetteer of India, History and Culture. 1988. Volume 2. Second edition. New Delhi: Publications Division, Ministry of Information and Broadcasting, Government of India.

Geertz, Clifford. 1963. "The Integrative Revolution: Primordial Sentiments and Civil Politics in the New States." In *Old Societies and New States.* Edited by Clifford Geertz. New York: Free Press of Glencoe.

———. 1973. *The Interpretation of Culture.* New York: Basic Books.

Gellner, Ernest. 1983. *Nations and Nationalism.* New York: Basil Blackwell.

Ghoshal, U. N. 1959. *A History of Indian Political Ideas.* London: Oxford University Press.

Glazer, Nathan, and Daniel P. Moynihan, eds. 1975. *Ethnicity: Theory and Experience.* Cambridge, MA: Harvard University Press.

Glazer, Nathan, and Reed Ueda. 1983. *Ethnic Groups in History Textbooks.* Washington, DC: Ethics and Public Policy Center.

Gledhill, Alan. 1967. *Pakistan: The Development of Its Law and Constitution.* Second edition. London: Stevens.

Goonatilake, Susantha. 1985. "The Formation of Sri Lanka Culture: Reinterpretation of Chronicle and Archaeological Material." In *Ethnicity and Social Change in Sri Lanka.* Colombo: Social Scientists Association.

Government of India. 1963. Official Languages Act.

Goyal, Shankar. 1996. *History Writing of Early India: New Discoveries and Approaches*. Jodhpur: Kusumanjali Prakashan.

Greenburg, Edward S., and Thomas F. Mayer, eds. 1990. *Changes in the State: Causes and Consequences*. Newbury Park, CA: Sage.

Greeney, Vincent, and Parween Hasan. 1998. "Public Examinations in Pakistan: A System in Need of Reform." In *Education and the State: Fifty Years of Pakistan*. Edited by Pervez Hoodbhoy. Karachi: Oxford University Press.

Greenfeld, Liah. 1992. *Nationalism: Five Roads to Modernity*. Cambridge: Harvard University Press.

Greenstein, Fred. 1965. *Children and Politics*. New Haven: Yale University Press.

———. 1968. "Political Socialization." In *The International Encyclopaedia of the Social Sciences*. Volume 14. New York: Macmillan and Free Press.

Gross, Feliks. 1998. *The Civic and the Tribal State: The State, Ethnicity and the Multiethnic State*. Westport, CT: Greenwood Press.

Guha, Ranajit, ed. 1997. *A Subaltern Studies Reader, 1986–1995*. Minneapolis: University of Minnesota.

Guha, Ranajit, and Gayatri Chakravorty Spivak, eds. 1988. *Selected Subaltern Studies*. New York: Oxford University Press.

Gujral, Ragini. 1984. "The Military, War and National Integration: Symbolic Treatment of the Military and War for Purposes of National Integration in Indian Mass Media." Ph.D. diss., University of Illinois at Urbana-Champaign.

Gunawardena, R.A.L.H. 1985. "The People of the Lion: Sinhala Consciousness in History and Historiography." In *Ethnicity and Social Change in Sri Lanka*. Colombo: Social Scientists Association.

———. 1995. *Historiography in a Time of Ethnic Conflict*. Colombo: Social Scientists Association.

Gunawardena, Victor. 1989. "Provincial Councils System: A Critical Perspective." In *Ideas for Constitutional Reform*. Edited by Chanaka Amaratunga. Colombo: Council for Liberal Democracy.

Gupta, D.C. 1978. *Indian Government and Politics*. Fourth edition. New Delhi: Vikas.

Gurr, Ted Robert. 1988. "War, Revolution, and the Growth of the Coercive State." *Comparative Political Studies* 21, no. 1.

Haas, Ernst B. 1958. *The Uniting of Europe*. Stanford: Stanford University Press.

Hardgrave, Robert L., Jr. 1979. *India: Government and Politics in a Developing Nation*. Second edition. Delhi: Freeman.

Hart, Janet. 1996. *New Voices Within the Nation: Women and the Greek Resistance, 1941–1964*. Ithaca: Cornell University Press.

Hasan, Abrar. 1985. "Pakistan Resolution 1940, and Future Constitutional Framework." *Sind Quarterly* 13, no. 3: 38–48.

Hay, Stephen, ed. 1988. *Sources of Indian Tradition, Volume Two: Modern India and Pakistan*. Second edition. New York: Columbia University Press.

Heesterman, J. C. 1985. *The Inner Conflict of Tradition*. Chicago: University of Chicago Press.

Henige, David P. 1974. *The Chronology of Oral Tradition: Quest for a Chimera*. Oxford: Clarendon Press.

Hennayake, Shantha K. 1993. "Sri Lanka in 1992: Opportunity Missed in Ethno-Nationalist Crisis." *Asian Survey* 33, no. 2: 157–164.

Hobsbawm, Eric. 1983. "Introduction: Inventing Traditions." In *The Invention of Tradition*. Edited by Eric Hobsbawm and Terence Ranger. Cambridge: Cambridge University Press.

———. 1990. *Nations and Nationalism Since 1780: Programme, Myth and Reality*. Cambridge: Cambridge University Press.

Hobsbawm, Eric, and Terence Ranger, eds. 1983. *The Invention of Tradition*. Cambridge: Cambridge University Press.

Holsti, K. J. 1992. "International Theory and War in the Third World." In *The Insecurity Dilemma*. Edited by Brian L. Job. Boulder: Lynne Rienner.

Holt, John C. 1987. "The Radical Egalitarianism of Mahayana Buddhism." In *Equality and the Religious Traditions of Asia*. Edited by R. Siriwardena. London: Pinter.

Hoodbhoy, Pervez, ed. 1998. *Education and the State: Fifty Years of Pakistan*. Karachi: Oxford University Press.

Hoodbhoy, Pervez Amirali, and Abdul Hameed Nayyar. 1985. "Rewriting the History of Pakistan." In *Islam, Politics and the State: The Pakistan Experience*. Edited by Asghar Khan. London: Zed Books.

Hooson, David, ed. 1994. *Geography and National Identity*. Oxford and Cambridge, MA.: Blackwell.

Horowitz, Donald L. 1985. *Ethnic Groups in Conflict*. Berkeley: University of California Press.

Huntington, Samuel P. 1968. *Political Order in Changing Societies*. New Haven: Yale University Press.

———. 1993. "The Clash of Civilizations." *Foreign Affairs* 72, no. 3.

Hussain, Karar. 1988. "Sind: The Rise and Growth of Nationalism." *Sind Quarterly* 16, no. 3: 26–31.

Hussain, Mushahid, and Akmal Hussain. 1993. *Pakistan—Problems of Governance*. Delhi: Konark.

Hutchison, John, and Anthony D. Smith, eds. 1994. *Nationalism*. Oxford: Oxford University Press.

"Ilaignar Padaiye! Ezhu!" (Youth force! Arise!). 1962. *Dravida Nadu*. November 18.

"Imposition of Hindi." 1963. *The Hindu*. May 3.

Inden, Ronald. 1989. *Imagining India*. Oxford: Basil Blackwell.

Indrapala, K. 1980. "Tamil Text-Books." In *School Text Books and Communal Relations in Sri Lanka*. Edited by Reggie Siriwardena, K. Indrapala, Sunil

Bastian, and Sepali Kottegoda. Colombo: Council for Communal Harmony Through the Media.

Irschick, Eugene F. 1986. *Tamil Revivalism in the 1930s*. Madras: Cre-A.

———. 1994. *Dialogue and History: Constructing South India, 1795–1895*. Berkeley: University of California Press.

Islam, Nazrul. 1989. *Pakistan and Malaysia: A Comparative Study in National Integration*. New Delhi: Sterling.

Ismail, Qadri. 1992. "'Boys Will Be Boys': Gender and National Agency in Frantz Fanon and LTTE." *Economic and Political Weekly*. August 1–8.

Jacob, Philip E., and Henry Teune. 1964. "The Integrative Process: Guidelines for Analysis of the Bases of Political Community." In *The Integration of Political Communities*. Edited by Philip E. Jacob and James V. Toscano. Philadelphia and New York: Preceptor and J. B. Lippincott.

Jacob, Philip E., and James V. Toscano, eds. 1964. *The Integration of Political Communities*. Philadelphia and New York: Preceptor and J. B. Lippincott.

Jahan, Rounaq. 1972. *Pakistan: Failure in National Integration*. New York: Columbia University Press.

Jain, S. K. 1994. "Secular, Not Federal, Victory." *Indian Express*. April 8.

Jalal, Ayesha. 1995a. "Conjuring Pakistan: History as Official Imagining." *International Journal of Middle East Studies* 5: 27.

———. 1995b. *Democracy and Authoritarianism in South Asia*. New Delhi: Cambridge University Press.

Jaszi, Oscar. 1961. *The Dissolution of the Habsburg Monarchy*. Chicago: University of Chicago Press.

Jatoi, Hyder Baksh. 1995. "Pakistan and Betrayal of Sindh." *Sind Quarterly* 23, no. 1: 17–36. First published in 1978, vol. 2, as "Sindh and Karachi."

Jauhari, Manorama. 1968. *Politics and Ethics in Ancient India*. Varanasi: Bharatiya Vidya Prakashan.

Jayawardena, Kumari. 1990. *Ethnic and Class Conflicts in Sri Lanka*. Colombo: Sanjiva Books.

———. 1993. "Some Aspects of Religious and Cultural Identity and the Construction of Sinhala Buddhist Womanhood." In *Religion and Political Conflict in South Asia*. Edited by Douglas Allen. Delhi: Oxford University Press.

Jeganathan, Pradeep. 1994. "Reinterpreting History" *Thatched Patio* 7: 1.

Jeganathan, Pradeep, and Qadri Ismail, eds. 1995. *Unmaking the Nation: The Politics of Identity and History in Modern Sri Lanka*. Colombo: Social Scientists Association.

Jennings, Sir Ivor. 1953. *The Constitution of Ceylon*. Third edition. Bombay: Oxford University Press.

Jinnah, M. A. 1950. "Address of Quaid-i-Azam Mohammed Ali Jinnah to the Constituent Assembly of Pakistan on his election as President (11th August, 1947)." In *Speeches of Quaid-i-Azam in the Constituent Assembly of Pakistan (1947–1948)*.

Johnston, R. J., David B. Knight, and Eleanore Kofman, eds. 1988. *Nationalism, Self-Determination and Political Geography*. London: Croom Helm.

Jones, Adele M. E. 1993. *Educational Planning in a Frontier Zone: Dependence, Domination and Legitimacy*. Aldershot: Avebury.

Jones, E., and J. Eyles. 1977. *An Introduction to Social Geography*. London: Oxford University Press.

Jones, Mary McAllester. 1991. *Gaston Bachelard, Subversive Humanist*. Madison: University of Wisconsin Press.

Joyo, Mohammad Ibrahim. 1985. "The Call of Sind—1970." *Sind Quarterly* 13, no. 2: 16–18.

Kailasapathy, K. 1985. "Cultural and Linguistic Consciousness of the Tamil Community." In *Ethnicity and Social Change in Sri Lanka*. Colombo: Social Scientists Association.

Kalansooriya, Ranga. 1998. "Muslim Grievances Must Be Structurally Addressed: Interview with Rauf Hakeem (General Secretary, Sri Lanka Muslim Congress)." *Daily News* (Colombo). April 3.

Kanapathipillai, Valli. 1990. "July 1983: The Survivor's Experience." In *Mirrors of Violence: Communities, Riots and Survivors in South Asia*. Edited by Veena Das. Delhi: Oxford University Press.

Kautilya. 1987. *The Arthashastra*. Translated by L. N. Rangarajan. New Delhi: Penguin.

Kaviraj, Sudipta. 1993. "The Imaginary Institution of India." In *Subaltern Studies VII: Writings on South Asian History and Society*. Edited by Partha Chatterjee and Gyanendra Pandey. Delhi: Oxford University Press.

Kazi, Aftab. 1987. *Ethnicity and Education in Nation-Building*. Lanham, MD: University Press of America.

———. 1991. "Education, Ethnicity and Socialisation in Pakistan." *Sind Quarterly* 19, nos. 1, 2, 3.

Kedourie, Elie. 1970. "Introduction." In *Nationalism in Asia and Africa*. Edited by Elie Kedourie. London: Frank Cass.

Keohane, Robert. 1984. *After Hegemony*. Princeton: Princeton University Press.

Keyes, Charles F., ed. 1981. *Ethnic Change*. London: University of Washington Press.

Khan, A. Sattar. 1993. "The Role of Sindh in the Pakistan Movement." *Journal of the Research Society of Pakistan* 30, no. 1.

Khan, Asghar, ed. 1985. *Islam, Politics and the State: The Pakistan Experience*. London: Zed Books.

Khan, Darya. 1989. "A Sindhi View" *Sind Quarterly* 17, no. 4.

Khan, Jahangir. 1995. "Split and Prosper." *Economic Times*. January 9.

Khan, Mohammad Asghar. 1984. "Thoughts on Sind." *Sind Quarterly* 12, no. 2.

Khory, Kavita R. 1995. "National Integration and the Politics of Identity in Pakistan." *Nationalism and Ethnic Politics* 1, no. 4.

Khuhro, Hameeda. 1978. *The Making of Modern Sind: British Policy and Social Change in the Nineteenth Century.* Karachi: Indus.

Khuhro, Hamida. 1992. "The Separation of Sind and the Working of an Autonomous Province." *Sindhological Studies* (Summer): 43–66.

Kirby, Andrew. 1989. "State, Local State, Context, and Spatiality: A Reappraisal of State Theory." In *The Elusive State: International and Comparative Perspectives.* Edited by James A. Caporaso. Newbury Park, CA: Sage.

Knight, David B. 1982. "Identity and Territory: Geographical Perspectives on Nationalism and Regionalism." *Annals of the Association of American Geographers* 72.

Kodikara, Shelton U. 1996. "Ethnonationalism in South Asia: A Comparative Regional Perspective." In *Refugees and Regional Security in South Asia.* Edited by Lok Raj Baral and S. D. Muni. New Delhi: Konark.

Kohli, Atul, ed. 1988. *India's Democracy.* Princeton: Princeton University Press.

Kohn, Hans. 1951. *The Idea of Nationalism.* New York: Macmillan.

Kothari, Rajni. 1970. *Politics in India.* New Delhi: Orient Longman.

Krasner, Stephen D. 1989. "Sovereignty: An Institutional Perspective." In *International and Comparative Perspectives.* Edited by James A. Caporaso. Newbury Park, CA: Sage.

Krishna, Sankaran. 1993. "Cricket, Nationalism and the Subcontinental Fan." *Pravada* 2, no. 2.

Krishnan, G. V. 1995. "New Party Will Be Launched in Tamil Nadu Today." *Times of India.* August 15.

Kumar, Arun. 1976. "Curtain on DMK Rule." *India Today.* February 15.

Kumar, Krishna. 1996. *Learning from Conflict.* Hyderabad: Orient Longman.

Kymlicka, Will. 1998. "Is Federalism a Viable Alternative to Secession?" In *Theories of Secession.* Edited by Percy B. Lehning. London and New York: Routledge.

LaPalombara, Joseph. 1963. *Bureaucracy and Political Development.* Princeton: Princeton University Press.

LaPalombara, Joseph, and Myron Weiner, eds. 1966. *Political Parties and Political Development.* Princeton: Princeton University Press.

The Laputan Flapper. 1959. "New State of Singapore Is Born!" *Homeland* 2, no. 52 (June 7): 7.

Lari, Suhail Zaheer. 1994. *A History of Sind.* Karachi: Oxford University Press.

Laski, Harold J. 1921. *Studies in the Problem of Sovereignty.* New York: H. Fertig. Reprint 1968.

———. 1960. *A Grammar of Politics.* London: George Allen & Unwin.

Lawton, Dennis. 1975. *Class, Culture and the Curriculum.* London and New York: Routledge and Kegan Paul.

Lee, Raymond, ed. 1986. "Ethnicity and Ethnic Relations in Malaysia." Occasional paper no. 12, Monograph Series on Southeast Asia, Center for Southeast Asian Studies, Northern Illinois University, Dekalb.

Lerner, Daniel. 1958. *The Passing of Traditional Society: Modernizing the Middle East*. New York: Free Press.

Levy, Marion J., Jr. 1966. *Modernization and the Structure of Societies*. Princeton: Princeton University Press.

Lewellen, Ted C. 1992. *Political Anthropology: An Introduction*. Second edition. Westport, CT, and London: Bergin & Garvey.

Little, David. 1994. *Sri Lanka: The Invention of Enmity*. Washington, DC: U.S.I.P. Press.

Loganathan, Ketheshwaran. 1996. *Sri Lanka: Lost Opportunities*. Colombo: Centre for Policy Research and Analysis, University of Colombo.

Lovett, Sir H. Verney, K.C.S.I. 1932. "The Indian Governments, 1858–1918." In *The Cambridge History of India, Volume VI: The Indian Empire 1858–1918*. Edited by H. H. Dodwell. New York: Macmillan; Cambridge: Cambridge University Press.

Machiavelli, Niccolo. 1992. *The Prince*. Translated by N. H. Thomson. Dover Thrift Editions. New York: Dover.

Madison, James. 1999. "Federalist Paper No.10." *The Federalist Papers*. Edited by Clinton Rossiter. New York: Mentor.

Maheshwari, S. R. 1996. "Abuse of Article 356." *Indian Express*. December 22.

Majumdar, R. C., and K. K. Datta. 1963. "Administrative System." In *The History and Culture of the Indian People: British Paramountcy and Indian Renaissance*. Volume 9, Part 1. Edited by R. C. Majumdar. Bombay: Bharatiya Vidya Bhavan.

Majumdar, R. C., H. C. Raychaudhuri, and Kalikinkar Datta. 1973. *An Advanced History of India*. Third edition. Delhi: Macmillan India.

Malik, Iftikhar H. 1993. "Ethnicity and Political Ethos in Sindh: A Case Study of the Muhajireen of Karachi." In *Ethnicity, Identity, Migration: The South Asian Context*. Edited by Milton Israel and N. K. Wagle. Toronto: University of Toronto.

Malik, Mohammed Sayeed. 1994. "Rulers and Governed." *Sunday Observer*. January 23.

Malkki, Liisa. 1997. "National Geographic: The Rooting of Peoples and the Territorialization of National Identity Among Scholars and Refugees." In *Culture, Power, Place: Explorations in Critical Anthropology*. Edited by Akhil Gupta and James Ferguson. Durham and London: Duke University Press.

Mani, Lata. 1990. "Multiple Mediations: Feminist Scholarship in the Age of Multinational Reception." *Feminist Review* 35 (Summer).

Mani, V. R. 1993. "The Emasculation of Dravidian Parties." *Times of India*. October 30.

———. 1995. "Tamil 'Protection Force' Launched." *Times of India*. October 31.

Mann, Michael. 1985. "The Autonomous Power of the State." *Archives Europeennes de Sociologie* 25, no. 1: 185–213.

————. 1986. *The Sources of Social Power, Volume I: A History of Power from the Beginning to* A.D. *1760.* Cambridge: Cambridge University Press.

————. 1988. *States, War and Capitalism: Studies in Political Sociology.* Oxford: Basil Blackwell.

Manogaran, Chelvanayagam, and Bryan Pfaffenberger. 1994. *The Sri Lankan Tamils: Ethnicity and Identity.* Boulder: Westview Press.

Maoz, Zeev. 1989. "Joining the Club of Nations: Political Development and International Conflict, 1816–1976." *International Studies Quarterly* 33: 199–231.

March, James C., and Johan P. Olsen. 1984. "The New Institutionalism: Organizational Factors in Political Life." *American Political Science Review* 78: 3.

Marenin. 1990. "The Police and the Coercive Nature of the State." In *Changes in the State: Causes and Consequences.* Edited by Edward S. Greenburg and Thomas F. Mayer. Newbury Park, CA: Sage.

Marthandam, Nambi. 1993. "Is Revolution Brewing?" *Pioneer.* January 31.

Mateke, P. 1992. "Curzon and the Idea of Transfer of Sind to Punjab." *Sindhological Studies* (Summer).

Mathews, Bruce. 1985. "The Sri Lankan Buddhist Philosophy of History and Its Relationship to the National Question." *Ethnic Studies Report* 3: 2.

Mayer, A. J. 1977. "Industrial Crises and War Since 1870." In *Revolutionary Situations in Europe, 1917–1922.* Edited by C. L. Bertrand. Montreal: Interuniversity Centre for European Studies.

McGilvray, Dennis B. 1982. "Mukkuvar Vannimai: Tamil Caste and Matriclan Ideology in Batticaloa, Sri Lanka." In *Caste Ideology and Interaction.* Edited by D. B. McGilvray. Cambridge: Cambridge University Press.

McGowan, William. 1992. *Only Man Is Vile: The Tragedy of Sri Lanka.* Calcutta: Rupa.

Mearns, Gordon P. 1991. *Malaysian Politics: The Second Generation.* Singapore: Oxford University Press.

Mehkri, G. M. 1994. "Sindh and Muhajirism—Some Candid Thoughts— Glaring Facts and Gaping Realities." *Sind Quarterly* 22, no. 4.

Merritt, Richard L. 1970. "Perspectives on History in Divided Germany." In *Public Opinion and Historians: Interdisciplinary Perspectives.* Edited by Melvin Small. Detroit: Wayne State University Press.

Migdal, Joel. 1988. *Strong Societies, Weak Societies.* Princeton: Princeton University Press.

Miller, Catherine, and Al-Amin Abu-Manga. 1992. *Language Change and National Integration : Rural Migrants in Khartoum.* Khartoum: Khartoum University Press.

Mishra, Vibhuti Bhushan. 1987. *Evolution of the Constitutional History of India, 1773–1947: With Special Reference to the Role of the Indian National Congress and the Minorities.* Delhi: Mittal.

Misra, B. B. 1990. *The Unification and Division of India.* Oxford: Oxford University Press.

Mitrany, David. 1946. *A Working Peace System: An Argument for the Functional Development of International Organization.* London: National Peace Council.

Modelski, George. 1964. "Kautilya: Foreign Policy and International System in the Ancient Hindu World." *American Political Science Review* 58, no. 3: 549–560.

Montville, Joseph V., ed. 1990. *Conflict and Peacemaking in Multiethnic Societies.* Lexington, MA: Lexington Books.

Moore, Barrington, Jr. 1966. *The Social Origins of Dictatorship and Democracy: Lord and Peasant in the Making of the Modern World.* Boston: Beacon Press.

Moore, Sally Falk, ed. 1993. *Moralizing States and the Ethnography of the Present.* American Ethnological Society Monograph Series no. 5.

"More, Not Merrier." 1998. *Indian Express.* July 1.

Morris-Jones, W. H. 1967. *The Government and Politics of India.* New York: Anchor.

Morrow, Raymond Allan, and Carlos Alberto Torres. 1995. *Social Theory and Education: A Critique of Social and Cultural Reproduction.* Albany: SUNY Press.

Mukarji, Nirmal. 1992. "A More Federal India." *The Hindu.* March 18.

Munshi, K. M. 1967. *The President Under the Indian Constitutions.* Bombay: Bharatiya Vidya Bhavan.

Murari, S. 1992. "Leaving PMK Alone Is the Wisest Course." *Deccan Herald.* October 4.

"Namadhu Pani" (Our task). 1962. *Dravida Nadu.* November 11.

Namboodiri, A.V.S. 1994. "Salutary but Not Perfect." *Deccan Herald.* March 24.

Nandy, Ashis. 1985. *The Tao of Cricket.* New Delhi: Penguin India.

Nanjundaswamy, M. D. 1992. "The Centre's Cat's Paw." *Times of India.* January 19.

National Steering Committee on Textbook Evaluation. 1994. *Recommendations and Report II.* New Delhi: National Council of Educational Research and Training.

NCERT. 1988. *Guidelines and Syllabi for Upper Primary Stage Classes VI–VIII.* New Delhi: NCERT.

———. 1994. *Ancient India: A Textbook of History for Class VI.* Eighth reprint edition. New Delhi: NCERT.

Nef, J. U. 1959. *War and Human Progress: An Essay on the Rise of Industrial Civilization.* Cambridge: Harvard University Press.

Nehru, Jawaharlal. 1959. *The Discovery of India.* New York: Anchor.

———. 1985. *Letters to Chief Ministers, 1947–64.* Edited by G. Parthasarathi. Delhi: Oxford University Press.

"Nehru's Blind Spot—The South." 1958. *Homeland* 2, no 8 (August): 3.

Nettl, J. P. 1968. "The State as a Conceptual Variable." *World Politics* 20.

Newburg, Paula. 1995. *Judging the State: Courts and Constitutional Politics in Pakistan*. Cambridge: Cambridge University Press.

Newton, Scott. N.d. "Approaches to the Phenomenology of Ethnicity." *Thatched Patio*.

Nithiyanandan, V. 1987. "An Analysis of Economic Factors Behind the Origin and Development of Tamil Nationalism in Sri Lanka." In *Facets of Ethnicity in Sri Lanka*. Edited by Charles Abeysekera and Newton Gunasinghe. Colombo: Social Scientists Association.

Noorani, A. G. 1991. "The Five Federal Flaws." *Indian Express*. October 15.

Nyang, Sulayman S. 1974. *The Role of the Gambian Political Parties in National Integration*. Sahel documents and dissertations.

Obeyesekere, Gananath. 1993. "Dutthagamini and the Buddhist Conscience." In *Religion and Political Conflict in South Asia*. Edited by Douglas Allen. Delhi: Oxford University Press.

———. 1994. "Ethnicity and Pluralism in Sri Lanka." *Thatched Patio* 7, no. 2.

Olwig, Karen Fog, and Kirsten Hastrup, eds. 1997. *Siting Culture: The Shifting Anthropological Object*. London and New York: Routledge.

Organski, Kenneth. 1965. *The Stages of Political Development*. New York: Alfred A. Knopf.

Oye, Kenneth A. 1986. "Explaining Cooperation Under Anarchy: Hypotheses and Strategies." In *Cooperation Under Anarchy*. Edited by Kenneth A. Oye. Princeton: Princeton University Press.

———, ed. 1986. *Cooperation Under Anarchy*. Princeton: Princeton University Press.

Paddison, Ronan. 1983a. "Intergovernmental Relationships and the Territorial Structure of Federal States." In *Pluralism and Political Geography: People, Territory and State*. Edited by Nurit Kliot and Stanley Waterman. London and Canberra: Croom Helm; New York: St. Martin's Press.

———. 1983b. *The Fragmented State: The Political Geography of Power*. Oxford: Basil Blackwell.

———. 1988. *The Fragmented State: The Political Geography of Power*. New York: St. Martin's Press.

Palanithurai, G. 1989. *Changing Contours of Ethnic Movement: A Case Study of Dravidian Movement*. Department of Political Science Monograph Series 2. Tamil Nadu: Annamalai University.

———. 1994. *Caste Politics and Society in Tamilnadu*. Delhi: Kanishka.

Pandian, J. 1987. *Caste, Nationalism and Ethnicity: An Interpretation of Tamil Cultural History and Social Order*. Bombay: Popular Prakashan.

Pandian, M.S.S. 1992. *The Image Trap*. Newbury Park, CA: Sage.

Panhwar, M. H. 1990. "The Economic Plight of Sindh Under Pakistan." *Sind Quarterly* 18, no. 2: 37–61.

Pant, A. D., and Shiva K. Gupta, eds. 1985. *Multi-Ethnicity and National Integration*. Allahabad: Vohra.

Paranavitane, Senarat. 1993. "Aryan Settlements: The Sinhalese." In *University of Ceylon History of Ceylon.* Volume 1. Edited by Senarat Paranavitane.

Parekh, Bhikhu. 1986. "Some Reflections on the Hindu Tradition of Political Thought." In *Political Thought in Modern India.* Edited by Thomas Pantham and Kenneth L. Deutsch. New Delhi: Sage.

————. 1995. "Jawaharlal Nehru and the Crisis of Modernisation." In *Crisis and Change in Contemporary India.* Edited by Upendra Baxi and Bhikhu Parekh. New Delhi: Sage.

Parsons, Talcott. 1951. *The Social System.* Glencoe, IL: Free Press.

Parsons, Talcott, and Edward A. Shils, eds. 1951. *Toward a General Theory of Action.* Cambridge: Harvard University Press.

Parthasarathy, R. 1992. "A Seditious Act." *The Hindu.* September 20.

Perera, Sasanka. 1991. "Teaching and Learning Hatred: The Role of Education and Socialization in Sri Lankan Ethnic Conflict." Ph.D. diss., University of California, Santa Barbara.

Pfaffenberger, Bryan. 1990. "Ethnic Conflict and Youth Insurgency in Sri Lanka: The Social Origins of Tamil Separatism." In *Conflict and Peacemaking in Multiethnic Societies.* Edited by Joseph V. Montville. Lexington, MA: Lexington Books.

Pieterse, Jan Nederveen, and Bhikhu Parekh, eds. 1995. *The Decolonization of Imagination: Culture, Knowledge and Power.* London: Zed Books.

Powell, Avril. 1996. "Perceptions of the Past." In *The Transmission of Knowledge in South Asia.* Edited by Nigel Crook. Delhi: Oxford University Press.

Prasad, Krishna. 1994. "Countdown to Confrontation." *Sunday Observer.* January 23.

Premdas, Ralph R., S.W.R. de A. Samarasinghe, and Alan B. Anderson, eds. 1990. *Secessionist Movements in Comparative Perpective.* London: Pinter.

Pye, Lucien, and Sidney Verba, eds. 1965. *Political Culture and Political Development.* Princeton: Princeton University Press.

Pylee, M. V. 1980. *Constitutional History of India, 1600–1950.* Second revised edition. Bombay: Asia Publishing House.

Qadri, A. Jamil, ed. 1988. *Intra-Societal Tension and National Integration (A Psychological Assessment).* New Delhi: Concept.

Radcliffe, Sarah, and Sallie Westwood. 1996. *Remaking the Nation: Place, Identity and Politics in Latin America.* London and New York: Routledge.

Raghavan, C. 1993. "Anything but Secessionist." *The Hindu.* August 22.

Ragsdale, Tod Anthony. 1989. *Once a Hermit Kingdom: Ethnicity, Education, and National Integration in Nepal.* New Delhi: Manohar.

Rajadurai, S. V. 1993. *(H)Indu (H)Indi India.* Madras: Manivacakkar Pathipakkam.

Rajadurai, S. V., and V. Geetha. 1996. "DMK: Cultural Limits to Political Consensus." In *Region, Religion, Caste, Gender and Culture in*

Contemporary India. Volume 3 of *Social Change and Political Discourse in India, Structures of Power, Movements of Resistance.* Edited by T. V. Sathyamurthy. Delhi: Oxford University Press.

Rajagopalan, Swarna. 1993. "Regime Maintenance in Two Pre-Modern Indian Polities." Unpublished.

———. 1997a. "National Integration in India, Sri Lanka and Pakistan: Constitutional and Elite Visions." *Nationalism and Ethnic Politics* 3, no. 4: 1-38.

———. 1997b. "Tamil Is My Mother; India is a Feeling in My Heart." Paper presented at the South Asia Conference, Madison, Wisconsin, October.

———. 1997c. "A Traveller's Collection of Tales." *Nethra* (International Centre for Ethnic Studies, Colombo) 1, no. 4.

———. 1998. "National Integration: The State in Search of Community." Ph.D. diss., University of Illinois at Urbana-Champaign.

———. 1999. "Internal Unit Demarcation and National Identity." *Nationalism and Ethnic Politics* 5, nos. 3–4: 191–211.

———. 2000. "Demarcating Units, Re-distributing Authority: Pakistan, India, Sri Lanka." In *Re-distribution of Authority: A Cross-Regional Perspective.* Edited by Jeanie J. Bukowski and Swarna Rajagopalan. Westport, CT: Praeger.

Rajanayagam, Dagmar-Hellmann. 1994. "Tamils and the Meaning of History." In *The Sri Lankan Tamils: Ethnicity and Identity.* Edited by Chelvadurai Manogaran and Bryan Pfaffenberger. Boulder: Westview Press.

Rajayyan, K. 1982. *History of Tamil Nadu, 1565–1982.* Madras: Raj.

Ramachandran, S., ed. 1975. *Anna Speaks: At the Rajya Sabha 1962–66.* New Delhi: Orient Longman.

Ramamurti, P. 1987. *The Freedom Struggle and the Dravidian Movement.* Hyderabad: Orient Longman.

Ramaswamy, Sumathi. 1993. "En/gendering Language: The Poetics of Tamil Identity." *Comparative Study of Society and History* 35.

———. 1997. *Passions of the Tongue, Language Devotion to Tamil India, 1891–1970.* Berkeley: University of California Press.

Random House Webster's College Dictionary. 1992. New York: Random House.

Rangarajan, Mahesh. 1995a. "Devotional Dravidian Movement in T.N." *Times of India.* March 22.

———. 1995b. "Star Crossed Trek." *Telegraph.* October 21.

Rao, B. Shiva. 1957. *Select Documents.* Volume 3.

Rao, V. G. Prasad. N.d. "Three Kazhagams in Tamil Nadu," *Times of India.* April 21.

Rasler Karen, and William Thompson. 1989. *War and State Making: The Shaping of Global Powers.* Boston: Unwin Hyman.

Ratnagar, Shereen. 1996. "Ideology and the Nature of Political Consolidation and Expansion: An Archaeological Case." In *Ideology and the Formation of Early States.* Edited by Henri J. M. Claessen and Jarich G. Oosten. Leiden: E. J. Brill.

"Reconstructing Nations and States." 1993. *Daedalus*, special issue 122, no. 3 (Summer).

Report of the Commission on Centre-State Relations. 1988. Volume 2: *Government of India, Ministry of Home Affairs.* New Delhi: Government Press.

Richards, John. 1993. *The Mughal Empire.* Cambridge: Cambridge University Press.

Richards, John, ed. 1981. *Kingship and Authority in South Asia.* Second edition. Madison: University of Wisconsin.

Rizvi, S.A.A. 1987. *The Wonder That Was India.* Volume 2. London: Sidgwick & Jackson.

Roberts, Michael. 1990. "Noise as Cultural Struggle: Tom-Tom Beating, the British, and Communal Disturbances in Sri Lanka." In *Mirrors of Violence: Communities, Riots and Survivors in South Asia.* Edited by Veena Das. Delhi: Oxford University Press.

———. 1994. *Exploring Confrontation.* Chur, Switzerland: Harwood Academic.

Rockman, Bert A. 1989. "Minding the State—Or a State of Mind? Issues in the Comparative Conceptualization of the State." In *The Elusive State: International and Comparative Perspectives.* Edited by James A. Caporaso. Newbury Park, CA: Sage.

Rokkan, Stein. 1969. "Models and Methods in the Comparative Study of Nation-Building." *Acta Sociologica.*

———. 1975. "Dimensions of State Formation and Nation-Building: A Possible Paradigm for Research on Variations Within Europe." In *The Formations of National States in Western Europe.* Edited by Charles Tilly. Princeton: Princeton University Press.

———. 1981. "Territories, Nations, Parties: Towards a Geoeconomic-Geopolitical Model for the Explanation of Variations Within Western Europe." In *From National Development to Global Community: Essays in Honor of Karl W. Deutsch.* Edited by Richard L. Merritt and Bruce M. Russett. London: Allen Unwin.

Rokkan, Stein, and Derek Urwin. 1983. *Economy Territory Identity: Politics of West European Peripheries.* London: Sage.

Rosenau, James N. 1989. "The State in an Era of Cascading Politics: Wavering Concept, Widening Competence, Withering Colossus, or Weathering Change?" In *The Elusive State: International and Comparative Perspectives.* Edited by James A. Caporaso. Newbury Park, CA: Sage.

Rosenau, James N., and Ernst-Otto Czempiel, eds. 1992. *Governance Without Government: Order and Change in World Politics.* Cambridge: Cambridge University Press.

Rostow, W. W. 1960. *The Stages of Economic Growth.* New York: Cambridge University Press.

Rothchild, Donald S. 1970. *Citizenship and National Integration: The Non-African Crisis in Kenya.* Volume 1, Study 3, of *Studies in Race and Nations.* Denver: University of Denver.

Roy, Beth. 1994. *Some Trouble with Cows: Making Sense of Social Conflict.* Berkeley: University of California Press.

Rudolph, Lloyd I., ed. 1984. *Cultural Policy in India.* Delhi: Chanakya.

Rudolph, Lloyd I., and Susanne Hoeber Rudolph. 1982. "Cultural Policy, the Textbook Controversy and Indian Identity." In *The States of South Asia: Problems of National Integration.* Edited by A. Jeyaratnam Wilson and Dennis Dalton. Honolulu: University of Hawaii Press.

———. 1985. "The Subcontinental Empire and the Regional Kingdom in Indian State Formation." In *Region and Nation in India.* Edited by Paul Wallace. New Delhi: Oxford University Press.

Rudolph, Susanne Hoeber, and Lloyd I. Rudolph. 1984. "Rethinking Secularism: Genesis and Implications of the Textbook Controversy, 1977–79." In *Cultural Policy in India.* Edited by Lloyd I. Rudolph. Delhi: Chanakya.

Ruggie, John Gerard. 1993. "Territoriality and Beyond: Problematizing Modernity in International Relations." *International Organization* 47, no. 1: 139–174.

Runciman, David. 1997. *Pluralism and the Personality of the State.* Cambridge: Cambridge University Press.

Rupesinghe, Kumar. "Ethnic Conflicts in South Asia: The Case of Sri Lanka and the Indian Peace-keeping Force (IPKF)." *Journal of Peace Research* 20, no. 4: 337–350.

Sabine, George H., and Thomas L. Thornton. 1973. *A History of Political Theory.* Fourth edition. Delhi: Oxford University Press.

Sack, Robert David. 1980. *Conceptions of Space in Social Thought.* Minneapolis: University of Minnesota Press.

———. 1986. *Human Territoriality: Its Theory and History.* Cambridge: Cambridge University Press.

Salamat, Zarina. 1992. *Pakistan, 1947–58: A Historical Review.* Islamabad: National Institute of Historical and Cultural Research.

Salgado, Nirmala S. 1987. "Equality and Inequality in the Religious and Cultural Traditions of Hinduism and Buddhism." In *Equality and the Religious Traditions of Asia.* Edited by R. Siriwardena. London: Pinter.

Samaddar, Ranabir. 1995. "Territory and People: The Disciplining of Historical Memory." In *Texts of Power: Emerging Disciplines in Colonial Bengal.* Edited by Partha Chatterjee. Minneapolis: University of Minnesota.

Samaraweera, Vijaya. 1973. "The Colebrooke-Cameron Reforms." In *The University of Ceylon, The History of Ceylon.* Volume 3. Edited by K. M. de Silva. Peradeniya: University of Ceylon.

Sarkaria Commission Report. See *Report of the Commission on Centre-State Relations.*

Sastri, K.A.A. Nilakanta. 1976. *A History of South India*. Madras: Oxford University Press.

Sathananthan, Sachithanandam. 1998. "Self-Determination: A Ceylon Tamil Perspective." *Accord: An International Review of Peace Initiatives* (August). Accessed at http://www.c-r.org/cr/acc_sri/self_determ.htm on March 10, 2001.

Sathyamurthy, T. V. 1997. "Political Changes in Tamil Nadu." *Review of Development and Change* 2, no. 1 (January-June).

Sayed, G. M. 1984. "Sind: The Beginnings of Discontent and Disillusionment." *Sind Quarterly* 12, no. 1: 6–9. First published in 1949.

Schaeffer, Robert. 1990. *Warpaths: The Politics of Partition*. New York: Hill and Wang.

Schermerhorn, R. A. 1970. *Comparative Ethnic Relations: A Framework for Theory and Research*. New York: Random House.

———. 1978. *Ethnic Plurality in India*. Tucson: University of Arizona Press.

Schneider, Jane, and Rayna Rapp, eds. 1995. *Articulating Hidden Histories: Exploring the Influence of Eric R. Wolf*. Berkeley and Los Angeles: University of California Press.

Schwartzberg, Joseph E., ed. 1978. *A Historical Atlas of South Asia*. Chicago and London: University of Chicago Press.

Schwarz, Henry. 1997. *Writing Cultural History in Colonial and Postcolonial India*. Philadelphia: University of Pennsylvania Press.

Scott, James C. 1985. *Weapons of the Weak*. New Haven: Yale University Press.

"Secret Documents on One Unit: A Conspiracy." 1989–1990. Parts 1, 2 and 3. *Sind Quarterly* 17, nos. 3–4, and 18, no. 1.

Sen Gupta, Bhabani. 1996. *India—Problems of Governance*. Delhi: Konark.

Shah, Sayid Ghulam Mustafa. 1978. "Sind: Causes of Present Discontent: A Socio-Political Analysis." *Sind Quarterly* 6, no. 2: 1–8.

———. 1983. "Sind: Causes of Present Discontent. An Urdu Conference Is Patriotic, a Punjabi Conference Is Patriotic, but a Sindhi Conference Is Unpatriotic!" *Sind Quarterly* 11, no. 4.

———. 1984. "Sind: Causes of Present Discontent. Sindhi Leadership, Its Hopes and Hazards." *Sind Quarterly* 12, no. 1: 1–9.

———. 1985. "Sind—Conflagration of Martial Laws and Its Resurrection from Ashes—I." *Sind Quarterly* 15, no. 1.

———. 1988. "Muhajirism, a Suicidal Nationalism: Some Forebodings and Some Caution." *Sind Quarterly* 16, no. 2.

Sharma, Arvind, ed. 1991. *Essays on the Mahabharata*. Leiden: E. J. Brill.

Sharma, R. S. 1989. *Origin of the State in India*. D. D. Kosambi Memorial Lectures (1987). Bombay: University of Bombay.

Sharma, Ramesh Chandra, Atul Kumar Singh, Sugam Anand, Gyaneshwar Chaturvedi, and Jayati Chaturvedi. 1991. *Historiography and Historians in India Since Independence*. Agra: M. G. Publishers.

Sharma, Suman. 1995. *State Boundary Changes in India: Constitutional Provisions and Consequences.* Chandigarh: Deep & Deep.

Sharma, Yog Raj. 1992. *State Autonomy and National Integration: Identity Crises of the Sikhs.* Jammu, India: Vinod.

Shastri, Ameeta. 1983. "Evolution of the Contemporary Political Formation of Sri Lanka." *South Asia Bulletin* 3, no. 1.

Shastri, Amita. 1992. "Sri Lanka's Provincial Council System: A Solution to the Ethnic Problem?" *Asian Survey* 32, no. 8.

Shekhar, G. C. 1992. "Reviving an Old Cause." *Telegraph.* October 3.

Shivaprakash, G. S. 1992. "Opening a Pandora's Box . . . ." *Deccan Herald.* October 26.

Short, John Rennie. 1993. *An Introduction to Political Geography.* London: Routledge.

Sigel, Roberta S., ed. 1970. *Learning About Politics.* New York: Random House.

Simmel, Georg. 1956. *Conflict.* Translated by K. H. Woldff. Glencoe, IL: Free Press.

"Sindhi as the Official Language of the Province of Sind." 1982. *Sind Quarterly* 10, no. 1: 22–34.

Singer, Marshall R. 1990. "Prospects for Conflict Management in the Sri Lankan Ethnic Crisis." In *Conflict and Peacemanking in Multiethnic Societies.* Edited by Joseph V. Montville. Lexington, MA: Lexington Books.

———. 1992. "Sri Lanka's Tamil-Sinhalese Ethnic Conflict." *Asian Survey* 32, no. 8.

Singh, Gurmukh. 1994. "Autonomous Councils Better Than New States." *Times of India.* October 12.

Singh, L. P. 1989. *National Integration.* New Delhi: Centre for Policy Research.

Singh, Satya Narain. 1992. *Political Ideas and Institutions Under the Mauryas.* Patna and New Delhi: Janaki Prakashan.

Siriwardena, R., ed. 1987. *Equality and the Religious Traditions of Asia.* London: Pinter.

Siriwardena, Reggie, K. Indrapala, Sunil Bastian, and Sepali Kottegoda. 1980. *School Text Books and Communal Relations in Sri Lanka.* Colombo: Council for Communal Harmony Through the Media.

Siriweera, W. I. 1985. "The Duthugamani-Elara Episode: A Reassessment." *Ethnicity and Social Change in Sri Lanka.* Colombo: Social Scientists Association.

Sivathamby, Karthigesu. 1979. "Hindu Reaction to Christian Proselytization and Westernization in 19th Century Sri Lanka." *Social Science Review*, no. 1.

———. 1987. "The Sri Lankan Ethnic Crisis and Muslim-Tamil Relationships—A Socio-Political Review." In *Facets of Ethnicity in Sri*

Lanka. Edited by Charles Abeysekera and Newton Gunasinghe. Colombo: Social Scientists Association.

Skocpol, Theda. 1979. *States and Social Revolutions: A Comparative Analysis of France, Russia, and China*. New York: Cambridge University Press.

Smith, Anthony D. 1991. *National Identity*. Reno: University of Nevada Press.

Smith, Graham, ed. 1995. *Federalism: The Multiethnic Challenge*. London and New York: Longman.

Snidal, Duncan. 1986. "The Game Theory of International Politics." In *Cooperation Under Anarchy*. Edited by Kenneth A. Oye. Princeton: Princeton University Press.

Snyder, Jack. 1991. *Myths of Empire: Domestic Politics and International Ambition*. Ithaca: Cornell University Press.

Sobhan, Rehman. 1993. *Bangladesh: Problems of Governance*. Delhi: Konark.

Sommer, R. 1969. *Personal Space: The Behavioral Basis of Design*. Englewood Cliffs, NJ: Prentice-Hall.

Sorabjee, Soli J. 1994. "A Landmark Judgment." *The Week*. April 3.

Spaeth, Anthony. 1993. "The People of the Lion." *Seminar,* no. 401 (January).

Spear, Percival. 1970. *A History of India*. Volume 2. Harmondsworth, England: Penguin Books.

Special Correspondent. 1996. "Gowda Rules Out Fresh Reorganisation of States." *The Hindu*. August 18.

Spivak, Gayatri Chakravorty. 1985. "Subaltern Studies: Deconstructing Historiography." In *Subaltern Studies IV: Writings on South Asian History and Society*. Edited by Ranajit Guha. Delhi: Oxford University Press.

"Sri Lanka: Provincial Council Elections and Devolution." 1993. *Thatched Patio*, special issue (International Centre for Ethnic Studies, Colombo). 6, no. 5.

Srinivas, M. N. 1994. "Tamil Nadu Past and Present." *Times of India*. March 17.

Srinivasan, Amrit. 1990. "The Survivor in the Study of Violence." In *Mirrors of Violence: Communities, Riots and Survivors in South Asia*. Edited by Veena Das. Delhi: Oxford University Press.

Stalin, Joseph. 1994. "The Nation." In *Nationalism*. Edited by John Hutchinson and Anthony D. Smith. Oxford: Oxford University Press.

"The State." 1979. *Daedalus*, special issue, 108, no. 4.

"Statehood Is the New Panacea for Backwardness." 1996. *Indian Express*. September 19.

Streusand, Douglas E. 1989. *The Formation of the Mughal Empire*. Delhi: Oxford University Press.

Subrahmanian, N. 1996. *The Tamils (Their History, Culture and Civilization)*. Chemmancherry: Institute of Asian Studies.

Subramanian, Narendra. 1999. *Ethnicity and Populist Mobilization: Political Parties, Citizens and Democracy in South India*. Delhi: Oxford University Press.

Subramanian, P. 1994. *Social History of the Tamils 1701–1947*. New Delhi: D. K. Printworld.

Subramanian, T. S. 1995. "An Upbeat Meet." *Frontline*. July 28.

Suntharalingam, R. 1974. *Politics and Nationalist Awakening in South India, 1852–1891*. Tucson: University of Arizona Press.

Sura. 1962. "Ellai Kaappom" (We will protect the frontier). *Dravida Nadu*. November 4.

Sura, Kavignar. K. 1962. "Arappuratchi" (Moral revolution). *Dravida Nadu*. September 16.

Suryanarayan, V. 2000. "India as a Safe Haven?" *Frontline*. December 23.

Syed, G. M. 1999. *A Nation in Chains*. Sind: G. M. Syed Institute of Social Sciences. First published in 1974. Accessed at http://members. unlimited.net/~saghir/saeen/nation/saeen-book5.htm on July 14, 1999.

Sylvester, Christine. 1994. *Feminist Theory and International Relations in a Postmodern Era*. Cambridge: Cambridge University Press.

Tahir, Tanvir Ahmad. 1990. "Pakistan Resolution and Politics in Sind." In *Pakistan Resolution Revisited*. Edited by Kaneez F Yusuf, M. Saleem Akhtar, and S. Razi Wasti. Islamabad: National Institute of Historical and Cultural Research.

Tambiah, S. J. 1986. *Sri Lanka: Ethnic Fratricide and the Dismantling of Democracy*. Chicago: University of Chicago Press.

———. 1988. "Ethnic Fratricide in Sri Lanka: An Update." In *Ethnicities and Nations: Processes of Interethnic Relations in Latin America, Southeast Asia, and the Pacific*. Edited by Remo Guidieri, Francesco Pellizzi, and Stanley J. Tambiah. Houston: Rothko Chapel.

Tamilnadu Textbook Corporation (TTC). 1995a, *Social Science 6*. Madras: TTC.

———. 1995b. *Social Science 7*. Madras: TTC.

———. 1995c. *Social Science 10*. Madras: TTC.

Tamir, Yael. 1993. *Liberal Nationalism*. Princeton: Princeton University Press.

Tanvir, Mubarak Ali. 1985. "The Development of Local Government in Sind During Pre-Partition Period." *Sindhological Studies* (Summer): 32–41.

Taussig, Michael. 1997. *The Magic of the State*. New York: Routledge.

Taylor, Charles. 1994. "The Politics of Recognition." In *Multiculturalism: Examining the Politics of Recognition*. Edited by Amy Gutmann. Princeton: Princeton University Press.

Tennekoon, Serena. 1987. "Symbolic Refractions of the Ethnic Crisis: The Divaina Debates on Sinhala Identity." In *Facets of Ethnicity in Sri Lanka*. Edited by Charles Abeysekera and Newton Gunasinghe. Colombo: Social Scientists Association.

Thapar, Romila. 1963. *Asoka and the Decline of the Mauryas*. New Delhi: Oxford University Press.

———. 1966. *A History of India*. Volume 2. Baltimore, MD: Penguin.

———. 1975. *The Past and Prejudice*. Delhi: National Book Trust.

————. 1978a. *Ancient Indian Social History: Some Reinterpretations.* New Delhi: Orient Longman.

————. 1978b. *Exile and the Kingdom.* Bangalore: Mythic Society.

————. 1984. *From Lineage to State.* Delhi: Oxford University Press.

————. 1987. *The Mauryas Revisited.* S. G. Deuskar Lectures on Indian History (1984). Calcutta: Centre for Studies in Social Sciences.

————. 1993. *Interpreting Early India.* New Delhi: Oxford University Press.

————. N.d. *Dissent in the Early Indian Tradition.* M. N. Roy Memorial Lecture 7. Dehradun: Indian Renaissance Institute.

Thomson, Janice E. 1989. "Sovereignty in Historical Perspective: The Evolution of State Control over Extraterritorial Violence." In *The Elusive State: International and Comparative Perspectives.* Edited by James A. Caporaso. Newbury Park, CA: Sage.

Tilly, Charles. 1975a. "Western State-Making and Theories of Political Transformation." In *The Formation of National States in Western Europe.* Edited by Charles Tilly. Princeton: Princeton University Press.

————, ed. 1975b. *The Formation of National States in Western Europe.* Princeton: Princeton University Press.

————. 1985. "War Making and State Making as Organized Crime." In *Bringing the State Back In.* Edited by Peter Evans, Dietrich Rueschemeyer, and Theda Skocpol. Cambridge: Cambridge University Press.

Tiruchelvam, Neelan. N.d. *The Politics of Decentralisation.* Colombo: International Centre for Ethnic Studies.

Tonyo, Mohammad Bachal. 1991. "Ethnicity in Sindh and National Cohesion." *Sind Quarterly* 19, no. 2.

Torsvik, Per, ed. 1981. *Mobilization, Center-Periphery Structures and Nation-Building.* Bergen: Universitetsforlaget.

Tyabji, Badr-ud-din. 1985. "Warning from the Past." *Statesman.* December 20.

Udayavinan, E. E. 1962. "Viduthalai Kannvizhikkum" (Freedom will stare us in the eye). *Dravida Nadu.* October 28.

"Ulootthanai Virattiduvom!" (We will drive out the deceiver!). 1962. *Dravida Nadu.* December 23.

"Ungal Pangu" (Your share). 1962. *Dravida Nadu.* November 25.

"Unholy Mess: Ayodhya." 1993. *Seminar,* no. 402 (February).

United News of India. 1999. "Lanka to Introduce Tamil in Sinhala Schools." *Indian Express.* September 17. Accessed at http://www.expressindia.com/ie/daily/19990917/ige17019.html on September 17, 1999.

"Uttarkhand: Fresh Look Needed." 1996. Editorial, *The Hindu Online.* August 13.

"Uttarakhand, Not the Last." 1996. *Indian Express.* August 17.

"Vaari Vazhangugal" (Give generously). 1962. *Dravida Nadu.* November 4.

"Vadukkodai Resolution." 1976. In M. Somasundaram, ed. 1999. *Reimagining Sri Lanka: Northern Ireland Insights.* Appendix I. Colombo: International Centre for Ethnic Studies, pp. 194–201.

Vajreshwari, R. 1966. *A Handbook for History Teachers.* Bombay: Allied.

Van den Hoek, A. W., et al., eds. 1992. *Ritual, State and History in South Asia: Essays in Honour of J. C. Heesterman.* Leiden: E. J. Brill.

Varma, Kewal. 1991. "Assault on the Indian Union." *Telegraph.* September 21.

Veeramani, K. 1981. *The History of the Struggle for Social and Communal Justice in Tamil Nadu.* Madras: Dravidar Kazhagam.

Venu, A. S. 1987. *Anna and the Crusade.* Madras: Nakkeeran Pathipakkam.

Verma, Prativa. 1988. *Social Philosophy of the Mahabharata and the Manu Smrti.* Delhi: Classical.

Vincent, Andrew. 1987. *Theories of the State.* Oxford: Basil Blackwell.

Viswanathan, V. N. 1994. "Dravidian Movement: An Epiphenomenal Study." In *Caste, Politics and Society in Tamil Nadu.* Edited by G. Palanithurai. Delhi: Kanishka.

Waever, Ole, Barry Buzan, Morten Kelstrup, and Pierre Lemaitre. 1993. *Identity, Migration, and the New Security Agenda in Europe.* New York: St. Martin's Press.

Walimbe, Y. S. 1990. *Political and Moral Concepts in the Santiparvan of the Mahabharata.* Delhi: Ajanta.

Walker, R.B.J. 1993. *Inside/Outside: International Relations as Political Theory.* Cambridge: Cambridge University Press.

Walker, R.B.J., and Saul H. Mendlovitz. 1990. *Contending Sovereignties: Redefining Political Community.* Boulder: Lynne Rienner.

Wallace, Paul, ed. 1985. *Region and Nation in India.* New Delhi: Oxford University Press.

Waseem, Mohammad. 1989. *Politics and the State in Pakistan.* Lahore: Progressive.

———. 1990. "Pakistan Resolution and Ethnonationalist Movements." In *Pakistan Resolution Revisited.* Edited by Kaneez F Yusuf, M. Saleem Akhtar, and S. Razi Wasti. Islamabad: National Institute of Historical and Cultural Research.

———. 1997. "Ethnicity and Religion in South Asia: The Pakistan Experience." Paper presented at Regional Centre for Strategic Studies Workshop on Ethnicity, Migration and Environment, Kandy, Sri Lanka, March 7.

Washbrook, D. A. 1989. "Caste, Class and Dominance in Tamil Nadu: Non-Brahmanism, Dravidianism and Tamil Nationalism." In *Dominance and State Power in Modern India.* Volume 1. Edited by Francine Frankel and M.S.A. Rao. Delhi: Oxford University Press.

Weiner, Myron. 1965. "Political Integration and Political Development." *Annals of the American Academy of Political and Social Science* 358 (March).

Westholm, Anders, and Richard G. Niemi. 1992. "Political Institutions and Political Socialization: A Cross-National Study." *Comparative Politics* 25 (October).

Wheare, K. C. 1964. *Federal Government.* New York: Oxford University Press.

Whittlesey, Derwent. 1939. *The Earth and the State: A Study of Political Geography.* New York: Henry Holt.

Wickremasinghe, Nira. 1995. *Ethnic Politics in Colonial Sri Lanka, 1927–1947.* New Delhi: Vikas.

Wight, Martin. 1952. *British Colonial Constitutions 1947.* London: Oxford University Press.

Wijesinghe, P.R.H. N.d. *Eight States in Sri-Lanka: The Internal Divisions.* Trincomalee: National Development Handbook.

Wilson, A. Jeyaratnam. 1982. "Sri Lanka and Its Future: Sinhalese Versus Tamils." In *The States of South Asia: Problems of National Integration.* Edited by A. Jeyaratnam Wilson and Dennis Dalton. Honolulu: University of Hawaii Press.

———. 1988. *The Break-Up of Sri Lanka: The Sinhalese-Tamil Conflict.* Honolulu: University of Hawaii Press.

———. 1994. *S.J.V. Chelvanayakam and the Crisis of Sri Lankan Tamil Nationalism, 1947–1977.* Honolulu: University of Hawaii Press.

Wilson, A. Jeyaratnam, and Dennis Dalton, eds. 1982. *The States of South Asia: Problems of National Integration.* Honolulu: University of Hawaii Press.

Winichakul, Thongchai. 1994. *Siam Mapped: A History of the Geo-Body of a Nation.* Honolulu: University of Hawaii Press.

Wiswa Warnapala, W. A. 1993. *The Sri Lankan Political Scene.* New Delhi: Navrang.

Wolpert, Stanley. 1993. *A New History of India.* Fourth edition. New York: Oxford University Press.

Wright, Theodore P., Jr. 1981. "Center-Periphery Relations and Ethnic Conflict in Pakistan: Sindhis, Muhajirs, and Punjabis." *Comparative Politics* (April): 291–312.

Young, Crawford, ed. 1993. *The Rising Tide of Cultural Pluralism.* Madison: University of Wisconsin.

Index

About the Book

What makes a national community out of a state? Addressing this fundamental question, Rajagopalan studies national integration from the perspective of three South Asian communities—Tamils in India, Sindhis in Pakistan, and Tamils in Sri Lanka—that have a history of secessionism in common but with vastly different outcomes.

Rajagopalan investigates why integration is relatively successful in some cases (Tamil Nadu), less so in others (Sind), and disastrous in some (Sri Lanka). Broadly comparative and drawing together multiple aspects of political development and nation building, her imaginative exploration of the tension between state and nation gives voice to relatively disenfranchised sections of society.

Swarna Rajagopalan is a postdoctoral fellow at the James Madison College of Michigan State University. Her publications include *Redistribution of Authority: A Cross-Regional Perspective* (coedited with Jeanie J. Bukowski).